TRANSFORMED!

"What *Good to Great* does for companies, *Transformed!* does for people."
—JACK CANFIELD, BESTSELLING AUTHOR OF *THE SUCCESS PRINCIPLES: HOW TO GET FROM WHERE YOU ARE TO WHERE YOU WANT TO BE*

"The Wrights' book is about transformation that taps human potential at all levels. The strength and commitment of the people they coach and train is proof of their effectiveness."
—DR. MUHAMMAD YUNUS, GRAMEEN BANK FOUNDER & NOBEL PEACE LAUREATE, 2006

"I've seen the results of their science-based, proven technologies in leaders and folks from all walks of life, and the results are unique and powerful. The integrity, critical thinking, and accomplishments of their students are remarkable."
—BRAD ANDERSON, FORMER CEO OF BEST BUY

"Thanks to Dr. Judith Wright and Dr. Bob Wright, we now have a powerful and comprehensive toolkit for personal and global awakening. If you are ready to activate your visionary birthright, read and apply what you learn in this 'must-absorb' new book. You will absolutely see significant changes in every domain of your life."
—BARNET BAIN, FILM PRODUCER, *WHAT DREAMS MAY COME*, *THE CELESTINE PROPHECY*

"It is so wonderful to see the work being done by Bob and Judith Wright to get people in touch with their deep inner selves, full of divine potential. We are not put on Earth simply to eat, drink and 'be merry' and yet few acknowledge this crucial truth while there is still time to do much more. Only in the last stages of life do people tend to realize that eating and drinking have not made them either 'merry' or even fulfilled on any level. I am so proud of the Wrights for their commitment to helping people blossom and unfold into the divine beings they truly are, and infusing them with courage, conviction, and concrete tools to live that infinite potential. The more people who undergo their trainings and carry that message into the world, the brighter the future—on individual levels and on a global level—will look."

—H. H. Pujya Swami Chidanand Saraswatiji Maharaj,
President and Spiritual Head of Parmarth Niketan Ashram,
Rishikesh, India

"Are you ready for a real makeover? This is not a reality show nor a self-help book of the past, it is your reality and hope for a new life. In their new book, Judith and Bob serve a feast of tips and techniques for self-transformation. Their recipe is a blend of the spices of life—find your passions—and anchoring them in nutritional staples of our diet—to helping others create a better society, better communities, and better-performing organizations. Their energizing style and engaging stories invoke a double shot of efficacy on your path to the possibilities for your dreams."

—Richard Boyatzis, Distinguished University Professor,
Departments of Psychology, Cognitive Science and Organizational Behavior, Case Western Reserve University; Adjunct Professor of Human Resources, ESADE; Co-author with Dan Goleman and Annie McKee of the international bestseller Primal Leadership, and Co-author with Annie McKee of Resonant Leadership and Becoming a Resonant Leader

"The Wrights truly understand transformation and transformational processes. I like that they ground their work in scientific findings, and they keep abreast of research literature across a wide range of fields. This is a terrific guide to personal transformation."

—Ronald E. Riggio, Ph.D.
Henry R. Kravis Professor of Leadership and Organizational Psychology,
Kravis Leadership Institute, Claremont McKenna College,
and Co-author of Transformational Leadership

"The Wrights are fundamentally transforming the field of 'Transformation Psychology.' Their research and practice reveals the foundations of power, happiness, and meaning in life. As practitioners, they share their genuine interest in people and have an exceptional capacity to simply and understandably communicate what they have learned. Transformed! is written clearly and memorably. They explain their theories and give practical examples and case studies. Transformed! is a must-read for practitioners and lifelong learners alike in order to create blueprints for spectacular living. Reading *Transformed!* fueled my continuing process of positive transformation."

—Dr. Bernard Luskin, President-Elect,
The Society for Media Psychology and Technology of
the American Psychological Association (APA);
Educator and founder of multiple accredited schools;
practicing licensed psychotherapist, research psychologist

"Want a great career, relationships, spiritual life? Then become *Transformed!* The Wrights' personal transformation process is truly unique. Their science-based, proven technologies help build leaders by transforming oneself from the inside out."

—David Mager, Co-COO, Deepak HomeBase
and Author of *Street Smart Sustainability: The Entrepreneur's Guide
to Profitably Greening Your Organization's DNA*

"A tour-de-force 'owner's manual' for living a great life. *Transformed!* is a thoughtful, step-by-step, and practical guide. Eminently readable, the book brilliantly balances real-world examples of transforming individuals with the scientific underpinnings that govern the forces at work within each and every one of us. Instead of settling for the temporary, superficial change that is the province of many a self-help book, Drs. Bob and Judith Wright show how each of us can systematically transform ourselves in deep and sustainable ways. Ignore this book only if your ambition is to lead a safely dull and unfulfilled life."

—M. Salahuddin Khan,
Author of *Sikander*, former CTO & CMO of Navteq, Managing Principal
of QMarket Associates, Management Consulting

"Rarely do we see brilliant research combined with inspiration and practical exercises in one body of work. If you've wondered how the latest in neuroscience, behavioral economics, and positive psychology can converge to produce transformation and if you have to pick one book to read and recommend . . . this is it."

—Marcia Wieder, CEO/Founder, Dream University

"Any organizational leader who intends to have a positive, lasting impact in our changing world must commit themselves to their own personal transformation. Bob and Judith Wright have made it their lives' work to discover what it takes to transform from the inside out and live a great life, personally and professionally. What they have put together here is a profound source of inspiration and a practical guide for anyone on that path."

—Robert White, Principal, Extraordinary People LLC
and Author of *Living an Extraordinary Life*

"Drs. Judith and Bob Wright's book breaks the mold from rhetoric to real life miracles. It inspires people to dream, to adventure and connect with what really matters in order to have a truly meaningful life."

—Dr. Ray Blanchard, Visionary Leader,
co-producer of The ANSWER to Absolutely Everything,
co-author of the bestseller The Art and Science of Success

"Judith and Bob Wright excel at connecting the dots between dreams and deliverables. Highly mutual and grounded in practicality, their tools and strategies have catalyzed key personal transformations in me that have been essential for growth and success in business and the world. I have deep respect for how they build on solid historical traditions of human development and transformation while also integrating the latest research and thinking from a range of modern scientific fields."

—Matt Booty,
Former President and CEO of Midway Games, Inc.

"Today, tragically, many people resign themselves to a life of achievement instead of fulfillment, entertainment instead of deep satisfaction, amusement instead of joy, and sensory pleasure instead of love. They believe this is 'as good as it gets.' The unique greatness of the work being done by Robert and Judith Wright is that they not only inspire people to reach for more, but they actually show people how to find it. . . . The Wrights weave together ancient wisdom and modern neuropsychology to explain why so many of us are resigned to living as seeds and, thankfully, how to get that seed to sprout and blossom!"

—Dr. Sadhvi Bhagawati Saraswati,
Parmarth Niketan Ashram Administrator, Rishikesh, India

"I've been a reader of personal development books for what seems like forever. All good and interesting, but not necessarily actionable. The Wrights are all about results, and I feel like living proof! Change—really, transformation—is no longer just good theory, but it's real! The roadmap described in this book is gold—and my career, my marriage and relationships, and my sense of purpose are all huge beneficiaries."

—Thomas Terry,
Former CEO, J.P. Morgan Benefit and Retirement Strategies

"I came to Wright during the bottom of the economic recession in 2008 experiencing a deep sense of hunger and humiliation without business prospects. I now lead within two highly successful start-up ventures and enjoy an exciting, powerful, and vibrant life. The key principles captured in this dynamic book guide my insights and priorities every day."

—Kirk Hallowell, Ph.D., author of *The Million Dollar Race: An Insider's Guide to Winning Your Dream Job*

"Dr. Bob and Dr. Judith Wright stand on solid ground. Not only do they integrate leading thinkers in psychology, education, behavioral economics, and neuroscience, but they have the rare gift of operationalizing theory and research so that people can use it to transform their lives. Personally, professionally, spiritually, and in my relationships, my life is richer and more satisfying because of this program. The model and process that they share in this book work at a foundational level, thereby creating a natural gravitational pull toward greater health and abundant living. This makes the difference between knowing something in your head vs. living it in your heart!"

—Laura Barrows, Psy.D.

"Bob and Judith are sharing with us their treasure chest of transformation. These principles and strategies work. I have experienced the transforming power of Evolating for more than twenty years as the Wright's have been developing and refining their theories and methodologies. I am experiencing the life-enriching results of Evolating in all areas of my life, including my own growth work, my marriage, my family, my counseling practice, and my ministry. I am seeing the Wright principles of transformation being multiplied exponentially every day in the lives of the people I care about. These principles impact all my relationships, most importantly my relationship with God and faith. Read this book and start enjoying more transformation in your life."

—Rich Blue, Founder and Clinical Director of the Center for Christian Life Enrichment and Founder of 2nd Order Ministries

"The *Transformed!* process has had a significant impact on me, and generations of my family. My mother and father, my wife, my children, and many friends have all participated in the program and achieved amazing results, including increased satisfaction and fulfillment, clarity in purpose and direction, and significant positive change. This methodology and program work. I am a better husband, father, friend, and employer. If you have ever given up on a dream, or feel limited by your beliefs, the Wrights' process can help. Get out of your cage. Maximize your potential. Dedicate your life."

—Richard B. Lyons, M.B.A., CEO & President, Lyons CG

"I have transformed my life in so many ways—the Evolating model works! Through this program I have created a satisfying marriage, increased my salary with jobs with greater responsibility and scope, completed my doctorate, and become the first non-M.D. to chair my hospital's ethics board. What an amazing journey!"

—DENISE DELVES, R.N., C.N.M., ED.D.

"While the word *transformation* is bandied about a lot these days, the transformation described in these pages is real and lasting. I see possibilities in my life and what I can achieve that I could not even begin to see before. I credit the dedicated work of Drs. Judith and Bob Wright for their model that is not only one of personal development, but one of transformation for humanity."

—CHRISTINA CANRIGHT, PRESIDENT, CANRIGHT COMMUNICATIONS

"Drs. Bob and Judith Wright have delineated the process whereby humans can transform and become what is possible for each one of us. By demystifying the process, the Wrights have truly provided a great service. The Wrights' methodology can help anyone create a more meaningful and fulfilled life."

—MICHAEL ZWELL, PH.D., CEO, ZWELL INTERNATIONAL

"*Transformed!* gives people the way, and not just the words, for becoming our best and most empowered authentic self."

—SONIA CHOQUETTE, AUTHOR OF *GRACE, GUIDANCE & GIFTS: SACRED BLESSINGS TO LIGHT YOUR WAY*

TRANSFORMED!

TRANSFORMED!

THE SCIENCE *of* SPECTACULAR LIVING

JUDITH WRIGHT *&* BOB WRIGHT

TURNER

Turner Publishing Company
www.turnerpublishing.com

Transformed!: The Science of Spectacular Living

Cover design: Eric Masi
Book design: Glen Edelstein
Author photos: Daniel DuVerney

Library of Congress Cataloging-in-Publication Data

Wright, Judith, 1951-
Transformed! : the science of spectacular living / Judith Wright & Bob Wright.
    p. cm.
Includes bibliographical references.
ISBN 978-1-61858-075-7 (pbk)

1. Change (Psychology) I. Wright, Robert J., 1948-II. Title.
BF637.C4W75 2013

158.1--dc23

Here's to the rebels:

the honest ones,

the ones living courageously with heart,

following their yearning,

the ones who see the matrix and go against the grain

for the right reasons.

They look for deeper truth.

See when others fear to open their eyes.

They go beyond the status quo and do the things their heart demands of them.

They make waves,

rock the boat,

live to their highest.

You can criticize them, disagree with them,

but you must deal with them.

They lead the way to unleashing the potential of humanity.

They can't be found in flocks.

They follow in the steps of the great ones from Gandhi to Teresa.

They are the ones living spectacular lives.

They are Transformers.

CONTENTS

INTRODUCTION

"I'VE LOST 25 POUNDS without really trying," Rebecca told us at her graduation last night. "I am making more money and I have gotten a promotion. I could never have imagined being so comfortable talking in front of 100 people before this year. And after years of trying to get my alcoholic husband to sober up and join me, I have developed the strength to go off on my own and am enjoying life. So often overlooked as the shy one, my friends now look to me as an example. I am so excited about my future—I can't imagine ever stopping this life of adventure." Rebecca's words and others' were powerful reminders of why we conducted the research that led us to write *Transformed!*

Another group was completing our Year of Transformation program and they were each telling their guests how they had learned, grown, and changed over the one year since they had begun the program. From all walks of life, educational backgrounds, and faiths, these graduates had made major leaps in their life projects. They had attended an introductory weekend, four additional weekend trainings, and weekly classes that introduced them to four curricular areas synthesized from over thirty years of curriculum, research, and development and integrating the best of applied human emergence technologies. Our work focuses on a student's life project, which gives meaning to everything they do and unifies the diverse areas of their life. It draws from a broad range of approaches to human excellence, from the ancient Greeks to current neuroscience and behavioral economics. It also incorporates strong doses of Mezirow's transformative education, Alfred Adler's lifestyle enhancement, and the existentialists' emphasis on personal responsibility and choice, along with a developmental psychology perspective that gives direction to each person's growth activities. In the weekly training sessions, students report on assignments they used during the week to challenge themselves to expand their behaviors, thoughts, and feelings throughout the day. Living their lives as experiments, and growing throughout the week, students experience consistent progress into expanded satisfaction, effectiveness, and fulfillment. Receiving a new lesson and new assignment, they then embark on the next week's adventure.

Years of research, including our doctoral studies, have led to an understanding of how to best sequence each week's lesson and assignment so it builds on those of the previous week. Everyone who participates in the curriculum learns and grows, but some—like Rebecca, quoted at the beginning—transform. The outward manifestations of her transformation were many: shy to outgoing, dependent to independent, and living in financial scarcity to abundance. The word *transformation* is no trite exaggeration for us—it signifies a real shift in state and way of being.

Transformation is not the domain of any age or social sector. One of the graduates hobbled to the front of the room using her walker: "I just had the best year of my 70 years on the planet. I am more excited than I ever dreamed possible. I thought I was on the way out, but I am charging into life, maybe not on my feet but definitely with my heart. I am so excited by so many things now—contributing to others, tramping through the woods, experiencing full joy, and not giving in to retirement. I used to be quiet and withdrawn, but with every day that comes I am more outgoing and talkative."

IN THEIR OWN WORDS

Transformation is facilitated by taking stock of where you are and where you are going. Each student in our Year of Transformation program writes two reports each week on what they are learning and how they are growing. Learning is defined as what they know now that they didn't know before, and growing is doing something they would not have done previously. The changes in beliefs, thoughts, and actions may seem simple but are remarkable all the same.

As each quarter comes to a close, a quarterly review grounds what students learned and the skills they developed in their growth at the end of each quarter. Then at the end of the year, each student captures their growth in a year-end essay that is amazing and exciting.

Below is the year-end report of a scientist whose study of science had been coupled with his careful, low-risk lifestyle—a lifestyle that changed dramatically. Within two years of this essay, he was recruited to be second in charge of research at a name-brand consumer products company with the intent that in a few years, he would head the research function.

Noah
38-year-old Senior Manager, Research & Development

Noah's Year-End Essay

These were some of the claims made by my false self before I started the Year of Transformation program: "I have a perfect life. I know how to handle every situation. I am nice to everyone. I am liked by everyone. I can provide advice on any topic to everyone. I have a successful career and a perfect family. I have a superior sense of morality over others. I do not need any change."

I started out skeptical. My friend claimed it would enhance my already great life. I still wondered, "If I have a perfect life, what difference could this year possibly make?" The first weekend training showed a glimpse of possibilities I had never imagined.

My first quarter was **Purposeful Living and Spiritual Development**. What can I possibly learn about spirituality from these people? I asked myself. Will it be the Christian version of spirituality? Should I be threatened as a Muslim? . . . I was in for a surprise. The weekend was really powerful and I already had one mistaken belief shifted by realizing that spirituality doesn't come solely from religion. This shift brought about the potential for opening up spirituality in every aspect of my life. I also discovered some insights into my relationship of fear, instead of a relationship of love, with God. I now believe He loves us—loves me.

I started to understand my place in the universe and what my purpose in life should be. Just knowing that I have a special place and purpose in this universe helped me strengthen my faith in creation. I am created for a purpose by a God who loves me and bestowed upon me the gifts that I need to discover and develop. With this in mind I know that I am NOT a part of some probability theory that equates the chances of my existence. I am a special creation with a purpose. It's up to me to find my purpose and use the gifts given to me to help me towards that goal.

My second quarter was **Nourishment and Self-Care.** The initial belief that was busted was that self-care was about buying more things for myself. My Infiniti G35 all of a sudden had a totally different meaning. I took a look back and thought through the circumstances under which I had bought that car a couple of years ago. In order to feel good, I "had" to buy that car and I made every justification as to why I needed it.

As the quarter progressed, I began realizing the importance of my emotions. The concept of going through my pain to be fully nourished, that really resonated with me. The journey to joy goes through pain.

I started to recognize my fears instead of running away from them. This is the time when I applied for a position that I was afraid to apply for, which I eventually got.

I had a lot of fear going into **Family and Intimacy**, my third quarter. There are certain fears and pain that I was running away from. Even identifying my family's rules and beliefs was challenging, realizing that I will continue to project my belief through others, whether it's my wife, my siblings, or perhaps even my newborn child. The other realization was how I always desired to have a more forceful mother who would stand up for herself and go after her dreams and desires. I projected that "wish" onto my wife and would get upset when I didn't see that happening. As a result of that realization, I shifted my actions. I dug into several historical pains. After building up a lot of feelings and emotions throughout the quarter, I finally broke into tears with my mother, mostly from the pain over the loss of my father 22 years ago. I felt like it was the first time I fully expressed that sadness. I also had a heart-to-heart conversation with her regarding her goals and my vision for her. That was the first time I had a conversation like that with her in my life.

I was really looking forward to the fourth quarter, **Personal Power**. I quickly learned how much I was using my passive-aggressiveness in the past and not fully going for what I desired. I learned to value and use both my direct, aggressive power and my receptive power. I started to bust the belief of "I'm not worthy" and used the other assignments to develop a stronger relationship with my wife and others around me. In one particular instance, my criticism of my wife led to a much deeper conversation and some locked-up and buried part of her life surfaced. We were able to talk about historical pains and then developed a joint vision. I must say that was the most powerful part of this quarter.

My journey this year was like learning a new language—first basic vocabulary and then practicing it in a safe environment. Then I started taking some risks and now I'm at a point where I know that running away from pain and fear will not get me closer to my greater vision.

During the last year, I have had some of the biggest increases in salary, and that is without a promotion. I have been able to recognize my victimhood at work and was able to identify a responsible course of action rather than blaming my management. I made bold moves like scheduling a meeting with the CEO and President just to talk about my development. *[Note: Noah works for one of the largest consumer products companies in the world.]* I stepped out of my comfort zone and applied for a really challenging role in a different part of the company. Everything in this position was different than what I had done in the past, from technology to business to people to managing a small division to managing direct reports.

There was fierce competition and I constantly second-guessed my abilities but I stuck with it. I focused on feeling and facing my fears and fully expressing my talents. In the end, they awarded the position to me, and I am really enjoying it. It's in line with my wildest dreams and goals—and my higher vision. Now I am more engaged, influential, and visible—a powerful leader at work. I have been able to provide direct and honest feedback, which led colleagues to ask me to be their mentor at work, and I take a lot of pride in it.

This was the first year my wife and I lived together. By recognizing our fears and not avoiding pain, we grew closer together and got to know each other much better. We had our baby during this year, and we have been able to discuss our feelings and fears. There's much ahead of us, but I feel like we have developed a good baseline. I also had heart-to-heart conversations with all of my seven siblings and my mother about my true feelings. This is also a work in progress.

Even with the successes, I know I am just scratching the surface, but at least I know that there is a surface to be scratched and I can celebrate that success.

Year-end essays tend to boil many moves down into one report. And although the year-end results are amazing, you can see how it really is a journey of many steps when reading quarterly essays.

Below is one of the quarter-end essays from a married Ph.D. student in Economics.

Darren
29-year-old Ph.D. student in Economics

Darren's End-of-Quarter Essay

Assignments I really struggled on: *Asking for What I Want* and *Displease with Ease*

This quarter, I discovered how much I ignore my own wants, and even convince myself that many of my wants don't exist. This goes a long way toward ensuring that I don't always get what I want. Throughout the quarter, I became more aware of my wants in the moment, uncovering previously hidden wants, and going for things that I want. I have enhanced my ability to identify my wants faster and more accurately in the moment.

I also learned that I have a limiting belief that I need to be liked to have value. This made the *Displease with Ease* assignment particularly difficult. I think I see myself being so capable, and at the surface the assignment seemed so much easier than actually implementing it in practice. I had such an aversion (like a complete block) to doing it, out of intense underlying fear of not being liked.

This fear has also kept me from being fully expressive in the moment. I've held back anger and hurt out of fear of upsetting or scaring someone. I had one big breakthrough and shocked myself in a fight with my wife. I expressed what I wanted with a vehemence that got her attention—and mine. I realized that, even though I was aware of the anger before I expressed it, I did not realize how much there was until I began expressing it. That was a huge learning moment.

I have had a fear of being open and honest with my mother

and sister. My relationship with both of them has improved over the course of the quarter. I've been less withholding from my mother, telling her more things about my life rather than focusing on the things I am proud of or what I selectively want her to know about. She does not do a great job of understanding my needs. But as I've gotten better at identifying and expressing my wants, I've discovered that she is very receptive to them. I also spoke truths to my sister, telling her some previously unexpressed upsets, as well as some responsible criticism. The conversation was very productive.

And no matter what an individual's life circumstances, it's clearly never too late to start. Following is a weekly report from the 70-year-old woman we quoted at the beginning of this introduction, from just one of her weekly reports.

Roberta
70-year-old retiree

Roberta's Weekly Essay

What did you learn?
I learned how powerful it is to be aware of my thoughts and to stop myself midstream. Every day I am more and more aware of how much power I have by being present. I find amazing insights come to me when I'm in the flow. By doing this work I feel so much more in touch with myself and with God.

Successes:
When I went to the doctor this week he was very impressed with my enthusiasm. I told him about my assignment and how empowering this whole program has been. He said, "I can see it and hear it in your voice." We talked about how much this has impacted my immune system and I agreed. I told him I can feel

my body being energized when I am fully conscious. I told him this may sound like some new-age stuff but what is happening to me is so amazing I want to share it with everyone.

Mistaken beliefs challenged or shifted:

I am so in awe of the power of just being aware moment-by-moment and how it can shift me to a new place. I am striving to improve, and I can feel this powerful presence guiding me. My son and daughter have both said they have never seen me so excited and empowered.

Yesterday I sat in my quiet spot and really cried and felt the pain for so many things and knew that I was truly loved. A lot of pain is over my family turmoil, which has been huge. But I know when I feel all of it fully, it truly leaves a space for the beautiful love and peace. Feelings truly are divine and to be honored. I was raised with my mother putting me down and telling me I was weak for showing my feelings. I knew she was wrong, but it took me a long time to honor them.

In spite of all the pain in my family I can see how my children and I are communicating more fully. We tell each other the hard truths. My daughter and son are engaging so much more fully now, which is beautiful. I love my life. I love myself. And, I now know I am loved.

Transformation is the result of going on the adventure of being fully human, fully conscious, fully responsible—living life as if every moment matters. In addition to our acknowledgments at the end of the book, we want to recognize our students, those intrepid and trepid adventurers who inspire, push, and support us in this work.

Transformed! is their story.

Judith and Bob Wright
July 26, 2012

TRANSFORMED!

CHAPTER ONE

THE TRANSFORMATIONAL IMPERATIVE

Everyone has inside himself a piece of good news!
The good news is that you really don't know how great you can
be, how much you can love, what you can accomplish,
and what your potential is!
—ANNE FRANK

YOU HAVE A BASIC INALIENABLE RIGHT—the right to discover and fulfill your potential. And, to exercise that right, you must transform and evolve from who you've been to who you could become.

This sentiment has echoed throughout the millennia as man has sought to discover what makes a good life. For the ancient Greeks the good life was *areté*—often translated as *virtue,* but more accurately, it means reaching your highest potential. The goal of life for the ancient Greeks wasn't happiness or contentment, but rather human flourishing—*eudaimonia*—the actualization of our distinctive function and capacities and living up to our potential.

Every religion and every spiritual teacher—whether Muhammad, Jesus, Buddha, or the saints as they followed the call to unknown lands and possibilities—teaches us to develop the disciplines to live good lives, to become enlightened and aware, to break through illusion (what the Hindus call Maya), to align with higher principles, to make the most out of our lives, and to become the best people we can be.

The existential philosophers from Kierkegaard to Nietzsche resonate with the vision of the ancient Greeks. Valuing human experience and human potential, they emphasize the importance of living authentically, which for them means that we live true to who we could be, not to who we have been.

Inspired by Nietzsche's will to power and self-mastery, Alfred Adler, founder of the school of individual psychology, proposed a self-perfecting drive: the desire we all have to fulfill our potential, to come closer and closer to our ideal.

Abraham Maslow, the father of humanistic psychology, saw our desire for self-fulfillment as the drive for self-actualization, to realize our potential.

Positive psychologists and economists alike study the good life, discovering that it entails engaging, finding meaning, and having the opportunity to improve our lives. They have definitively proven that it is not what we buy or have, but who we are and what we experience, that brings us satisfaction.

Current cultural messages reflect these sentiments, whether it's the U.S. Army's appeal to "be all that you can be" or Oprah's "live your best life."

From philosophers to psychologists, religious leaders to reformers, educators to economists, and soldiers to superstars, we hear the call to transform and fulfill our potential—the ubiquitous human imperative.

WE ARE DESIGNED TO TRANSFORM

And amazingly, not only are we called to transform, but neuroscience research today definitively demonstrates that we are also uniquely designed to transform, to fulfill our potential. Deep within us, both in our hearts and in our minds—literally in the makeup of our brain's structures—reside the drivers and tools of transformation.

We have the amazing gift of neuroplasticity: the ability to build new neural circuitry, new selves, and new lives. We can literally change our brains and our minds, and what we believe, who we are, and how we live. We can transform.

The very fact that we have neuroplasticity lets us know that we possess these amazing capabilities. Our transformation circuits are only activated, however, with our conscious choice and intent, through the stimulation of novelty and focused attention, as well as through our yearnings and emotions, which signal to our brains, "Pay attention, this matters!" Such attention not only rewires the circuitry of our brains, but it also affects the expression of our genes.

We are designed to seek, to be curious, to discover. When we are thrilled about the world of ideas and divining meaning, our seeking circuits are firing, activating one of the pleasure centers in our brains. We are in a state of eagerness and directed purpose—a state we human beings love to be in. This thrill of anticipating a reward motivates us to act.

Yet while this is exciting, we will only be fully satisfied and transform when we activate the other pleasure center of our brains— our satisfaction center—which occurs only when we seek and then engage in activities and ways of being that touch our deeper yearning.

We are designed to be explorers, and when we explore, our brains light up with pleasure. It is the novelty, not the outcome, that most delights our brain and activates our neuroplasticity. Our brains are never "happier" than when we are learning new things, stretching just beyond our current capacities. This is where we build new circuitry and develop mastery.

Our brains respond with a flurry of neuronal activity when we open our minds to new possibilities, free ourselves of limiting beliefs, and perceive ourselves and our world in new and empowering ways. By acting on this new awareness and stretching right to the edge of our abilities, we activate our neuroplasticity to build new circuitry—to transform how we think, what we believe, what we do, and who we are.

And yet another powerful tool of transformation resides within us. When we activate the most recently evolved part of our brain—our frontal lobe (our prefrontal cortex), transformational magic occurs. The frontal lobe is the seat of our intention, our will. Our dedication and focused attention spark this structure of the brain into action.

Our consistent focus on our highest values increases blood flow to the frontal lobe, and the more we focus on our yearning and our values, the more we transform.

WE ARE DESIGNED TO CONSCIOUSLY ENGAGE IN OUR OWN TRANSFORMATION

We *do* have the force within us. It is the power of transformation.

In childhood, we begin to dream of possibilities—*I want to be an astronaut, I want to be an explorer, I want to be a rock star, I'm going to be a (you fill in the blank) when I grow up.* The continual evolution of childhood is just the beginning of the design's capabilities. Think about how a child is always changing—with every developmental stage, every experience. Each new experience interacting with the previous self, leading to the unfolding of his or her design, reveals still more elements of the child's uniqueness. And what a delight it is to witness this unfolding of each child becoming himself or herself! It's as if each of the child's growth changes reveals a new, yet more essential, self.

The template of possibilities does not end with childhood. The same is true of adulthood: the more we transform, the more of ourselves we become. But the transformational design changes in adulthood. This capacity to learn, grow, and transform that came so naturally as a child now comes under our conscious control and can only be activated by our intentional attention and choice, and the exercise of our free will.

This change of childhood's native transformational force is part of the design. We are designed, as adults, to create ourselves, and to chart our destinies by consciously engaging in our own transformation—what we call *evolating.* Our technical term for the *Transformed!* process, *evolating* (from the Latin *evolare*) refers to a flying up or out, an unfurling. As opposed to *evolution,* which is a gradual adaptation to something that already exists, *evolating* is consciously creating that which doesn't yet exist, emerging from an inner direction as opposed to an outer need. It is a continual process of flying up from one way of being to a greater one, from one way of living to a greater life. It leads to discontinuous leaps—leaps of transformation.

JUDITH'S STORY: HOW I LEARNED TO TRANSFORM AND SO CAN YOU

I have been a leader and high achiever since I took the stage in my first dance recital when I was three years old. By the age of ten I knew *Robert's Rules of Order,* and by twelve, I was the youngest participant in an International Red Cross Leadership camp for high-school juniors and seniors, where I was voted head of the multinational group. I continued as a leader in high school, becoming the drum majorette of a championship marching band, a student council officer, editor of the yearbook, and class valedictorian. I continued to amass awards in college, graduating *Phi Beta Kappa* and *summa cum laude.* I married a man who looked like Sylvester Stallone and had a genius I.Q., but I still was not fulfilled and did not know what was missing.

The Rehabilitation Act of 1973 provided for demonstration grants to help people with disabilities get through college. I was 23 when Mott College made me the head of a national demonstration grant program for students with disabilities to successfully complete college. It was a great opportunity to do something that had never been done before—design, set up, and manage a program to provide a model for other colleges to emulate. I *was* the department, running everything from administration to counseling to community outreach. I learned sign language in order to communicate with students who were deaf, and my world was opened beyond anything I had ever imagined as I counseled students with extreme physical limitations, many of them in wheelchairs, with problems ranging from cerebral palsy to muscular dystrophy and spinal cord injury. I was learning more deeply about humanity, helping to write the state of Michigan's guidelines for serving people with disabilities, and appearing on television and radio—but I was still missing something.

My success at Mott led me to be hired with a joint appointment at the University of Illinois at Chicago and the State of Illinois for another national demonstration program in early childhood disabilities. It entailed program development, staffing, supervision, and work with families of children with a range of early childhood developmental disabilities such as developmental delay, severe cerebral palsy, retardation, spina bifida, and often even combinations of these. Remarkably, some parents thrived in the face of their difficult situation, while others needed great help just to cope and get by—some never recovering. The ones who were happy were accepting the challenges and actually transforming while the others were resisting the challenges and suffering endlessly.

While the program helped most of them transition eventually, it was at this point that I began to put together my two-plus-two's and to realize that there was something missing in my life. I had always accomplished my goals, getting bigger and bigger grants, but I was still not fulfilled, and many of these families and students from this and my prior job seemed happier than I was. Transformation had been forced on them, and they had embraced it.

What was it going to take for me? I had been fat—I haven't mentioned that yet, have I? Well, I had lost the weight—another goal accomplished—but I was still unfulfilled. While I was good with people—I had social skills, I was a leader who could read others, anticipate needs, and meet them, I was empathic—I didn't really read my own needs and meet them. I partied, I laughed, but I wasn't all that happy. I had enough social and emotional intelligence to feel, but not the facility to express for myself. I could hold my feelings back where needed but I couldn't stir them up for my own satisfaction. I still wasn't fully me, nor was I yet on the journey of discovery until this wake-up call: the realization that many folks who appeared less well-off than I were happier than I was.

I learned that I had focused on external success rather than my own inner yearnings for connection, to matter, to be real, to make a difference. I hadn't allowed my true feelings and truths to emerge. I started expressing anew to the man who is now my ex-husband, and I had my first big wake-up call: he could not handle me following my yearning—speaking my mind and expecting more—so our relationship ended. This led me to get coaching and take personal development classes. I was finally learning to follow my inner urges beyond goal achievement to the personal journey of transformation.

The next major event in my life occurred over 30 years ago, when I began dating a man who had been on a transformational journey, studying with the giants of psychology and spiritual teachers alike. He was unlike any other human being I had ever met. This man had truly dedicated himself to living consciously, discovering and expressing what he called the truth of his experience to his highest vision. Without knowing it, he was dedicated to transformation.

He had spent his life opening himself to new possibilities, new ideas, new paradigms—not just for intellectual enterprise but for the deep purpose of discovering and expressing who he was at the core. The first to challenge someone else on an assertion, he was also the first to open himself up to having his own beliefs and precepts profoundly challenged. His college years included living in multiple environments and countries, following the same pursuit—looking for deeper, ultimate truths. He threw himself into his career as an entrepreneur, becoming a therapist's therapist and growing a staff of dedicated professionals serving national firms from Borg Warner to Harcourt Brace with employee assistance, managed care, and other consulting. He has never stopped studying and learning, literally and figuratively leaving no stone unturned.

Our first date was in October of 1980. We were married in 1981, seven months later. Bob demanded I express my desires. Initially afraid of my inner feelings and uncomfortable with revealing myself, I fled, or turned and fought. Once we got done with our initial fights over this, I learned to yearn, to engage in new ways with him. The quality of my life was shifting dramatically. It was no longer just about achieving goals, but about meeting my deeper yearnings. And ironically, as I focused on becoming more of myself, I naturally accomplished even more than I had before. I now valued being fully present and the journey of discovering myself and others, not only with Bob, but with everyone I met. I have kept discovering new areas of myself as the relationship has deepened and broadened to the point where we are writing this book together—truly a transformational event for both of us. While this book is about research into great lives and transformation, if you look deeply, you will also notice a love story of two beings marrying their lives like the double helix—the whole time reporting on research into great and useful things for you.

I am so thankful for the research that yielded the *Transformed!* process because it gives me a way to understand and communicate my transformation and helps me look back to my days as an achiever who was a great learner and goal achiever, but not yet a Transformer. I can explain why I feel so much more satisfied and fulfilled, and how I can do things and be things I never imagined possible. I relish the opportunities I've had to share what I've learned in a range of forums: from *Oprah* to *20/20,* and *Today* to *Good Morning America,* as well as in one-on-one coaching sessions with corporate leaders and in larger presentations to diverse audiences. I am honored to support others from all walks of life on their journeys in ways I could never have imagined.

I am thrilled to be able to have a clear, reproducible process from which to share these discoveries with you and guide our mutual transformations going forward.

THE BENEFITS OF TRANSFORMATION—NO MATTER WHERE YOU ARE ON THE PATH

Whether you have been on a personal development path for some time or are just beginning, you will achieve things beyond your imagining as you apply the principles and lessons of *Transformed!*. We know this because we have helped thousands of people from all walks of life and all levels of education to create phenomenal life projects and live spectacular lives.

Note that we aren't saying we helped them quit smoking, lose weight, find a mate, achieve career success, or attain spiritual peace, though people have done all these things with this process and their work with us. More important, though, they have changed every aspect of their lives in ways that are nothing less than astonishing.

You may not be aware that more is available to you than just achieving a specific goal. There is a life out there waiting for you that right now may seem completely out of reach—or even something you haven't ever thought about. You may find it difficult to be excited about getting something you haven't imagined or aren't even conscious of wanting. But just below the level of everyday consciousness, each one of us has an inner drive or yearning to be more ourselves.

When you're on a transformational path you achieve more, you feel more, you experience more. No one is bored on this path. So much novelty and challenge exists when you transform that every day feels like an adventure. And while great, traditionally celebrated events happen because you're on this path—job promotions, marriage, kids, travel—you are also on a journey of inner discovery.

Be aware, too, that this is an ongoing process. What we mean is that you don't just benefit when you reach a goal, but you benefit over and over and over again. Too often, people make significant changes in their lives, feel good about their accomplishments, and then unthinkingly slide back to pre-change behaviors. They aren't vigilant about change and thus can't sustain the gains they've made. The *Transformed!* process doesn't allow that to happen. It requires transformation to become a way of life.

The benefits of transformation, then, are large and small, external and internal, focused and multifaceted, daily and for the rest of your life. And then there's the benefit of taking action. At Wright, a personal and professional development organization and graduate institute, we refer to the "assignment way of living," and by that we mean that our students are expected to act on what they learn, to practice new behaviors, to try new things, to be willing to take risks. The most common complaint about traditional seminars is that they end and the results are neither sustainable nor cumulative. Still others complain that traditional therapy is all talk, thought, and no action. As much as we believe in the value of reflection, meditation, and dialogue, we know that you have to take what you reflect, meditate, and dialogue on into the world. Sean, the Chief Information Officer for a global financial firm and one of our students in his first quarter of study, best expressed the benefit of making consistent small changes at a high velocity:

"I'm finding myself flowing with life and not holding so much anxiety. I'm not spending as much time worrying about the thing I need to do, I'm just doing it. I feel I am starting to get better at changing my behavior on the fly. The little changes make such a huge difference, and the more I can make these changes, the more powerful I become. I am feeling joy in this."

Our students believe in greatness and continuously seek it in every area of life. They dedicate themselves to discovering who they are and becoming who they can be. They knock the doors off their limited perceptions, challenge mistaken and limiting beliefs, and explore what is possible. While they celebrate each success, they are not satisfied with a simple achievement or incremental progress.

Our students participate consciously in the process of their ongoing transformation. They dedicate themselves to learning and living the skills of leading a great life project. They yearn for more than traditional values—they want those, too—but they want much deeper connection, much greater learning, growing, awareness, and consciousness. They crave a sense of belonging to something that really matters and makes a positive difference in every aspect of life. They crave unifying, meaningful ways of being and they live these things, each in their own unique expression.

DISCOVERING THE PROCESS

The transformation process that our students have used so successfully has evolved over time, and we were not ready to write about it until we conducted research to discover how some of our students made quantum leaps of transformation. We want to share with you how the process reached this stage.

Over time, we noticed that certain students experienced exponential change. Their capacities expanded exceptionally, as did their service to different communities, their joy of living, depth of relationships, career success, and satisfaction. They became far more spiritually dedicated in a wide range of religions, had major influence on amazingly diverse groups of people, and found themselves to be more loved and loving than they had ever been before.

Why them? The unique integration of coaching, seminars, peer training labs, and the assignment way of living generates significant growth in the vast majority of our students, who experience positive change in their lives, but this smaller group clearly was moving faster, deeper, and wider than anyone else. We engaged an outside researcher to help us get the study of these high performers going. We then took this initial data and dug deeply on our own to discover what these individuals were doing that allowed them to transform in such startling and inspiring ways. Though we'll share what this research revealed in detail in the next chapter, for now, we'd like to give you a quick preview of some traits they had in common. Our high performers:

* *Followed their deepest "urges" wherever they would take them.* These urges arose in the moment from a host of motivations: the desire to be seen and connect with others, to make a significant impact, to connect with a higher power.

* *Acted on these urges rather than just waiting, thinking about them, or talking about them.* Doing meant taking action in ways that were often a stretch, challenging, and sometimes scary.

* *Experienced the ongoing excitement of discoveries about themselves and others.* They rethought basic life assumptions and formulated new ones, bringing unconscious and limiting beliefs to the surface and creating new ones that gave them more options for learning and growth.

Further application of the research to still other Transformers revealed that this group of students shared traits with many of our transformational heroes: Winston Churchill, Martin Luther King, Jr., Gandhi, Mother Teresa, and Buckminster Fuller. Obviously, these amazing individuals existed before Wright did, yet the applicability of the *Transformed!* process to them and the parallels between them and our students were astonishing. They transformed themselves instinctively in the same way our high-performing students did by focusing on their life projects through our courses and coaching.

What if we could harness their transformative power? What if we could refine our process based on our observation of these students? Ultimately, that's exactly what we did. We didn't reinvent the wheel—the process we had already been using for years was highly effective for most students. But by integrating lessons learned from studying these transformative fast-trackers, we made it even more powerful.

What also helped us improve the process were the numerous breakthrough studies in various scientific arenas that have emerged in recent years. We have grounded our process in the work of positive psychologists, cultural evolutionists, neuroscientists, behavioral economists, and others. As a result, this is a process that is science-based as well as empirical. Throughout the book, you'll find references to the work of pioneering scientists.

At this point, you may be asking yourself the following question: Is it worth it? The real question is, "Are you worth it?" As we've noted, transformation requires work. More than that, it demands embracing learning, challenge, and even some emotional discomfort. People do it because the rewards are numerous, leading to a more genuine, fulfilled you.

WHAT TO EXPECT FROM YOURSELF

Whether you are already far down your path of transformation or just beginning, you need to expect two things from yourself. First, you need to expect courage. If this stuff were easy, everyone would be transforming. At various points, you're going to need courage to do what the process asks of you. If you're shy, you may need to speak out in group settings. If you're stuck in a particular routine, you may need to make an effort to leave that routine behind. If you're a rugged individualist, you may be required to reach out to others for feedback and support. We're going to ask you to take some risks and tackle challenging projects, so there's a level of discomfort you need to endure. This can be difficult, and so you'll need courage to push ahead.

Second, expect greatness. We are designed to live great lives. It is through being socialized that we limit our capacity. The good news is that we can reignite this natural capacity. We have no doubt that you're capable of greatness. This is not starry-eyed optimism but pragmatic certainty. We've coached and trained many people who have achieved spectacular results in every area of their lives. They have learned to transform—that is, to consciously reignite their capacity to live ever-greatening lives. We fully expect that by the time you're done reading, you will not only be inspired to live spectacularly, but you'll also have a process that will both set you on this ever-greatening path and keep you accelerating to cover ever greater distances.

CHAPTER TWO

TRANSFORMED:
THE SCIENCE OF PERSONAL CHANGE
AND TRANSFORMATION

Transformation feels as if some basic architecture is being remodeled rather than just new furniture being put in the house or moved from room to room. There is some deep structural change . . . that alters the backbone of existence.
—DAN SIEGEL

NO MATTER HOW HAPPY we are, how much we've grown, or how many changes we've made in our lives, we sense there is more. No matter how much we achieve, we feel the beckoning of our unfulfilled potential. Some part of us wonders, *Am I fulfilling my destiny? Living the life I am supposed to be living? Becoming who I could become? Is there a greater life—or a greater me—awaiting my discovery?* And, when our lives aren't going the way we want, we often hope that a better life is available.

The possibility of greatness is powerful, and it's why stories of transformation are so resonant. We delight in Harry Potter's developing magical ability, the Force within Luke Skywalker, the hidden courage of Frodo in *The Lord of the Rings*. We are inspired by the transformational stories of our heroes—Gandhi, from attorney to spiritual leader; Oprah, from an abused young girl to a media giant beloved by millions; Abraham Lincoln, from his humble roots in a one-room cabin to the White House.

But is this kind of transformation just the stuff of myths and legends, distant historical figures, or super-celebrities? Is transformation more ideal than real? Can regular people like you and me really change in significant and multifaceted ways? Is it possible to revolutionize *all* aspects of your life—your relationships, career, sense of self, spirituality, leadership, service?

If you're like most skeptics, you may think that buying this concept is akin to buying snake oil. In fact, your pantry may be stocked full of dusty bottles of this oil that never delivered on their promises. Maybe you took a workshop or course that talked about transformation but eventually left you feeling let down at best and deceived at worst. You may have started meditating, gone into therapy, or followed the teachings of a guru with the hope that a new you would emerge but found that while you made some changes, at the core you were the same. It's no wonder you have doubts and questions!

Here's the short answer. We've all been swindled, bamboozled, and hoodwinked—probably not out of a malicious intent by others, but out of our own ignorance and denial of what it takes for real transformation. We all want a quick fix, but buying into quick fixes is like a junk food binge, empty calories that never really satisfy. That's the bad news. The good news is that not only have we witnessed the real transformation of hundreds of individuals, but our research and hundreds of other scientific articles, books, and research studies validate the concept.

No, transformation is not easy. But it is completely possible. With sustained effort and effective use of your natural capacities, you can do it. Throughout this book we'll share the stories of students who have transformed, and the science-based process that facilitated their transformations. But now that we've thrown the word around so much—what is transformation?

Transformation is a metamorphosis from one state to another. It is not just doing things better. Despite popular belief, changing jobs or careers, going from being single to having a serious relationship, or moving from unhappiness to contentment are all just incremental moves. Not to disparage any of those life changes, but transformation is broader and deeper—and it lasts. When you transform, who you become is different from who you were—emotionally, cognitively, and spiritually. Transformation impacts the quality of every area of your life in positive ways—your relationships, career, sense of yourself, service, and spiritual life. We're not talking about a cosmetic difference. You can't just measure transformation in pounds lost or money gained or goals achieved. Think of the caterpillar transforming into a butterfly—one is utterly, completely, and absolutely unlike the other.

Here's a litmus test for transformation:

You do something that you could never have imagined yourself doing, become something you could never have imagined yourself becoming, and, ultimately, live a life greater than you could have ever imagined yourself living.

Transformation is a bold step into the unknown. Yes, the unknown is frightening. That is a large part of why so few venture into the land of true transformation. But it's also exhilarating and enlightening, leading to profound epiphanies. Even better, we are all capable of becoming butterflies, no matter how long we've been dragging our bellies across the ground. We are not talking about some formula for how you should be, but a process by which you unleash who you could be. This isn't just talk. We've seen it with our eyes, facilitated it with our process, and studied it with our research. But particularly for those of you who are skeptics and analyzers, we want you to know, scientifically, how we got here.

THE GROUNDBREAKING, EYE-OPENING STUDY

Over the years, in Wright programs, a small number of individuals have emerged who have not just learned and grown, solved their problems, and met their goals, but have also seized the opportunities and made quantum leaps in every area of their lives. They have absorbed our curriculum like people dying of thirst in the desert stumbling into an oasis—they were insatiable in their thirst for transformation. They resonated with our curriculum, a synthesis of theories and methods for developing human potential in all areas of life, drawing from the ancient Greeks to the existentialists; behavioral and social sciences; educational, developmental, Adlerian, humanistic, and positive psychology theories and methods; behavioral economics; neuroscience; and the best of other human emergence technologies.

These voracious learners stretched the methods we had carefully developed, forcing still more experimentation and evaluation and resulting in further enhancements in our process.

Looking at these outstanding learners, it was clearly time to engage in yet another round of assessment and curriculum development. While most of our students had learned new skills, grown in their capacities, and made improvements in their lives beyond what they anticipated, these particular students were setting a new standard. We were quite struck by the degree to which they stood out and were transforming their lives, despite participating in the exact same programs as the other students. These high-performing students include:

- *A non-verbal, number-crunching accountant* who became a widely respected author and thought leader in his field, called upon by Congress to provide expert testimony

- *A timid, conservative attorney* who put his job on the line by standing up in a meeting to point out his superiors' flawed strategy and has since become a highly respected COO in the finance arena

- *A couple on the brink of divorce,* at the point of filing papers at the attorney's office, who not only healed their marriage, but created an intimate, loving partnership and began leading couples' trainings to inspire other couples to have the relationship of their dreams

- *A Christian counselor* who touched people so profoundly that he became a minister and a thought leader in the church—deepening his marriage, growing his counseling business, and writing powerfully to enhance the faith and personal growth of others

- *A shy physician,* mother of two, who dealt successfully with divorce and the challenges of a rebellious adolescent while becoming increasingly assertive and experiencing love and intimacy with her new partner

- *A young academic* who went from hiding her true thoughts and feelings and focusing her life on making other people comfortable to becoming an empowering motivational speaker and an inspiration to other women

- *A beautiful party girl* who had been routinely wined and dined and was used to wrapping men around her finger, and then began to develop her inner beauty, changed her values and lifestyle, and returned to college to obtain a degree

Rather than making significant but incremental improvements in various areas of their lives, these students made quantum leaps. They experienced what psychologists refer to as second-order change: sustained life transformations that were not mere improvements but totally new behaviors, positively influencing everything from their relationships to their careers to their spirituality. They were making huge gains in fulfillment, self-esteem, and self-respect, and they were contributing to others in all areas of their lives.

At that moment, we knew we needed objective data on the phenomenon, so we brought in a well-known researcher from outside our culture, Dr. Bill Seidman, an expert in positive deviance research. Positive deviants, as they are known in statistical research, use the same resources as others but perform at extreme levels above the mean (two to three or more standard deviations). Dr. Seidman's research methodology assesses the key elements of positive deviant success and propagates their winning ways throughout a business or organization—including even major world corporations. We wanted him to help us uncover the secrets of our high performers.

Bill began by asking our students to identify the fellow students they saw as positive deviants. Throughout this process, the same names came up consistently, and they were the names of the students we'd identified as the ones making significant exemplary changes in their lives—the students who were transforming. Because Bill limits assessment groups to twelve, we narrowed the field of those identified by their peers as positive deviants down to twelve, and sent them for three days of intense interviewing with Bill. Armed with the objective data that he gathered in the interviews, we conducted our rigorous research using grounded research methodology to discover what these students were doing differently that had led to such dramatic results.

We were blown away by the practicality and elegance of the process our research revealed. It explained why some did not do as well and predicted who would exceed expectations. It gave guidance to help us enhance performance in both those who were struggling and those who were flying. Using our study as well as additional research in neuroscience, psychology, philosophy, and other areas, we have been able to clarify the process revealed by our research and create a useful model that provides a path for conscious engagement in one's own transformation. It harnesses the transformative power revealed by these positive deviants, whom we named Transformers. Just as important, the research revealed the affective and cognitive roadblocks faced on the path to transformation. From this information we continued to devise enhanced methods to overcome these obstacles.

Our research made the distinction between growth and transformation clear and provided a guide for those who really hunger for more in life. The research has guided us to bring together the best of neuroscience and performance studies into a dynamic process.

As with most valid models, the process generalized to a wider range of situations, people, and circumstances. As we expanded our research beyond our students, we gained insight into how human beings learn, grow, and ultimately transform. We were able to glean insights into why one person experienced radical and meaningful life shifts and another person didn't. Why was Josh able to grow and develop in startling ways but Joe struggled to do so? Why did Mary find a way to revamp and revitalize her relationships, her health, and her spirituality, while Jane could make meaningful changes in her career, but not really transform in her life as a whole? Certainly a given individual's attitude and prior experiences, as well as other factors, have an impact on whether he or she transforms. But we also learned that transformation is possible for just about anyone with the right process and assistance along the way. People can make quantum leaps: conformists can become revolutionaries; agnostics can become believers; neurotically shy individuals can become outgoing and engaged; cynics can become idealists. We're going to share the stories of the positive deviants from the study—and of many others who have now learned this powerful process—and we hope their transformations will inspire and amaze you as much as they have inspired and amazed us. Let's start with Laine:

Laine's life wasn't terrible. Like many of our students, she was a successful professional—in her case, her success had been in sales before receiving her doctorate in psychology and getting stuck in a dead-end agency position. She was growing, but she was not happy in her life. Shy, she struggled with relationships as well as with self-esteem. If you were to meet her back then, you would have said that Laine was a pleasant person, but somewhat unassertive and uncertain in her relationships. She sometimes even appeared somewhat cold and aloof. If you were one of her clients, you would have recognized that she was talented. And if Laine ever opened up to you—something she didn't do often—you would have discovered that she wasn't particularly happy or satisfied. Despite her successes, she felt as if she were just getting by. Divorced, Laine had fallen into a pattern of trying to please the guys in her life and neglecting to do or ask for things that would make her happy.

Fast-forward three years: Laine had now become a full-time therapist with her own successful practice. She was more genuine and authentic. Most would even call her warm and inviting. She was becoming a regular educational, inspirational speaker on the lecture circuit, developing a reputation as an expert on a range of subjects.

She was also dating a new man, the first time in her life that she'd had a serious relationship where it wasn't all give and no take. Their relationship was balanced and mutually rewarding, and Laine found herself talking to him with far greater honesty than she had ever talked to anyone. She could even criticize him and face the gut-wrenching fear of making requests that she feared would end the relationship.

The changes in Laine were obvious to those whom she had known over time, including her parents and her sister—her parents were so impressed at the changes she was making that they joined her on the journey of personal development and transformation, taking on issues in their relationship with one another that very few individuals in their seventies and eighties would even consider delving into. Her relationship with her sister deepened and the family as a whole developed a rewarding level of candor and intimacy with one another.

When her parents died within a few months of each other, it was terribly sad, but because truths had been told and nothing had been left unsaid, Laine and her sister were able to celebrate their family's love, what their parents had meant to them, and what they meant to each other as sisters, in a real, genuine way.

If you had met Laine three years earlier and not seen her again until now, you would wonder what had gotten into her. The mild-mannered pleaser of the past has been replaced by a vibrant, engaged woman who is unafraid to speak her mind. Laine used to speak haltingly and quietly, while she now articulates her thoughts clearly, with humor and equanimity and without apology. While elements of the "old" Laine remain—her newfound warmth more readily reveals a core sweetness and sincerity that have always been there—she has changed in so many ways that if you weren't around to witness the hard work that went into her evolution, you might think that only a Faustian pact could have transformed her so completely.

THE TRUTH ABOUT TRANSFORMATION: AN ANTIDOTE TO SNAKE OIL

Your story of transformation may not look like Laine's, but if you're serious about moving beyond change toward a radically fulfilling life, you'll need to understand the four primary truths and misconceptions about transformation.

Truth #1: Transformation occurs on many levels. It affects all of your life . . . not just one area.

People hire a life coach, attend a workshop, or go into therapy to solve a problem or achieve a goal. They focus on wanting to be happier, on not sabotaging relationships, or on getting ahead in their career. That's fine, but solving the problem or achieving the goal is change with a lowercase "c." We're not knocking it; in fact, we help facilitate it because it can provide significant, incremental improvement in a person's life. But it's not transformation, which is all-encompassing. The positive deviants we studied experienced changes in their feelings, their thoughts, their careers, their relationships, their personalities. Everything shifts. Everything from family to career takes on a new meaning. Transformation may result in moving from a job that pays $50,000 to one that pays over a million dollars a year, but it also takes place on less tangible but no less significant levels.

Consider Doug, an MBA and CPA with a high-profile background in a top global consulting firm. He came to us when his life seemed to be falling apart. His wife was threatening to leave him. He had fallen off the partnership track at work and he was seriously contemplating making a radical career shift to become an outdoor leadership instructor. At the time, this change of profession and location seemed transformative to Doug. But it was actually only an escape. We advised him to stay and learn the lessons life was presenting him with where he was, and, if he was going to leave his profession, to leave it as a success.

Going through the Transformed process, he became a Transformer, leading national policy in his field. His spiritual life blossomed, and not only did his wife stay with him but together they developed a deeply loving relationship and partnership and started a family together. The way he interacts with people today is light-years ahead of how he used to interact with them. Not only did he succeed in becoming successful right where he already was, but his career took off beyond his wildest imagination—he was recruited by the top boutique firm in his discipline and he authored the definitive technical book for accounting in his specialized area. He opened the Chicago branch office for another firm which, when it was later sold, led to him opening his own firm.

Partnering with the national and international standards boards, Doug exposed problems in corporate top executive compensation and accounting, transforming the nature of his work as he transformed himself. He risked his secure business by pushing for changes in corporate compensation practices, betting that he would be embraced by the boards of top corporations—which in fact became a reality. He later earned a doctorate, as did his wife.

Truth #2: There's no such thing as a quick fix; transformation is gradual.

When you understand how the brain works and what it takes to build new, lasting neural pathways, you realize that there is no such thing as a quick fix—and anything that offers one is misguided at best and fraudulent at worst. The odds are you've taken a class, been to a workshop, or experienced some other type of learning situation that provided useful ideas about how to transform your life, or some aspect of it. You've spent a few hours or perhaps a few days absorbing theories and exercises that struck you as valuable or maybe even epiphany-producing. You've learned a lot about yourself and what you need to do to change, and you're excited about putting this learning to work. Unfortunately, it's one thing to learn a valuable lesson; it's something else to put it into practice.

Bob learned to play the trombone when he was young. During our *Transform!* weekend training, he tells the audience that he's going to teach them how to play the trombone. He explains how to play the trombone through a quick summary and demonstration—showing how to buzz the lips together to create a higher note versus a lower note. He explains that they now know the essentials necessary to play the instrument and asks, "Who thinks they can now come up here and play the trombone?" Of course, no one says they can. There's a big difference between learning and doing. Even though Bob is no professional-level musician, no one could imagine playing as well as he without hundreds and maybe even thousands of hours of practice. And if playing a musical instrument is so demanding, what is required for radical, positive life transformation?

The transformational process presented in this book will include not just the conceptual model, but a wide variety of assignments and tools to put that model to work for you. Transformation requires daily work, making mistakes, coaching, reflection, and learning-by-doing. There are no shortcuts to transformation—only to temporary, superficial change. And that's the point. Transformation takes time and practice—a lot of both.

When we give in to the allure of a quick-fix solution for permanent, transformational change, we're not only lying to ourselves, we're short-circuiting the possibility of ever having true transformation. From instant messaging to the instant microwave, we are accustomed to fast and easy. So many people have been sold on quick fixes that they've been led to believe that a magic pill or formula exists for everything, including transformation. There is no magic bullet. The magic comes from hard, dedicated work, guided by effective strategy and tactics.

Truth #3: There is no right time. You don't need to want to transform.

This may seem counterintuitive, but most people start to change not because transformation is the goal but because they want to be happier, more successful, or more spiritual. As we noted, most people have more specific objectives than the generalized notion of transformation. You may require a more specific, short-term objective to get you on a transformational path. That's fine. Once you get on the path with the right process, the odds are you will want to progress toward living a great life, and only transformation can take you there.

Understand, too, that as a human being you have an innate drive to learn, to grow, and to transform. We define learning as coming to know something new, and growing as doing something you have never done before. We all want to explore our capabilities, to keep improving our relationships, to achieve more in our careers, to find more meaning in our daily lives. Dr. Diana Fosha, a leader in the new field of interpersonal neurobiology, writes that "People have a fundamental need for transformation. We are wired for growth and healing . . . We have a need for the expansion and liberation of the self, the letting down of defensive barriers, and the dismantling of the false self . . . In the process of radical change, we become more ourselves than ever before, and recognize ourselves to be so . . . [This] overarching motivational force . . . strives toward maximal vitality, authenticity and genuine contact. . . . Residing deeply in our brains are wired-in dispositions for [transformation]."

Most often the proof of this need manifests itself not in a deep desire but in its opposite. When we're not on a transformational path, we are nagged by the feeling that we should be doing something more, that we're missing out on things. We have a vague sense of lost opportunities. This is what the existential philosophers call "ontological guilt," and we try to drive it out of our conscious mind through soft addictions: watching television, gossiping, texting, shopping, and a hundred other things that distract us from the nagging voice in our head telling us that we should be doing more.

So don't feel you need to be driven to change every aspect of your life in order to start transforming. A vague dissatisfaction or inkling of desire will do. Most of our students began with small steps and accelerated their learning and growth over time.

Truth #4: Transformation is ongoing and all-encompassing.

> *I transformed my body by losing 100 pounds and working out every day.*
> *I transformed my mind with five years of therapy.*
> *I transformed my spirit through meditation.*
> *I transformed my low self-esteem into high self-esteem through a*

weekend workshop of intense role-playing, emotional stretching exercises, and coaching.

The "T" word is used regularly by a variety of self-improvement professionals and their patients, clients, and students. Too often, their versions of transformation, while desirable, are limited and temporary. For instance, therapy can be tremendously helpful, but it's much more focused on solving problems than on holistic, continuous change and the realization of full human potential. After all, the literal purpose of therapy is to return patients to a pre-morbid state—the condition they were in prior to the development of their problems. Similarly, diets and workouts may create a new physical you, but they don't touch all the other areas of your life.

Consider transformation from a statistical perspective. In 2008, 2.6 million kids played Little League baseball; the total number of professional baseball players playing that year: 1200. So the odds of a kid growing up to play in the majors are pretty slim. In the same way, people enter into all sorts of self-improvement programs and processes dreaming of a new life. They too have slim odds; some of them may experience a temporary but positive change in one area of their lives or they may solve a problem that's been hampering their careers or relationships or physical or mental well-being, but they are not likely to transform and live a great life.

Among Wright students, ninety-six percent report experiencing significant lasting change; twenty to forty percent experience transformation, and many of the rest are still in the process of change and/or transformation. Therefore, the process presented in this book provides you with much better odds than you'll receive elsewhere. It's not a guarantee that you'll transform, but it's the next best thing.

THE TRANSFORMATIVE PROCESS: THE SIX PHASES

Earlier we used a caterpillar-to-butterfly metaphor to illustrate the process of transformation, and for some of you, the journey from ungainly and crawling to beautiful and soaring may have been appealing. But others of you no doubt are aware that the transitional phase between caterpillar and butterfly can be a bit disconcerting. When the caterpillar is in its chrysalis—the silky threads that encase its body—it begins a process called histolysis in which it digests itself from the inside out. Essentially, it becomes a gelatinous mass before it reconfigures itself into a butterfly.

Thankfully, none of our students have become literal jellied blobs, but most of them have struggled with their transitions. This is to be expected. As you learn and grow and change in different ways, you may become anxious about what you're leaving behind. You may be scared by some of the actions you need to take in order to live a great life. You'll also experience many positive emotions, but it would be wrong to pretend that personal transformation is a smooth, easy path. Like life itself, it can be messy.

Fortunately, unlike the caterpillar, you're not alone and without a guide within your chrysalis. We've found that what facilitates transformation more than anything else is a viable process. What's scary is when you're afraid, alone, and in the dark. A tried-and-true process provides direction and support. All the positive deviants in our study leaned on the *Transformed!* process as they made meaningful changes in their lives. The clearly defined process acts as a compass to help you navigate the challenges of the transformational journey. As you'll discover, we will provide not only a description of the phases of the process but also related tools and stories designed to instruct and inspire you.

For now, though, we'd like to give you a sense of the phases of the process and how they work.

YEARNING: A desire or universal longing to create, to connect, to touch and be touched, to love and be loved, to be seen, to matter, to be heard, to contribute, to help and be helped. It arises momentarily and is gone, only to reappear for another brief time. Transformers tend to their deeper yearning, recognizing and acting on it more than others. Yearning is different from wanting—we want to make a lot of money, to be entertained, to look good. We all have wants, but yearning is a driver of transformation, while wants are drivers of goals and, at their most problematic, can also feed into our soft addictions. When we know what we yearn for, we possess the motivational energy and direction to take the next step in the process.

ENGAGING: Spontaneous, uncensored, in-the-moment responses to the urges generated by our deeper yearning. Engaging involves responding to, rather than ignoring or repressing, these urges. Obviously, we can't give in to every urge, but we do need to identify whether our urges relate to a true yearning, and if they do, we need to find ways to respond to them through our behaviors. We have to learn to act on our yearnings if we are going to start changing our behaviors in meaningful ways.

REVELATING: A term that describes both the awareness of ourselves and of new possibilities as well as the act of revealing ourselves in expression. Revelating can be inspirational, like discovering a new possibility for a course of action, or ominous, such as when we realize we are programmed. In this phase we realize we've been operating under a self-fulfilling prophecy managed by a "matrix" of mistaken beliefs and limited thinking that has been holding us back, restricting our happiness and fulfillment. As we start acting differently, revelating helps us start thinking differently.

LIBERATING: Stepping out of the cage of habitual living, doing the undoable and saying the unsayable. Liberating is doing something contrary to the limiting program, or matrix, discovered in revelating. Transformers develop a lifestyle of liberating. Directed by what they discover in the revelating phase, they consistently engage in new behaviors outside former habits and routines. In this phase, we are starting to transform our actions in significant ways—we are able to break away from old, limiting patterns, from how we acted in work settings to how we interact in relationships.

REMATRIXING: Doing it again and again to help build new neural pathways. Rematrixing is the watchword of Transformers. Liberating may feel great, but if we do not repeat those liberating moves intentionally and often, the transformation will stop dead in its tracks and we won't rematrix. We may believe we've transformed when we break from our routines and embrace a new way of behaving, but, in most cases, we have merely learned and grown. Essentially, rematrixing means reprogramming our brains—changing our beliefs and our behavior. Rematrixing capitalizes on our brain plasticity—research demonstrates that to transform ourselves, we need to create new neural pathways. Without rematrixing, lasting change and transformation won't happen. Rematrixing teaches us how to rewire our mind by practicing new ways of being—consciously, repetitively, and intentionally.

DEDICATING: This final phase is about a lifelong commitment to conscious, sustained, intentional action that goes beyond habitual behavior. This may not seem like much, but our research shows us it's what allows people to live continuously great lives. Dedicating means making an unbreakable commitment to transformation. When we are truly dedicated, we recognize that greatness doesn't come from settling or stopping with what we already have—it comes from continually yearning, engaging, revelating, liberating, and rematrixing.

Although we've listed these phases in order and each one will receive its own chapter, in real life they aren't always so neatly separated. On a given day, you may liberate, discover a new yearning, and engage anew. On other days, you may go to bed having revelated and awaken with yet another insight that causes you to access yet a deeper level of yearning. All of these activities can fit into rematrixing if you are dedicating. Or you may find yourself spending a lot more time on revelating than liberating or vice versa. What you'll learn to do is keep all the phases in mind since they are part of a whole. After a certain amount of practice, you'll find yourself able to draw on all six phases within the course of your daily routine.

In addition, understand that these six phases are continuous rather than finite. In other words, you're going to be cycling through them over and over. It's not as if you spend one day on dedicating and then you're done. You'll keep returning to it and the other phases, finding new assignments and applying them within new life contexts. In this way, you'll gradually integrate the phases into who you are—a critical achievement if you are to be a Transformer.

The Transformed! Process

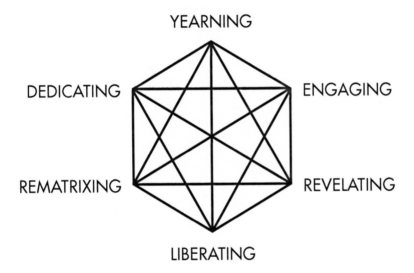

YEARNING

DEDICATING

ENGAGING

REMATRIXING

REVELATING

LIBERATING

THEORY AND PRACTICE

What's the difference between learning, growth, and transformation?

First: Learning is knowing something you didn't know before; growing is doing something you haven't done before; and transforming is becoming someone you wouldn't have imagined being before. The problem comes when people use the words interchangeably; they attend a great seminar, acquire mind-blowing concepts, and believe this knowledge has changed their lives—that they have transformed. In fact, they've learned, which is an essential *part* of transforming but not *synonymous* with it.

When you look at these three terms within the context of the phases, you can see the differences more clearly. Many coaching, seminar, therapy, and spiritual development methodologies tap a level of yearning and take participants through revelating—this involves learning. Other activities add liberating—this requires growth. Some help people begin to rematrix but fall short of transformation, lacking the technology to help their adherents master dedicating.

Transformation means becoming different, not just better. There is nothing wrong with better, in fact it can lead to transformation, but it is insufficient as a true catalyst of transformation on its own. In order for transformation to be a fact, we need to be doing something totally different so that we become materially changed. Many may seem to be transformed, but then they fall back, and their changes do not last. Our research revealed that these learners did not dedicate. Transformation requires maintenance—"use it or lose it" is a reality. While you may never again be a ninety-pound weakling, without transformation, you will likely be a camouflaged weakling, capable of fooling all but the truly transformed.

In the diagram below, you will see how transformation works. Learning takes place among the first three phases: yearning, engaging, and revelating. Growing requires the fourth: liberating. Transformation takes repeated, intentional action, thought, and feeling in rematrixing, and it must be maintained with dedication.

The Transformed! Process:
Growing vs. Transforming

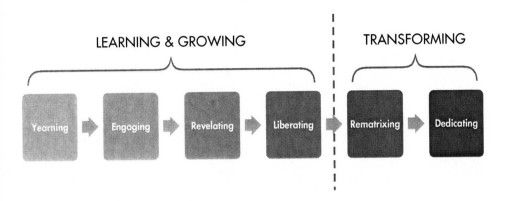

The *Transformed!* process can be used as a tool of self-evaluation and planning, as well as a map. It explains learning and growth, diagnosing what happens in successful as well as failed growth moves. It can help you to plan and strategize—providing a tool to predict successful approaches and minimize failed efforts.

By identifying the developmental phase you have completed, are currently in, or have yet to enter, you can assess your progress and where you still need to go. It works like any guide, helping you get your bearings. For instance, in many self-development programs, people stop short of their potential because they get stuck and don't realize they simply have to move to the next phase to get unstuck. With this graphic in hand, you're less likely to stop doing your personal development work because you didn't experience significant change after going through an introductory training course; you can see that you failed to use your yearning to propel you into the engaging phase.

This process is a continual engagement in the next level of what is possible for human beings. As you become a Transformer, you keep setting the bar higher, not only achieving increasingly ambitious goals, but also deriving increasing satisfaction from your achievements—as well as from your everyday moments.

At this point, you may be asking yourself: Is Transforming worth it? We have two answers for you, the first one scientific, the second, experiential.

BRAIN CHANGE

Until relatively recently, the conventional wisdom was that we are stuck with the brains we were born with. We assumed that the brain was static rather than dynamic and that we needed to accept our cognitive limitations. But an overwhelming body of new scientific research—especially in the area of neuroscience—has shattered these assumptions. This research makes a strong case for "brain plasticity" or "neuroplasticity"—the ability of the brain to reconfigure neural pathways based on experience and learning. From a transformational standpoint, what this means is that we can use our malleable minds to grow and develop as human beings. We can learn more effective ways of relating to people; we can escape our routines and establish new ways of living; we can master skills and explore jobs and careers that we thought we couldn't handle; we can push ourselves past the limits we artificially imposed on ourselves and stretch mentally, physically, emotionally, and spiritually.

Most people, however, never take advantage of their brain's plasticity. Transformers, in contrast, capitalize on it as a means to *rewire their mind* to become the person they previously never thought they could become. A unique you emerges naturally as you live the phases of the transformative process. The bottom line is that "rewiring your mind" is not hyperbole or something to be taken figuratively. Instead, it is absolutely literally possible, and you don't have to go into a science lab or rely on electrodes or a surgeon's scalpel to do it.

Daniel Siegel, an expert in interpersonal neurobiology and author of *Mindsight,* writes: "We know from findings of neuroscience that the mental and emotional changes we can create . . . are transformational at the very physical level of the brain." Siegel's perspective on focused attention translates directly to aspects of our findings that are the key to rewiring: that "by developing the ability to focus our attention on our internal world" (what we call yearning), "we are picking up a 'scalpel' we can use to resculpt our neural pathways [engage, revelate, liberate, and rematrix], stimulating areas of the brain that are crucial to mental health and well-being."

Neuropsychiatrist Dr. Jeffrey Schwartz reinforces this concept with what he calls "attention density." His belief is that if we want to create change in our lives, we must pay concentrated and consistent attention to all the issues surrounding a given change. Attention density activates brain circuitry and, over time and with repetition, it actually alters the structure of the brain. In this way, "the mind does change the brain."

Here are some additional pieces of research that, when taken as a whole, offer a powerful argument for using the mind to change the brain:

- *IQ can be raised by 21 points over four years.* In a *Newsweek* article published in early 2012, reporter Sharon Begley documented the work of cognitive scientist Cathy Price and other researchers. The researchers' findings indicated that not only can IQ be raised significantly through intense focus, but also that physical changes occur in the brain that correspond to an improved IQ.

- *Studies of monks found that the more they meditated, the more gray matter they developed* and the more long-lasting gamma wave activity they manifested. In studies of monks who have meditated for many years, Dr. Richard Davidson's research revealed that meditating monks' brains had increased gray matter in the structures associated with compassion, self-awareness, empathy, sense of self, and happiness. Dr. Andrew Newberg, an expert on the effect of prayer on brain activity, has found that intense prayer and meditation changes numerous structures and functions in the brain—and that these changes can impact values as well as perceptions.

▪ *Numerous studies demonstrate that brain plasticity can be increased even in aging adults.* An amazing example of this is the case of Pedro Bach-y-Rita as told in *The Brain That Changes Itself* by Norman Doidge. Bach-y-Rita, a Catalan poet and scholar, suffered a debilitating stroke from which none of his doctors felt he could recover. At the time, brain plasticity was yet to be discovered. Refusing this prognosis, his son George, a psychiatrist, dedicated himself to his father's full recovery. Day in and day out, for over a year, George helped his father practice the repeated micro-movements that helped form new neuronal connections to replace the necrotic ones damaged by the stroke. To the amazement of all, Pedro was eventually able to resume his teaching, writing, and vigorous outdoor activities.

The point of these studies is simple but profound: We possess the cognitive capability to change our brains and change our lives. Throughout these pages, we'll use terms like rewiring, reprogramming, and rematrixing to describe how we can capitalize on brain plasticity. By pushing ourselves to learn new things, to engage in activities we've never engaged in before, to stretch our capabilities by tackling projects that we once deemed too difficult, we change our brains and facilitate our own transformations.

WHY TRANSFORM?

We can provide 101 reasons why personal transformation is beneficial, but the best one of all is this: You will give birth to a greater you. Regardless of your age or personal development to date, you don't know who that greater you is, but you've probably had glimpses. You've thought to yourself, *If I only did x, I could have achieved so much.* Or you imagine having a different, much more satisfying relationship with your spouse, your children, your parents. Or you dream about all the good you might accomplish for humankind if only you had the right team or you didn't have all the responsibilities, the financial concerns, the self-doubt. Somewhere deep inside of you, you understand that you could be greater than you are.

Transformation is the path to releasing this greater person from the recesses of your mind and bringing him or her to life. There's nothing egotistic, inauthentic, or delusional in wanting to have a great life. In fact, it's a perfectly natural impulse. Cultural evolutionists such as Andrew Cohen and Ken Wilber talk about how people want to participate in their own evolution and reach the next level of development. We're not made to settle for good over great, to accept comfort instead of challenge. We all have a drive to explore and learn, but society or our own upbringing often dampen that drive, and we believe we can only do or achieve or be so much and no more.

If we were to ask you what you want out of life, we doubt that any of you would respond with, "Greatness." If you're like most people, you have very specific goals related to career, relationships, family, spirituality, and other areas of life. This process will help you achieve those goals— actually enabling you to surpass them—but that's a byproduct of the larger objective. Remember our earlier litmus test for transformation: *doing or becoming something that you could never have imagined doing or becoming.* At some point in the future, if you work at the process of transformation, you're going to find yourself doing the unimaginable. It may start with you being brutally honest with a scary, hypercritical boss, telling him why his strategy won't work. It might involve your going on a pilgrimage when you've never done anything resembling sacred travel before (or even ever thought of yourself as someone who would do such a thing). It might mean reconnecting with a loved one you haven't spoken with for twenty years. It might mean sticking with a job you hate until you master it. It might mean starting your own company when you've always worked for someone else.

But best of all, transformation will affect every single area of your life—your whole life project. What's truly exciting for us is watching people transform into what we refer to as their next most radiant self. If we could show you before-and-after pictures of students who have experienced what psychologists refer to as second-order change—a level of change that is much broader and deeper than the norm—it would be far more dramatic than the before-and-afters of people who have lost a hundred pounds. It's as if they've shed the disguises they've been wearing for years and revealed who they really are. It's as if they've changed from caterpillars to butterflies.

CHAPTER THREE

YEARN:
IGNITE YOUR TRANSFORMATION

We are desire. It is the essence of the human soul, the secret of our existence. Absolutely nothing of human greatness is ever accomplished without it. Not a symphony has been written, a mountain climbed, an injustice fought, or a love sustained apart from desire. Desire fuels our search for the life we prize.
—JOHN ELDREDGE

IF YOU'RE LIKE MOST PEOPLE, you know what you want. In fact, if pressed, you could probably rattle off a laundry list of wants: cars, houses, vacations, jobs, electronic devices, and so on. But when it comes to what you yearn for, you may draw a blank.

There's something vaguely old-fashioned about the term. It has an Old Testament ring to it. Or it sounds like what a heroine in a Victorian novel might say as she stares out the window of her Gothic tower waiting for a lost love to return. As a result, you probably haven't used "yearn" in a sentence recently. It feels awkward on your tongue, uncertain in your mind . . . and hardly the dynamic power and fuel of transformation.

When we talk of transformation, we are not talking about a formula but rather about something deeply personal that emerges from within—a unique, new you. Take a moment to reflect upon what you yearn for. Let your mind go blank and listen to your heart. Imagine if your soul had a voice and could articulate what it wants most in the world. Or, more simply, consider what you desire deeply, what would turn your good life into a great one.

Still nothing? That's okay. Yearning is a natural capacity you can develop.

Or maybe you've come up with a list of things you yearn for that are actually wants—you "yearn" to be rich, you "yearn" to travel around the world, you "yearn" for freedom, you "yearn" to have your boyfriend or girlfriend agree to marry you, you "yearn" for a gigantic television. It's okay, too, to mistake wants for yearnings—we all do it, but it rarely leads to transformation.

The good news is that we know what you yearn for—and it's exactly that yearning that generates transformation. The things you yearn for are the same things that everyone in the world yearns for. Specifically, we yearn:

- to matter
- to love and be loved
- to be seen
- to contribute
- to connect
- to belong
- to achieve mastery
- to be affirmed
- to connect with a higher power

There are different ways to parse these yearnings—Maslow's hierarchy of needs is one way to view them—and we'll look at them through various lenses, from stories of those who have learned to yearn effectively, to perspectives from a range of fields including education, positive psychology, neuroscience, and behavioral economics. But for now, recognize that these yearnings are universal, and that by getting in touch with them, you open your life to the possibility of greatness.

So all you have to do is memorize this list and you're set? If only it were that easy, we could limit the frustration of career dissatisfaction, the disappointment of unfulfilling relationships, and much general emotional pain and upset with a snap of our fingers. Getting in touch with what you yearn for is an attainable skill, but you need to learn the entire process. We know—the word "process" sounds dull and formulaic. But this particular process is neither of those things. Instead, it's challenging, exciting, and transformational.

The first step requires you to apply yearning to your own life. You see, even though we all yearn for the same things, this doesn't mean that we all do the same things to achieve what we yearn for. I may follow my yearning to connect through interactions with my team at work, while you may follow your yearning through intimate relationships. I may yearn to have an influence in the world and fulfill it through my career while you fulfill your similar yearning primarily through raising a family. I may pursue my yearning for a sense of mastery by public speaking while you pursue yours by both playing and teaching chess.

The opportunity to fulfill our yearnings exists in every moment of every day. That means that the power of transformation is available in every moment too, if only we would learn to access the fuel— our yearning. The trick that leads to our development is learning to recognize and respond to these moments consistently. And we're not talking about that once-in-a-lifetime desire—to take a round-the-world vacation or to retire. We can get what we yearn for during even the most mundane of routines—we can find great meaning while doing a home repair project, in the middle of the night when we can't fall asleep, or while driving across the state on a business trip.

We're all on different yearning paths, even though we are all headed toward the same ultimate destination. So it's a bit tricky to translate universal yearnings into our individual lives. To make it less tricky, let's analyze a much beloved movie and its protagonist who mistook his want for a yearning.

GEORGE BAILEY DID NOT YEARN TO TRAVEL

You have probably seen *It's a Wonderful Life*, the mid-forties Frank Capra movie starring Jimmy Stewart. It's a beloved movie for many reasons, including the way it taps into our yearning. Think about Jimmy Stewart's character, George Bailey, who's convinced that he yearns to travel to exotic places, that he can only truly be happy when he is freed from his responsibilities in Bedford Falls and can travel to the four corners of the earth.

He's relying on a false formula for fulfillment, but he is absolutely convinced it's the right one. It is only when that formula is proven false that he gets in touch with his deeper yearning to connect, care, love, and be loved. All George has to do is shift the way he views what he most desires—replacing his obsession with travel with the moment-by-moment desire to be fully alive, to be connected to friends and family, to be loved, to care for and love them in return—and suddenly, he is no longer antsy, stressed out, unhappy. In touch with his yearning, every moment becomes special—just being able to hold Zuzu's petals, a gift from his daughter that he thought had disappeared, is now a cherished moment for him, as he comes to derive tremendous meaning from even small gestures.

We all deserve to experience Zuzu's petals—not just one time but thousands of times in our lifetimes. Imagine having experiences every day that are truly fulfilling and meaningful, that provide you with such heartfelt, soul-stirring satisfaction that you want for little else. That's what happens when you know what you yearn for and you strive for it regularly—your life project becomes a journey of fulfilling your yearnings. Generally, breakthrough moments like George's "I want to live again" revelation are the result of many moments of yearning that have a cumulative effect. They build up to transformational moments like he had. However, often many of us have simply not been aware of our yearning, or have pursued in error the things we thought would satisfy it. Thus our yearnings have often gone unmet. And so to truly satisfy them, we must first address the errors we make in wanting.

MISWANTING: WHY I CAN'T GET NO . . . SATISFACTION

Unfortunately, when it comes to yearning, we are our own worst enemy. We are, as positive psychologists Daniel Gilbert and Timothy Wilson have noted, guilty of "miswanting." We convince ourselves that something will make us happy, but in reality that something does nothing more than provide a brief, temporary buzz. As a result, we ignore our deeper yearnings and focus on surface wants.

If you're skeptical about this last statement, understand that this is the way our brains are wired. Neuroscientists have identified different pleasure centers in the brain, and one is related to our wants or cravings and one to our feelings of deeper satisfaction. Dopamine is released in our brain when we anticipate and indulge our wants or cravings, while opioids are released when we meet deeper needs. We choose the dopamine over the opioids almost every time. We confuse dopamine's stimulation with satisfaction . . . and end up in a spiral of wanting without the fulfillment of the opioid-generating center of the brain. We want what we want, and we want it now! We don't engage in internal debates such as, "Should I eat that huge bowl of ice cream or should I strive to meet my deeper hunger to matter in the world?" We scarf down the ice cream without a moment's hesitation. We numb our tongue—and ourselves—to our deeper requirements.

In our workshops, we often do an exercise that illustrates the feelings we experience as we go after our wants. Try this exercise with a friend:

Take a moment and think of what you want in this particular moment in time. It can be anything in the world—from food to the latest smartphone to vacations to jobs to wealth. Have your friend set a timer for one minute, and then complete the sentence "I want _____," out loud, cramming in as many wants as you can within one minute, pretending that you can obtain every want you articulate in this time frame. When the timer goes off, switch roles. When you have both completed your minute, take a few seconds for both of you to simultaneously say out loud what you want as quickly as possible. Now, take a bit of time to reflect on how you feel. Then compare notes and share your feelings with each other.

If you're like most people, you'll feel "buzzed": energized, high, excited. This is the same feeling that you receive when you engage in these wanting behaviors. You feel that rush of anticipation when you eat a bag of cookies or when you buy that cool new outfit or when your day trading nets you a big gain. But this buzz is temporary. More to the point, it creates the illusion that this is what provides us with profound happiness. If you've ever bought a hot car, cool gadget, or other sexy high-ticket item, you know what we mean. In fact, there's a term for it: buyer's remorse. People spend weeks or months wishing and wanting, and when they finally achieve the object of their desire, it's a rush. Then it is all over, and the ensuing emptiness causes us to seek the next acquisition or goal. We had such high expectations, and yet somehow, they aren't met by actually possessing the object of our wanting.

That initial buzz does, however, enable us to avoid thinking about what we really yearn for. It allows us to focus on something more easily obtainable, something that will send a surge of dopamine through our brains. The same can be true of anticipated sporting events, television shows, dates, and almost anything. We may have been convinced that the cool car, latest techno-gadget, vacation home, designer dress, or plasma television was what would provide us with true happiness, but as it turns out, we are poor predictors of what makes us lastingly and fully happy. Positive psychologists call it poor affective forecasting.

Even more troubling, after we discover that the new plasma TV doesn't provide the long-term joy we expected, we fail to learn from our mistake. You would think we would recognize that vacations, electronic devices, and job promotions are not what provide us with sustained happiness after the second or third time, but we continue to miswant. In our minds, we tell ourselves that even though the job promotion or the beautiful house in the country failed to offer sustained satisfaction, perhaps it is really the luxury boat that we need to be happy; or the new trophy wife; or the latest version of the iPad; or the trip to Aruba.

The problem isn't just in our heads and the pleasure centers in our brains. We also become confused about what really makes us happy because of all the external messages we receive. Not to pick on Apple, but that company's advertising is so slick and sophisticated that it's easy to envision your life becoming infinitely better once you purchase their devices. Advertising, television shows and movies, romance novels, Web sites, and music videos all intensify our miswanting. Stressed out by a high-pressure job, trying to grapple with rebellious teenaged children, concerned about financial issues, we can fall prey to media messages that deify objects: a car, a diamond ring, and a cruise all appear to be transformative.

Therefore, you need to be able to differentiate what you want versus what you yearn for if you are to become a Transformer. Let's look at some techniques and tools for doing so.

THE "SO THAT" RED FLAG

Wanting is external, and yearning is internal. In other words, what you want resides outside the core of who you are. You want things, positions, cars, job titles, money. Yearning, though, goes to your essence: you yearn for mastery, for connection, to matter. What confuses matters, though, is that what you want is connected to what you yearn for. You may want to make a lot of money, but it's related to your yearning to touch and be touched, to be loved, or valued. On the outside, you want to make a lot of money because you believe that you'll be more desirable, or treated with more respect, or that others will envy you if you're wealthy. Deeper down, however, you long to have more contact with others, for them to love you for who you are, not what you have; or you long to make contributions to the lives of others. Becoming wealthy may provide you with a brief burst of happiness, but relatively soon, you'll experience a growing sense of dissatisfaction because you're not meeting your deeper yearning. This is a critical differentiator: meeting a want provides fleeting happiness while responding to a yearning provides longer-lasting and deeper satisfaction.

Wants can be very seductive and appear to be the key to this satisfaction.

Lucy, for instance, dreamed of becoming the first woman to be named managing partner of her corporate law firm. In Lucy's mind, this and only this was what she was striving for. She told herself it wasn't just for the prestige of the title or the money, but that she wanted to do it to open doors for other women. She dreamed of people talking about her as a pioneer, a groundbreaker.

Dreams are great, and they can motivate people to achieve significant goals, but even so, they often are merely wants in grand disguises. This doesn't mean you shouldn't pursue your dreams. Recognize, though, that we yearn for more than being the head of a firm or being viewed as an innovator.

At a deeper level, Lucy yearned to touch and be touched, to matter, and to have a sense of mastery. Her dream of becoming head of her law firm seemed on the surface to be related to that yearning, but even when her dream came true, there were problems. It didn't fully satisfy her—because she had not fully recognized or directly addressed her yearnings.

At first when Lucy became the managing partner, she was ecstatic, her friends threw a big party for her, and, as she said, "I was on a high for a week." But in the weeks that followed, Lucy came crashing down to earth—she found herself enmeshed in the details of being a managing partner and spending hours each day with what she viewed as petty problems, policy, and paperwork. She also found it difficult to put her policies into place because of resistance from other senior partners. Within a few months, she began to think that she had made a huge mistake as she realized that she disliked her new role.

It took some work on Lucy's part to recognize that her yearning was to touch and be touched and to matter, and upon that recognition—as we'll see later in the chapter—she began restructuring her life in many ways, both at work and at home.

Our point is that while some wants are easy to identify as wants—various objects like clothes and cars, for example—others are trickier to discern. Don't assume, therefore, that just because you've aspired to something for a long time or feel a burning desire to achieve a particular goal that it means it's more than a want. Lucy's example has hopefully disabused you of that assumption. Her original goals were driven by, but not directly informed by, her deeper yearning. She wanted to be managing partner so that she could have more power and control. She wanted more power and control so that she could make a difference in the firm. She wanted to make a difference in the firm so that she could be more important. She wanted to be more important so that she could touch others and matter to them—all of which she learned had been available the entire time, each step of the way in her career.

How can you determine whether something is what you want or what you yearn for? Ask yourself what a given want, aspiration, or goal will do for you. It may not be immediately obvious; however, if you keep looking beneath your wants, it can lead you to your deeper yearnings. Subject your fervent wishes and desires to the "So That" litmus test:

Take a piece of paper and write down three goals, or objects, or situations that you believe will make you enormously happy. Put this in the form of the following sentence: "I want ＿＿＿＿＿＿ so that ＿＿＿＿＿＿."

For instance:
"I want to be a CEO so that my dad will be proud of me."
"I want that new Jaguar so that people will respect me.
"I want to lose weight so that I look sexy."
"I want him to ask me out so that I feel good about myself."
"I want a promotion so that I can have more money."

In many cases, if your desire is a want, then you will be able to fill in the blank after "so that." And, each want leads to another. Wants are never the end of the line. If it's a yearning, however, you may have trouble coming up with a final statement of "so that." That's because what we yearn for is enough. Yearning is an end in and of itself. We yearn to see and be seen, to connect, to touch and be touched— we're not doing it for any reason other than the pure longing.

FROM WANTING TO YEARNING

Now, go back to your list and see if there are other levels of "so that's."

Keep going until there is no other so that—chances are you have now gotten to the yearning underneath your want or goal. For instance:

"I want a promotion so that I can have more money."

"I want more money in order to be able to have more fun and skydive more."

"I want to skydive so that I feel the thrill."

"I want to feel the thrill of skydiving so that I can feel alive."

"I want to feel alive . . . I *yearn* to feel alive."

Knowing the yearnings beneath your goals makes the achieving of them much more satisfying. And, ironically, focusing on the yearning in daily life leads to achieving many more goals than you imagined. While goals are fine, we don't have to wait until we get a raise and go skydiving to fulfill a deeper yearning such as feeling alive. Focusing on the deeper yearning leads you to be more present and engaged every day. Being more present and engaged, you are more likely to win that promotion—and a whole lot more. And, when you do achieve your goals, you will be much more satisfied.

Yearning is the heart of intrinsic motivation—the motivation to transform that comes from inside ourselves and is satisfying in and of itself; wants are extrinsic motivation—wanting something so that we get some other reward. With intrinsic motivation, not only are we more satisfied, but we also achieve more. Behavioral economics and motivational researchers have proven that intrinsic motivators result in higher achievement and enjoyment than extrinsic ones do. Spontaneous exploration, curiosity, greater creativity, and productivity are results of intrinsic motivation. It seems that intrinsic motivation is strongly related to what neuroscientists have identified as the satisfaction center in our brains, which is activated by our yearning. Both are scientific validation of the importance and the power of yearning versus wanting.

Another key differentiator between wanting and yearning involves specificity versus universality. You know it's a want when your wish involves a highly specific outcome, person, brand, or style. You want a Kate Spade bag, the newest iPad, Jimmy Choo shoes, to date Josh, to attend a professional baseball dream camp, to spend the summer in Greece. These are as opposed to the universal desires to matter, to make a difference, to have influence. Keep in mind too that you may express these universal desires in terms that are a bit different than ours. For instance, we talk about the yearning to make an impact; you may express it as a yearning to be seen and heard. Nonetheless, it's the same shared yearning, and that universality differentiates it from a more specific, individualized want.

UNIVERSAL YEARNINGS

Here are some of the universal yearnings we share as human beings. While you probably can relate to them all, say them out loud to see which have special resonance for you. I yearn...

Survival and a sense of existence
...to exist

A reflection of your existence
...to be seen
...to be heard
...to be touched

An appreciation of your existence
...to be loved
...to be affirmed
...to be respected

An expression of your existence
...to express
...to experience fully
...to learn, to grow
...to trust, to develop
...to touch
...to create

Exchange and connectedness with other people
...to be known
...to be understood
...to matter

...to know another person
...to be close
...to feel connected to others
...to make deep contact with another
...to be intimate
...to love

A sense of mattering
...to matter
...to be valued and to value
...to do what I came here to do on earth
...to make a difference
...to please God
...to fulfill my purpose
...to unfold my destiny

Ultimate union with the Divine
...to feel connected to the greater whole
...to be one with all
...to know God
...to feel union with the Divine

THE DIFFERENCE BETWEEN A GOOD AND A GREAT LIFE

Now let us return to lawyer Lucy and what happened when she made the transition from wanting to yearning.

Smart, empathetic, and attractive, Lucy was one of those people who seemed capable of getting anything she wanted. In fact, before she even graduated from her law school, she did what so many highly motivated individuals do: she made a list of goals. In the next decade, she focused on achieving these goals, devoting a great deal of time and energy to accomplishing them. Some of the goals were related to her career—she wanted to make partner at a major law firm before she was thirty-five, and she made it with two years to spare.

Lucy also wanted to marry "a stable, decent guy, someone who is a professional"; and she found him at age twenty-seven. And she wanted to have two kids before she turned thirty—she just made it to that goal. There were other smaller goals—a beautiful house in a particularly prestigious suburb, trips to Paris, London, Barcelona, and so on. All achieved.

But by the time Lucy turned forty, she had become increasingly dissatisfied with her life. Here she was, managing partner, at the top of her firm and profession. She couldn't quite figure it out, since everything was going well both personally and professionally. The feeling intensified over her first and only year as managing partner. As much as she tried to shake it off—she felt guilty for complaining since she had achieved so many of her goals—it wouldn't go away.

Within a year, she had talked to the partners' management committee and asked to be replaced. She recognized that she needed to make changes in her life, though she didn't know exactly what they needed to be. Feeling stuck and confused, Lucy came to us for coaching.

As part of the coaching process, Lucy began learning about herself. The more self-aware she became, the more Lucy realized that there was something beneath all her wants that she had been missing. Lucy yearned to touch and be touched, to matter, and to make a difference, and the higher she had gone in the firm, the less she seemed to matter. Everything from her choice of a husband to her career decisions had been dictated by societal standards. Measured by these standards, Lucy was leading a good life. Measured by her deeper sense of herself, however, she was nowhere near the great life she yearned for.

Lucy began to recognize the deeper yearnings that really motivated her, and she restructured her life. She began by trying to relate to clients not just on a business level but as individuals with a range of issues and concerns—about everything from the future of their companies to retirement to their own professional growth. When she broadened and deepened her approach, Lucy found she was making a much more significant contribution. This energized her; she felt as if she were truly partnering with her clients. In turn, her higher level of drive and commitment enhanced her performance. Lucy was adding value in a way she never had before. Her clients gave her more work and she attracted more clients to the firm. In the process, she added to her staff and became more interested in developing her people—she loved watching them learn and grow, and soon she was overwhelmed with associates clamoring to work in her group.

Resigning as managing partner was only a first step. Over the next few years, Lucy made additional changes in her life, and they all revolved around her yearning to touch and be touched and to matter. More subtly, she and her husband evolved their relationship— they had regular dates, provided each other with much more honest conversation and feedback, and helped each other grow both personally and professionally. Lucy cut back on her over-the-top exercise regimen, devoting more time to a personal project she had long wanted to make happen—coaching her children's teams and spending more one-on-one time with each of them. The kids looked forward to their special time each week with Mom.

The greatest surprise to Lucy was the deepening of her prayer life. She had been taught to pray as a child, but it had been more a matter of habit than a personal relationship with a higher power. The yearning for contact with the Creator was strong in her and she wondered how much of her earlier accomplishments had been driven by misguided attempts to meet that deep need. In ways both small and large, in every aspect of her life, Lucy was learning to be guided by her yearning.

Getting in touch with her yearning freed Lucy to be who she really wanted to be. Lucy was able to grasp what yearning meant to her and recognize it from one moment to the next. Let's look at how you can do the same.

URGES: YEARNING IN THE MOMENT

Like yearning, *urge* is a word you probably don't think much about. Consider that urges might not be what you assume they are, since people misuse the term frequently. For instance, urges are different than cravings: you crave a candy bar; you have the urge to sing a favorite Beatles song at the top of your lungs. The former is what we term a soft addiction—the need for instant but very short-lived pleasure, whether from a candy bar, a new outfit, or watching television. Urges originate in a deeper place, and they are very much in and of the moment.

Urges are impulses that arise from what we yearn for. Unlike cravings, they are highly individual and, at times, idiosyncratic. These urges bubble up from inside of us—they're not conscious decisions. Through early socialization, we learn not to give in to these urges but to govern them instead. We're taught that it's not socially acceptable to do whatever something inside of us is urging us to do. You can't break into song in the front row in the middle of a presidential inauguration address no matter how powerful your urge to do so might be. At the same time, this urge is related to a deeper yearning—you want to celebrate, to have a connection, to impact those in attendance. The point is, you can pay attention to this urge and identify the yearning that gave birth to it even when you do not act directly on it. There are innumerable urges coursing through us at any given moment. Just as a surfer doesn't catch every wave, we don't act on every urge, but we must become more aware of our urges if we are going to learn to honor our yearning.

There is a classic scene in the movie *Elf* in which the main character, Buddy, played by Will Ferrell, hops across the street on the crosswalk, carefully landing only on the white bars. Then he picks gum off the underside of a railing and delightedly chews it. Next, he circles repeatedly in a revolving door until he becomes sick to his stomach. He waves with enjoyment to a man he thinks is waving at him, but who is really hailing a taxicab. Finally, he enters the Empire State building, gets in an elevator, and presses a button for one floor. Intrigued by how the button lights up when he presses it, he presses another one . . . and then another and another until he has run his hands over all 102 floor buttons. Throughout this scene, he is following the urges that bubble up from his yearning to connect, engage, and discover.

Transformers do not necessarily do all the things Will Ferrell does in *Elf,* but they do recapture that delighted way of being and follow their delight a great deal more than others do. Following their urges, they become more spontaneous and their behavior becomes less edited. For all of us, just being aware of these urges helps us connect with what we yearn for and takes us in the direction of being Transformers.

Take a look at these common urges and see which ones you can recognize:

* hug someone spontaneously (rather than as part of a formal greeting)
* skip down the sidewalk
* blurt out a truth
* say hello to everyone in the elevator
* break into song
* tell someone how much you care about them in the middle of an ordinary situation (e.g., at lunch, or while playing tennis)
* smile at a stranger
* create and articulate your own prayer
* start dancing in the street
* make a sudden resolution

We could have listed thousands of examples of urges, but we want you to use this list of ten and consider what yearnings gave rise to them. Here is a list of some of the universal yearnings:

A. to matter
B. to love and be loved
C. to be seen
D. to contribute
E. to achieve mastery
F. to be affirmed
G. to connect with a higher power
H. to connect

Now, go back to the list of urges and match the letter of the yearning to the relevant urge. Here are some possible responses:

1. hug someone spontaneously (rather than as part of a formal greeting) B
2. skip down the sidewalk C
3. blurt out a truth D
4. say hello to everyone in the elevator A
5. break into song G
6. tell someone how much you care about them in the middle of an ordinary situation (e.g., at lunch, or while playing tennis) H
7. smile at a stranger F
8. create and articulate your own prayer G
9. start dancing in the street C
10. make a sudden resolution E

These aren't definitive answers. To some extent, the yearning described by the urge depends on who you are. While your dancing in the street may reveal how much you want to be seen and appreciated, it may reveal another person's need to express, connect, celebrate, or matter. The point of this exercise is to help you start thinking about your urges and linking them to yearnings. If you practice doing it consciously, you'll probably start doing it reflexively and be much more in touch with those things you yearn for.

HOW WE'VE LEARNED NOT TO YEARN

Have you ever thought about why we don't naturally yearn? Actually, we do yearn naturally. Put another way, why is it so difficult for us to identify and act upon our yearnings? Many reasons, but first and foremost, we don't want enough. Something prevents us from giving in to the urge, to the deeper desire, to our heart and soul's longing. We feel it, but then a voice in our head responds:

That's not OK.
I don't deserve it.
I'm being greedy.
Who do I think I am?
I'm such a dreamer; get real!
I can't afford it.
It's not me.
It's not time.
I'll do it someday.
If only I . . . , then maybe I could . . .

We're conditioned to suppress our yearning. As children, we lack the social awareness, impulse control, judgment, or skill to act appropriately or effectively on our urges. So based on adult and parental instructions and rebukes, we internalize many messages that unconsciously limit our impulses and urges. This restricts our ability to yearn and have appropriate and fulfilling desires as adults.

One of the biggest barriers to yearning is that we don't allow ourselves to want enough, but there are other blocks:

* *Miswanting,* which we've already discussed

* *Soft addictions,* which numb us to what we yearn for

* *Loss aversion,* the fear of leaving our comfortable routines behind for a more meaningful, more satisfying, but less familiar life

Don't let these or other obstacles stand in the way of attaining what you yearn for. As you move forward through the phases of the *Transformed!* process, remember that you're entitled to the possibility of a great life, and the only way to achieve it is through reawakening and developing your capacity to yearn.

THE GESTALT OF YEARNING: WHAT IT MEANS AND HOW YOU BENEFIT

Yearning allows you to be yourself in the fullest, deepest sense of that term. Getting in touch with what you yearn for will transform your life into an increasingly personal adventure into yourself and your world. As you read that sentence, you no doubt wondered, "How?"

By giving you the capacity to turn the most mundane moment into a fulfilling experience. Imagine yourself in a business meeting. You want your company to succeed and you fear that the strategy it is following will lead to failure. You have an urge to speak up. You yearn to contribute and to be well received. You are the least senior person in the room. It will look presumptuous if you speak up, but if you remain silent, the company will suffer.

That is exactly the bind Josh found himself in with a client. Josh had been working at getting in touch with his yearnings. He knew he had this powerful urge to contribute in areas of his life where he felt like a bystander, and so he saw this moment as an opportunity to respond to this yearning. He half-raised his hand and said that he believed the strategy was flawed, that they needed to deal with the CEO's limitations or it would not work. The room became silent. The chairman straightened and his contact gave him a dirty look. The silence deepened and finally, the chairman excused Josh from the meeting. At first, they told Josh they would not need his services anymore, but shortly, the chairman called him back and reengaged him to help them deal with the problem. From that point on, Josh's relationship with the client took off and he always attributes this one moment as the catalyst for his success as a consultant known for straight talk who speaks the difficult truths.

If you're not in touch with your yearnings, you may miss this type of moment. Instead of speaking up in the meeting, you might waste time and energy complaining to friends about how your company is being run by shortsighted leaders. Or you might miss that moment to love and to matter in your child's life when you're tucking her into bed and she wants to talk but your mind is jumping to all the "to do's" left at work. Or maybe you dash off a hurried peck on the cheek to your mate on your way out the door and miss the opportunity to really see and appreciate each other for a moment while nourishing your yearning to love and be loved.

When you are truly in harmony with what you yearn for, you experience every moment in a deeper and more fulfilling way. Most of us go through life having the buzz that comes with bursts of pleasure. We get high on responding to a want, and then we crash. This up-and-down cycle is not particularly satisfying. Instead, we end up living from one buzz to the next; this allows us to tolerate the time in between and masks the fact that our deeper longings aren't being met.

Now imagine the alternative. Consider what happens if you are continuously focused on what you yearn for and striving to get that yearning met. In our relationship, when I'm hurt because Bob dismissed something I said, instead of withdrawing, I can understand what is really going on: I yearn to be heard and to matter, and Bob's dismissal has implied to me that I don't matter. And I can find satisfaction in being in touch with my yearning, rather than getting into a fight with no clear outcome—clarifying my yearning helps me make my communication to Bob very clear: "I feel hurt and invalidated, like I don't matter." Many repeats of this conversation have dramatically decreased the frequency of Bob's dismissals of things I say. There are many other improvements in our relationship that have come from times when I have interpreted his comments and looks as dismissals, but because I've spoken up about it, I discover these particular moments are not, in fact, intended as dismissals, and we can get to the heart of things immediately, both in conversation and in my own mind. By my sharing my vulnerability, Bob and I connect directly as he softens his perspective and I acknowledge his point of view. We quickly find solutions to problems and avoid wasting precious emotional and intellectual energy.

Think about being able to feel like you're not wasting time. Think about deriving great satisfaction not just from one big accomplishment a year but hundreds of thoughts and actions—thoughts and actions that are all keyed into what you yearn for. Every aspect of your life—work, relationships, leisure time, family—moves to a higher level.

Elliott, for instance, is an editor we've worked with, and for a few years, he kind of liked his job and kind of was good at it. Yet there were times when he questioned whether this was the right position for him, even though it was a top editorial job with a prestigious publication. He was bored at times, and at other times felt that he wasn't contributing as much as he should. There were even instances when Elliott questioned his choice of profession—he wondered if he should go back to law school or maybe try teaching.

Yet once he understood what he yearned for—and especially how much he yearned to have the respect of others, mastery, and influence in the world—his attitude, enjoyment, and performance in his job changed. He began speaking more in editorial meetings, sharing his ideas. Before, Elliott had operated within his own unconscious limits around what he should talk about and what he should not; he had been careful not to offend anyone or to infringe on other people's territory. Even though he had strong ideas about the magazine's editorial direction, he had made an effort to speak coolly and calmly, often deferring to others, as he felt a junior editor should. But once Elliott understood and recognized his yearnings and the cost to his self-esteem of not following them, his attitude and approach changed. He was willing to challenge more senior editors whom he felt were keeping the magazine overly conservative and dull. He took initiative and spent weekends creating detailed strategies for changing aspects of the magazine, which he presented with tremendous conviction and authority. He became a much more hands-on, inspiring editor for his reporters, encouraging them to pursue the types of stories he felt were critical to the magazine's success.

Within a year, Elliott not only received two promotions, but he also found himself relishing his work in a way that he had never experienced before. It was as if he had been transported to a different magazine or even a different career—something that he knew was exactly right for him.

Like the "old" Elliott, we all do things we think we should do or that we're good at, but our activities and behaviors are often disconnected from the deeper, central, driving focus of Yearning. In relationships, we act in ways that often fritter away the precious time we have together. Our communication is less purposeful as we gossip or engage in shooting the breeze about trivial topics; we don't know how to have meaningful conversations and aren't conscious about how they can deepen the relationship. Or even worse, we become bogged down in bickering and petty misunderstandings, unable to talk about what matters.

YEARNING: A GUIDE FOR THE CHOICES WE MAKE

Transformers know that their yearnings provide them with a life compass. When they are at a crossroads or facing a difficult decision, their yearnings give them direction. If you're like most people, no matter how much you have learned and grown, you have experienced a feeling that you wanted to live an even more purposeful life; or you wanted to develop a more spiritual nature. And so you volunteered at a soup kitchen or you signed up for meditation classes.

Again, if you're like most people, you may have enjoyed the first few times serving food to the homeless or sitting cross-legged on a mat trying to clear your mind. But then you became bored or other events and activities prevented you from continuing with these endeavors. With yearning, we are talking about a driving force that can bring meaning to everything we do, if only we learn the skills to activate it.

When you're not acting out of your yearning, these altruistic or spiritual goals are pursued in isolation. In other words, they aren't tied to your intrinsic drives. You're seeking a single experience to fulfill you rather than finding thousands of fulfilling encounters and activities as part of your life project. It may be that instead of volunteering at a soup kitchen, you should be investing more fully in many different areas of your life, bringing greater meaning, and serving yourself as well as those whose lives you touch in the course of a day.

Tapping your yearning, then, is not an intellectual exercise, nor is it about what you think you should do or the right way to live. Instead, it's a discovery and celebration of deep-seated needs that come from your heart, that represent your soul's longing. You've encountered it before in brief glimpses—just before your eyes close and sleep comes, in the space between wakefulness and dreaming. It echoes within you, something you can't quite put a name to, but you know it's what you want most in the world.

Think of yearning as a companion to your days, a guide for your decisions, a compass toward satisfaction, fulfillment, and well-being— your guide to spectacular living.

CHAPTER FOUR

ENGAGE:
TRANSLATE YEARNING INTO ACTION

Love life, engage in it, give it all you got.
—MAYA ANGELOU

"I THINK YOU ARE LETTING your personal life interfere with your professional decisions." Toni said this to Jane, her best friend. Toni could barely believe she had said those words. Never before had she spoken so directly to Jane. For one thing, Toni had always been someone who preferred to please rather than confront. For another, Jane angered easily, especially when anyone criticized her boyfriend Bill. Jane had just informed Toni that she was turning down a great job in public relations because it would require her to do a lot of traveling—and she knew that Bill wouldn't like that she was away from home so much. Toni called her on it because she knew the real reason Jane was turning down the job was because Bill was overly possessive, and that's why he'd be upset if Jane took this job. Though Jane was angry at Toni for confronting her on this issue, she eventually got over her anger and recognized that Toni was doing what a good friend should do. More to the point, it was a breakthrough for Toni. For the first time as an adult, she had stepped out of her comfort zone of pleasing and entered her discomfort zone of confronting. As difficult as it was to do, she found herself feeling great afterwards despite Jane's anger—she had acted on her yearning to make a difference. It was a tremendously energizing feeling. When she confronted Jane, it was if she had tapped into some deep reservoir of power within her. Her entire being felt electric.

For people like Toni, when their yearning is followed by engaging, life becomes an adventure of discovery and fulfillment. It's not enough to just yearn; we have to act on that yearning. Yearning, no matter how deeply felt, doesn't lead to a great, satisfying life without engaging.

It is the moment-by-moment practice of engaging that helps you become more spontaneous and more present in each moment. You step outside your comfort zone, try new things, take risks, and turn your life from a routine into an adventure.

Engaging, as Transformers mean it, is more than the word as you currently think of it. You are likely wondering what it really means and asking yourself, *Aren't I already engaging? Geez, I'm busy enough, and I'm reading this. What more do I need to do to really have a satisfying, successful life?*

Think about this . . .

Are you engaged at work? As a parent? With your spouse or partner? When you take the train to work or when you go to church? When you jog in the morning and when you read a book at night? Are you engaged in your overall life project—not just a work project with a tight deadline or an interesting home project?

If you're like most people, you're scratching your head and wondering what we're really asking. Some of you may believe that engaging means paying attention. You listen to every word your husband says (and could even repeat it back). Some of you may think it means focusing on the task at hand. You concentrate on your work assignments and don't allow your attention to wander. These are all forms of engaging, but they are probably not full engagement because you have feelings, urges, and yearnings that you aren't bringing to bear.

Engaging is a deeper and wider concept than just listening or concentrating, though these are important elements of engaging. We'll define it in more detail shortly, but for the moment, understand that to be truly engaged, your yearning and your emotions must be involved. You may be completely focused on your new boss at work, a new date, or shopping at an exclusive new store, but even if you are totally turned on by your favorite designer's hot new collection, these activities don't satisfy a deeper yearning, and therefore your engagement takes place only on a superficial level. Worrying about the new boss, being curious about the new date or, sorry to say, even finding the hottest new designer shoes doesn't qualify as fulfilling a yearning, nor does being kind of high and buzzed constitute real emotion. Similarly, if your mind is into something but your heart is not, you're lacking the emotional involvement that distinguishes true engagement. Just as emotions help us sense what we yearn for, they are the litmus test for full engagement. We feel an experience deeply when we're fully engaged in it.

So when we ask if you're engaged, we're asking if you're involved in a given activity with your heart, mind, and soul. We're asking if you are so intimately connected to a given task that you are willing to step out of your comfort zone and push yourself to get it done right. We're asking if you're taking risks and stretching yourself in ways that might feel uncomfortable but also provide you with such a spark that you feel as if you could set the world on fire with a touch of your hand. Now think about these questions with that description of engagement in mind:

When you're at your job, does it feel like most of the things you do really matter? Do you feel joy as well as fear as you go about your activities? Do you find yourself having new ideas and learning new things continuously throughout the day?

When you have lunch with a friend, are you energized and moved by the depth of the conversation? Do you focus intently on speaking honestly and openly? Are you acutely aware of how what you say and the way you say it affects the other person? Are you aware of what your friend or partner is saying and feeling and its effect on you?

When you work out, are you highly conscious of how your mind, body, and spirit are responding to the exercise regimen? Are your thoughts and emotions racing along with your physical self? Do you see yourself and the world more clearly as you exercise?

Do you take risks during your days, whether it's sharing a more vulnerable truth, being more assertive about something that bothers you, asking for more responsibility at work, or following a spontaneous urge in the moment? Are you trying new activities? Are you willing to risk looking stupid, displeasing others, or even being rejected?

When you take a risk, do you feel more alive than you've felt in days, weeks, or months? When you try something challenging or new, do you have a surge of energy?

As you think about your answers, understand that your level of engagement exists on a continuum. At the far right of the continuum, your engagement is total and transformational. At the far left of the continuum, you are completely disengaged. You may be physically present and doing the work or talking the talk, but emotionally and cognitively you're somewhere else. Or you may be sitting under a tree and meditating or going for a long walk in the woods thinking deep thoughts, but that isn't being more engaged either—you may become more reflective, more thoughtful, and more mosquito-bitten, but you won't necessarily transform unless your yearning and emotions are engaged.

Engagement Continuum

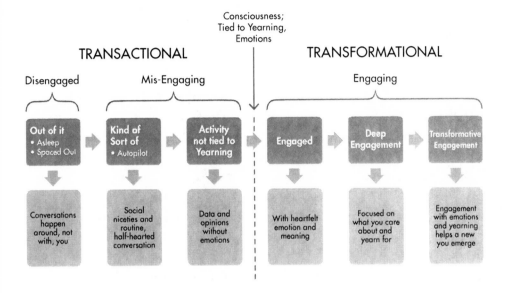

Don't worry about locating yourself on this continuum at the moment or be concerned if you're on the left side of it and don't know how to move to the right side. Our level of engagement varies daily and even hourly. With knowledge and practice, you'll have a better sense of where you are when you take a given action and how to engage more fully and deeply.

WHY TRAVEL THE CONTINUUM?

Transformers in our research reported enhanced marriages, multiple job promotions, better self-esteem, more personal influence, and much more. When you are on the right side of the continuum, you begin to fulfill your yearning and experience the gratification of doing things that deeply satisfy you, rather than things that distract you, numb your feelings, or address a superficial craving.

Perhaps best of all, engaging gets you juiced. To transform, you need energy, and engaging is like plugging into your own personal power socket. It creates the momentum necessary to keep you moving through the steps of the process. It serves as a catalyst for the journey that Transformers take, providing the impetus to get you moving in a new direction.

Research from the relatively new field of positive psychology—created in order to study and apply scientific methods to aspects of living fulfilling lives—provides compelling evidence for why engaging is key to our happiness and well-being. Sometimes described as leading "an engaged life" or being "in the flow," engaging is one of the key elements of authentic happiness. The key to being happy at work can be seen as intentional engaging—being curious, taking initiative, suggesting improvements, asking for additional work, helping others, and being creative.

It seems we are designed to derive pleasure from engaging. Neuroscientists have discovered that our brains light up in ways that result in positive experiences when we are engaging in new things. The novelty of engaging helps facilitate our brain plasticity and, ultimately, our transformation by activating the property of the brain that allows us to learn, grow, change, and fulfill our potential. Neuroscience shows that it is only by engaging—being aware, paying attention, and intentionally doing new things—that we learn, grow, and ultimately transform into someone doing something that would have been unimaginable without full engagement.

Gregory Berns, a professor of neuroeconomics at Emory University, found that it is through engaging in novel experiences, and not just being focused on the outcomes, that we experience true satisfaction. If that weren't enough, researchers in the field of high performance have found that deep engagement at work leads to enhanced productivity, and our research reveals that those who engage receive more promotions and higher pay!

It doesn't end there. When you consistently engage, you develop what researcher Angela Duckworth calls "grit"—the perseverance needed for long-term goals—which turns out to be a key predictor for success in all areas of life.

So how do we get all these benefits of engaging? Let's define what engaging is and isn't.

MYTHS AND REALITIES

Let's start out with what engaging is not by examining some common misconceptions or myths around engagement. Many activities masquerade as engagement.

First, people often mistake activity and attention for engagement. You may believe yourself to be very much engaged as you surf the Internet or watch a favorite soap opera, or you may be incredibly busy at work as you struggle to complete ten projects at once. But being frenetic or concentrating on every word that your favorite actor in the soap opera says doesn't put you on the right side of the engaging continuum. That's because your actions aren't designed to satisfy a yearning but are instead repressing the yearning and are driven by what psychologists Gilbert and Wilson call "miswanting." In miswanting, you yearn to discover new things but mistakenly think that activities like surfing the Internet will get you there, or you yearn to feel important and mistakenly think that over-busyness will satisfy that desire. But in fact the activities you choose are suppressing these underlying yearnings.

Second, some people believe that they're really engaged when they act upon a magical solution to their problems. Doug thought that by quitting his job and becoming an Outward Bound instructor, he would transform his life. He was sure that by taking this risk and being a guide in the wilderness—a huge leap from his corporate job—he would be operating at a highly conscious level, emotionally and cognitively engaged.

Yet he wasn't. Instead, Doug was simply escaping from his problems. Being an Outward Bound instructor sounded good to him, but it wasn't what he yearned for. Nature provided an escape from the daily challenges of his life; he was guilty of miswanting—thinking that being an Outward Bound instructor would be his secret to happiness. Now that Doug is facing his daily challenges with deeper yearning guiding his engagement, his career is blossoming.

While vacations can yield new perspectives and creative responses to daily challenges, escapes are never avenues for deep engagement. People take fabulous vacations, sign up for meditation classes, and decide to become deep-sea divers or pottery artists, thinking that this will provide the engagement their regular job or their current relationship lacks. They convince themselves that they will be completely tuned in as they tour the great cathedrals of Europe, or that when shaping wet clay on a wheel, every fiber of their being will be involved in the process. In truth, though, they remain on the left side of the continuum. They are using travel and creativity to avoid deeper yearning in daily life.

When your motivation is to escape, a high level of engagement does not lead to the fullest development and transformation. It does not engage your emotions fully since you are leaving behind significant unfinished business. Keep in mind that engaging involves getting *into* things, not getting *away* from it all.

Third, people assume they're engaged when they're focused single-mindedly, and sometimes obsessively, on achieving a goal. Christina was a business executive who was "engaged" in climbing the highest mountain peaks in North America. There was no question that when Christina was training for these climbs and when she was actually on the mountain, she thought of little else except getting in shape and navigating her way to the top. These endeavors demanded her complete physical and mental focus; her survival was dependent on it. Yet when Christina wasn't training for or climbing these mountains, she was inactive and indulgent; she'd gain over thirty-five pounds each year— pounds she would shed prior to the next annual climb. These pounds represented the real lack of engagement in Christina's life. Christina ate to avoid her trouble at work. A top saleswoman for major companies, she would climb to the top of the sales heap at each company, too, only to be fired despite stellar results because she would upset so many people with her negative attitude.

So Christina was not fully engaged. While she had stunning powers of concentration when it came to climbing, this was only one part of her life; her career had plateaued and her marriage teetered uncertainly due to her lack of broad engagement. Being deeply engaged in one area and disengaged in five others doesn't work. If you're like Christina, your obsessive focus in that one area probably stems from miswanting. Her climbs allowed her the illusion of engagement so she could avoid dealing with all the substantive issues in her personal and professional worlds. If she were in touch with her yearning, she would recognize that what she really wants is to matter and have impact at work and at home, and she would translate that yearning to all dimensions of her life.

So engaging isn't a single-minded focus on one goal or area of life and it's also not escape or activity. Nor is it any type of soft addiction. Soft addictions, by definition, limit us to continuous partial attention. We are there, but not fully there, when we over-party, zone out, overeat, or get buzzed from mindlessly surfing the Internet or shopping (not to mention when we drink or do drugs). Our actions are reflexive or reactive—knee-jerk responses that come up almost without our conscious awareness and don't flow from our yearning.

Another common compulsion that obscures true engagement is working hard. In other words, we throw ourselves into our work with such mindless fervor that it helps us avoid dwelling on anything but work, including our deeper yearning. Often, our careers stall because we work hard but not smart. By smart, we mean following our deeper yearning, taking appropriate risks, learning, growing, and advancing as a result.

Now that we've covered what engaging is not, let's turn to what engaging is. We've already defined it to some extent: when you're engaged, the action you take is driven by your yearning, it's informed by your emotions, and it exists on a continuum. But let's identify some key approaches to engaging that might give you a better sense of what it looks like:

- **DEVELOP TRUE GRIT.** Engaging is focused, continuous

involvement—what Duckworth calls "grit"—as opposed to flitting from one thing to the next. Often we engage and then disengage. In other words, we see our engagement as temporary—a way to achieve a goal rather than to fulfill a deeper yearning to succeed, influence our world, and be affirmed. With engaging, we become totally involved in a work project, knowing that its successful completion will help us get a strong sense of personal fulfillment as well as a bonus or a promotion. By consistently engaging and reengaging, we develop the grit Duckworth says is marked by perseverance—a key quality that we need to transform our lives.

- **SEEK NOVELTY.** True engagement means you seek out experiences that are new and different. Falling into the habit of doing the same thing the same way means that you're probably operating on autopilot—you're getting things done, but there isn't any risk or learning involved. So though you're engaged in a task in the most basic sense of that word, you're not engaged at a sufficiently high enough level for it to really matter.

- **MAKE MISTAKES.** Transformers are not just willing to make mistakes and displease others; they also celebrate the learning mistakes engender. If this strikes you as counterintuitive—if it seems like these actions will distance you from what you yearn for—understand that taking risks and failing is the best way to learn. And, in order to please yourself, you may have to displease other people. Your boss may not like it if you disagree with him, but to do the work in a way that has impact, you may have no other choice. Obviously, you don't want to turn yourself into a mistake-making, displeasing machine; this is a path toward failure and misanthropy. Fortunately, making a few key mistakes and taking a few stances that run counter to others you care about is usually sufficient to jump-start the learning process.

- **PREPARE FOR HURT.** With engagement, we experience embarrassment and hurt, and out of this comes genuine humility. As you take action in ways that are true to your yearning, you say and do things at times that others don't appreciate or approve of. Like a child who is acting authentically and follows his urge to tell the teacher what he thinks of an assignment, you too may find yourself being misunderstood, rejected, or reprimanded. Bob has a great story that illustrates this point:

I yearn to belong, and participating in a network with idealistic business folks and heavy-hitters in the consciousness-raising business scene helps me meet this yearning. We had an annual "rebels" meeting where we met to talk about what was wrong with our organization and what should change. One key member, a Marxist businessman whom I respect, was in this meeting, and I was absolutely certain we were on the same page.

The executive director dropped in on our rebels group, and there was silence. The conversation became very surface-oriented and artificial. People began holding back, and his very presence in a "rebels'" meeting reduced the vehemence of people's expressions. I pointed out that the conversation had changed and that what he was doing had led to a dead conversation. After doing so, I was shocked to discover that all my fellow rebels discounted me, insisting that nothing had changed. They made nice, siding with the "establishment."

I was profoundly hurt, but I also learned a great deal about myself and groups. After reflecting on the situation, after licking my wounds, I took responsibility and began figuring out what had taken place. I realized I had been too confrontational. I also learned that many people talk the talk but are unwilling to stand and be counted. As a result, I grew more savvier and, hopefully, stronger.

This is a significant truth about engagement: you may be hurt, but you must not let this hurt prevent you from engaging anew. As you gain in your commitment to transforming, you also gain in resilience. Once you discover that getting embarrassed or turned down isn't the end of the world, you develop both a recognition of your own limitations and an awareness of your own inner strength. We've heard people speak up in meetings and get shot down, and they say, "Well, that was a mistake. I'm never doing that again." In fact, they need to push past the hurt, allow themselves to feel humbled, learn from it, and engage again. If you're never getting hurt, then you're not engaging at a high enough level.

- **LEARN AND GROW.** As we noted earlier, learning is knowing something you didn't already know and growing is doing something new. If you go back to the continuum, you'll notice that on the left side, it's possible to engage partially or at a low level and still learn. You may be paying close attention when you're with a friend or child or your spouse, or you may be really into a new career and devoting a great deal of time to it. Yet even if you're learning something about the other person or acquiring new skills, you're not necessarily growing. The right side of the continuum leads to new behavior as well as new knowledge. People who engage on the right side of the continuum possess another quality articulated by Stanford psychology researcher Carol Dweck, which is a "growth mindset." They don't just want to learn new things; they want to use that learning to function at a higher level, both personally and professionally. They're actively seeking opportunities to interact with the world in fresh ways, recognizing that, no matter how good they already are, they can always become even more communicative, adventurous, and inventive.

When you think of all these traits of engaging, you may realize that they describe a way of being that you probably embraced when you were a small child. Little kids engage fully and transformationally with the world around them. They are willing to make mistakes, they are vulnerable to being hurt, and they love novelty. Most of all, they are attuned to their urges, and they respond to them without censure. They are brilliant at taking action based on their yearning. As they grow up, though, they learn to hold back, avoid hurt, and live life on the safe side.

So really, we're asking you to return to a way of doing things that you embraced as a child. Obviously, you need to be discerning in your choices. Just as a surfer can't try to ride every wave that comes his way, you cannot respond to every single impulse. You need to act within your skill set, guided by your deepest yearning—while employing a healthy risk-benefit analysis mindset. In other words, pick your spots to let your urges dictate your behaviors and you'll move to the right on the engaging continuum.

ENGAGING HERE AND THERE, AND FINDING ADVENTURE EVERYWHERE

Every area of life becomes more exciting as you learn to recognize yearning and engage more. Your life becomes juicier, richer, and more challenging as you move to the right on the continuum. You find yourself engaging in more activities in more ways and more profoundly than you ever thought possible. Giggles will follow sighs as you alternately delight and astound yourself by following your urges. Many people who do not understand the process of transformation overthink their lives, believing that they need to become more aware and thoughtful in order to be more conscious in their relationships or participate more fully as parents or in other familial settings. It is often quite the opposite. Deeper awareness is not available until we risk and follow our yearning with engaging. Continual engagement and adjustment causes us to evolve our ways of being in all areas of life and in a million small ways as well.

Deeply engaged individuals keep building on their engaging behaviors so that they enliven every activity—a walk in the park becomes a communion with nature in which you delight in the beauty around you; shopping for food for dinner becomes a creative endeavor as you give yourself permission to experiment and try new recipes and flavors and make mistakes; listening to a challenging piece of music becomes an exercise of focus as you keep committing yourself to understanding the piece while letting it reveal itself to you; a commute to work becomes an adventure in discovery, where saying hello to your doorman turns into a meaningful conversation about parenting, a visit to the coffee shop becomes an exploration into the dreams of the barista, and an encounter with a parking attendant becomes an opportunity to support his career aspirations. In this way, engaging becomes an essential behavior no matter what you're doing, and it lifts all areas of your life up like a rising tide lifts all boats.

Jenny provides us with a good example of the dramatic effect that engaging can make in your life. As a professional musician, Jenny had engaged fully with her music from a young age. She was an internationally recognized jazz musician. When she played the piano, she was involved in her playing with heart, body, and soul. She took risks and was willing to endure hurt and rejection. As a musician, she learned and became more proficient.

But Jenny began to recognize that her engagement was limited to music—she was not engaging in all areas of her life. She became dissatisfied with a life that was merely good; she wanted it to be great. And so Jenny began working at being more present in her relationships with a variety of people, taking chances and speaking honestly rather than overediting her thoughts and words so she wouldn't say anything offensive or wrong. Her love life deepened, as did her friendships and her music. She began asking more of herself and of others, which gave her access to a depth and enjoyment that up to that point she had only experienced in her jazz music.

She began taking different parts of her life more seriously too, spending more time and cognitive and emotional energy doing and learning in the spiritual realm as well as on the business side of her music. As a result, Jenny deepened her relationships, resulting in marriage and having children. She moved on from solely being a jazz pianist, transforming into being an entertainer. She broadened her musical repertoire, studying with samba and rock experts, and she also founded and runs a highly successful, top-ranked entertainment firm. Work activities she formerly looked down upon, such as playing weddings, have become joyous celebrations of life for Jenny and the various bands she has organized and manages.

She continues to deepen her relationship with God and works on achieving greater intimacy in all her relationships, especially with her husband. Her full and wide-ranging engagement has been transformational throughout all areas of her life. As one person said about Jenny, "She lights up a room. You feel better for just having been around her. It's like she's the music, not just what comes out of her piano."

A SCIENTIFIC BASIS FOR DOING AND FEELING, NOT JUST THINKING

A wide range of research corroborates our own discoveries that engaging requires you to take action—to talk and question, to participate, to take risks, to try new things, to operate outside your comfort zone. Many people, including some very smart people, have a lot going on in their minds but are unable to translate all this mental activity into action. Or they take action, but only within the confines of their regular routines, rarely doing or saying anything that varies from what they've always done or said. In these situations, it's very difficult to take action in ways that are congruent with their yearning, to experience emotional involvement in their words and deeds and to learn and grow.

If you need further evidence that real engaging is worth the effort, consider that prominent scientists offer highly motivating evidence that you have to engage in two distinct areas—feeling and doing. They make it clear that intellectual engagement is insufficient. You have to recognize and honor your emotions and get off your *kiester* and act! In his bestselling book, *Emotional Intelligence*, Daniel Goleman beautifully illustrates that, while engagement begins with yearning, it also requires us to "get out of our heads" by adding emotion to otherwise purely intellectual thought.

We (Bob and Judith) were at a talk by Peter Senge, the renowned MIT systems scientist and author of *The Fifth Discipline*, for a group of highly successful entrepreneurs. After finishing his lecture and beginning a question/answer period, Peter asked the participants if they had learned anything in his talk. The response was a resounding

"Yes." Senge challenged this response, saying that the group will not have learned anything until we had actually *done* something differently. Catcalls erupted from the crowd. He earned the group's ire, yet he was conveying an essential truth about learning—we have to act to truly learn.

"Learning by doing" is how we really acquire knowledge and skills, according to a growing body of scientific evidence. It posits that action builds new capabilities for the implicit memory to draw upon, and that it is implicit memory—that which is not consciously available—that governs most of what we do. Russian psychologist and educational theorist Lev Vygotsky, in fact, suggested that all learning is based on engagement. He proposed that we learn by actually doing things before we know how to do them, and that—contrary to common belief—learning is not something that happens in our heads unaccompanied by action.

Current neuroscience research shows that neurons are continually wiring together and that we must repeatedly fail before we establish the neural pathways of a new desired behavior.

Now ask yourself these questions:

Can you recall how many times you failed before consistently learning to tie your shoes?

How about learning to ride a bike? Did thinking really help much? You may have reassured yourself but you still needed to "get the feel of" riding.

How about learning a foreign language? You can't just read it to speak it.

We do not learn and grow by analysis alone. Developing new neural pathways requires engagement, and engagement requires making mistakes until behavior becomes automatic. Salespeople will tell you the same thing—you have to keep at it until you begin to hit your stride and maintain rapport. Consulting firms bring in analysts as assistants and keep them away from the client until they have seen enough and made enough basic, safe mistakes to deliver consistent results in work product as well as client relationships.

In one study, Carol Dweck illustrated the cause-and-effect relationship between effort and success. She notes that the test scores of children in the study who were praised for engaging and trying hard improved by 30 percent while those of children praised just for being smart declined by 20 percent. Dweck explains that rewarding effort and engagement increases our sense of self-efficacy—our belief in our capabilities—and helps us develop the growth mindset necessary for a great life.

Given Dweck's findings, think about these questions:

How do you feel when your boss only acknowledges you when you achieve great results and never seems to notice the hard work that you put into it?

How do you feel after completing an activity in which you've invested yourself fully; when you've put a lot of time and emotion into dealing with a situation or solving the problem?

How do you feel when you just coast through or operate on automatic pilot (even if the outcome is favorable)?

IF ENGAGING IS SO GOOD FOR ME, WHY DON'T I DO IT?

Considering all the evidence that engaging is good for us both internally and externally, why do we so often resist it? The simple answer is this: because transformation isn't easy. For a lot of reasons, we take the path of least resistance. But to help you engage more often and more deeply, we'd like to provide you with a checklist of common resistance factors, followed by an explanation of each. Keep this list handy so you can guard against letting one or more of them turn you into a watcher rather than an engager:

Blocks to Engaging

- Poor Affective Forecasting

- Dread

- Loss Aversion

- Pseudo-Engaging (Soft Addictions)

- A Lack of Self-Efficacy

- Continuous Partial Engagement

- Fear of Being Hurt or Rejected

As you read through the explanations below, ask yourself *how* you experience all of the blocks in the above list—not *if* you experience them. Transformers are ever-vigilant for these blocks and have life teams—people who support them and point out when they are being sabotaged by one of these blocks. These blocks can appear in a wide variety of life areas, including your physical health, family relationships, and work. They can be difficult to detect, so let's go through each of these resistance factors and explain how they stand in the way of engagement.

In the course of a typical day, each of these blocks are active for most of us. We awaken and worry about things that likely will not happen—this is *poor affective forecasting*. We live in constant *dread* of the boss or something else that's lurking in our subconscious. We hold back on making a comment to our boss or a friend out of *loss aversion*, for fear of losing the job or the relationship. We then become enmeshed in doing a job that we disagree with or think could be done better, thereby demonstrating *pseudo-engagement*. You know you can do the job better than the loudmouth at the next desk, but you hold back out of *limited self-efficacy*. You never hit your full potential, not because of all the excuses you use but because of *continuous partial engagement* as you fragment yourself. Underneath all of it is *fear of rejection*.

These blocks can be seen even in highly successful athletes, top executives, entrepreneurs, and other experts. Their work may be fine, but all of these experts operate in some area of their lives from limiting patterns. These patterns always show up in one or more areas, be they relationships, physical health, or even spiritual life.

POOR AFFECTIVE FORECASTING is a fancy name to describe how we imagine worse outcomes than are probable. We catastrophize potential outcomes of an action. We imagine more painful emotional outcomes than positive ones. We make extreme statements internally, telling ourselves that if we take that risk at work, we'll regret it for the rest of our lives. We predict to ourselves that if we give in to our yearning to matter by speaking up, we will be rejected and lose our jobs. We imagine a vacation to a third-world country will be a disaster and we'll be miserable because of the possibility of disease, discomfort, and so on. Essentially, we resist engaging because we mire ourselves in dire predictions about how we'll feel.

DREAD is a nameless terror of doing something new or outside our comfort zone. It is more nebulous than poor affective forecasting. It is a state of constant fear. It is not the specific fears of our poor affective forecasting, rather it's an ever-present dark cloud. Therefore, our resistance in the form of dread may not have a specific name or cause, but it prevents us from engaging in yearning-driven activities. Dread takes place on an unconscious level. It lurks beneath the surface and steers us away from activities that are unfamiliar, keeping us stuck.

LOSS AVERSION has to do with not wanting to give up what we already possess, even if what we possess isn't particularly satisfying. We resist taking a job that might allow us to make a huge impact in the world because we don't want to give up the well-paying job even though we are underemployed in that job. Or we resist praying, meditating, or engaging in other spiritual pursuits because we fear we will be met with derision by friends. Or we may even sense that if we were to connect with a higher power, it might change our lives and cause us to give up a lot of the things we have and do. In some instances, what we don't want to lose is our everyday, familiar numbness! Engaging in activities that meet our yearning is guaranteed to penetrate our anesthetized state.

PSEUDO-ENGAGING is related to loss aversion in that they both have to do with soft addictions. Like rearranging the deck chairs on the *Titanic,* pseudo-engaging is an activity that misses the point and keeps us involved in it with no meaningful outcome. Pseudo-engaging means that we are deep into a soft addiction that may look like engaging but is really an activity like surfing the Web or playing video games. With these diversions we feel as if we're committed to an activity with every fiber of our being. In reality, we're committed only on a surface level and our yearning is not being satisfied. We can devote our lives to playing tic-tac-toe, spend every waking moment playing it, be the best in the world at it, but even if we win 10,000 games in a row, it likely won't make an iota of difference in our own lives or anyone else's.

A LACK OF SELF-EFFICACY can best be understood via the children's story of *The Little Engine that Could.* In the story, the little engine was able to make it up a steep incline by repeating to itself, "I think I can, I think I can, I think I can." As with many universally beloved children's stories, there's a lesson for all of us in it. Self-efficacy is more than self-confidence or self-esteem. It's not just a generalized feeling that we're okay, but rather it's a specific belief in our ability to take effective action. This belief is accompanied by engagement; it is not some idle thought or superficial self-dialogue—if you are not doing, you do not really believe. When we lack self-efficacy, we tell ourselves, *I don't think I can do it. I'm not capable. It's just too hard.* We doubt our ability to travel to a foreign country, to take on a new career or job, to establish a relationship with someone who seems "out of our league," to reestablish a valued relationship with a loved one, or to awaken the spiritual part of ourselves. We resist, therefore, because "we think we can't, we think we can't, we think we can't." In our coaching, we occasionally encounter folks who think they have self-efficacy but are continually making excuses. Excuses are a sign you lack self-efficacy. The little engine took action. Even though the hill was steep, it kept going.

CONTINUOUS PARTIAL ENGAGEMENT (CPE) looks like engagement but isn't. Multitasking often translates into doing a lot of things simultaneously but not very well or with much engagement. CPE is a poor substitute for full engagement, but people gravitate toward it because it fosters the illusion of being involved, important, and busy. CPE is the domain of multitaskers, of electronic communicators, and of people who run around like the proverbial headless chicken. You've had dinner with these individuals, and, while you're talking to them, they're texting and studying the menu and scanning the restaurant for people they know. By doing two or more activities simultaneously, you can create the buzz of busyness, but you lack the focus to engage in a meaningful way. In this way, you offer de facto resistance to this step in the *Transformed!* process.

FEAR OF REJECTION, of looking stupid, and of being humiliated can be understood within the context of Bob's earlier story about how he spoke up during his network meeting. Getting shot down when you say something—whether in your professional or personal life—can prevent you from ever wanting to do the same thing again. You're hurt, especially when you expected a positive outcome and it turned out to be negative. Yet as Bob noted, you have to get up, dust yourself off, learn from the experience and do the same thing again. If you fear rejection, you'll never ask the person who will turn out to be your one true love out on a date; you'll never try a job or career that will provide you with the ideal opportunity to influence others; and you'll never try to help those who are less fortunate than you are—all because you fear that you will be rejected.

All of these resistance factors can be overcome with the right mindset and toolkit. Let us help you create one of each.

LIFE AS AN ADVENTURE

As you attempt to engage in each moment of your life, remember to keep the Engaging Continuum handy to chart your location on it at any given moment in time. Keep it with you for at least a week. For instance, you may find yourself in a workshop you judge as excruciatingly boring, but in fact you are making it boring by not engaging. Boredom is a symptom of non-engagement. As you hike through the woods, you may notice that you are not engaged with your children and you then engage with them by making the walk an adventure of discovery—of the woods as well as of each other and how each of you experiences the walk.

Make it your goal to move to the right side of the Engagement Continuum no matter what you're doing. Admittedly, this can be challenging in certain areas of your life. But if you keep your position on the continuum in mind and make a consistent effort to engage when you're at work, at home, traveling, in a religious setting, or anywhere else, you'll likely find yourself moving to the right.

How do you make a good-faith, consistent effort to engage? Here are some suggestions regarding attitude and activities:

DAILY LIFE ASSIGNMENTS. We call it the "assignment way of living." We choose an assignment each morning that causes us to do at least one new thing that day. Life assignments stimulate yearning and engagement. They will cause you to look at ways to make the mundane meaningful—engaging more fully in your daily activities, whether being more present when you tuck your child into bed at night, pushing yourself to finish that project with deadlines and rewards, or even making a game of cleaning the toilet. In addition, choose assignments that cause you to take risks and step outside your comfort zone. You may take small steps like following a different route home or ordering something new at Starbucks, or larger adventures like sharing a heartfelt truth with your spouse or asking for that well-deserved raise. Here are four kinds of assignments with examples under each type:

- *Nourishment and Self-Care Assignments*
  - Identify the emotions you are feeling every hour
  - Identify your wants and needs throughout the day
  - Ask for things—big and small, tangible and intangible, low-risk to outrageous

- *Family and Intimacy Assignments*
  - Identify the beliefs that limit you or hold you back that you have in common with other members of your family—and discuss them
  - Act contrary to a limiting belief

- *Personal Power Assignments*
  - Speak up. Share your agreements or disagreements at least once an hour—whether at home, at work, with family, or with friends
  - Share aloud with others something you dislike
  - Be silent and notice what happens around you—discover the significant power in silence

- *Purposeful Living and Spiritual Development Assignments*
  - At least once a day, share something that really matters to you with someone
  - Ask people what higher purpose they wish to have in their lives

Here are some other assignments to alter your ways of thinking, feeling, and doing:

CHOOSE A GROWTH MINDSET. Make a conscious choice of a growth over a fixed mindset. Most of us have a fixed mindset. Oh, we don't mind learning something new or even taking a class or seminar periodically, but we're not passionately curious and really stretching ourselves on a daily basis. We aim for a goal, achieve it, and are content to coast for an indefinite period afterwards. In other words, we engage as a short-term tactic to get what we want. We may engage to become a black belt in karate, to secure a plum position with our organization, or to find a romantic partner. Once we get what we want, though, we disengage. What we're suggesting here is adopting a growth mindset if you want to sustain engagement past an end point.

SAY WTF (WHAT THE F**K). Pardon our language, but nothing quite gets the point across better than that specific phrase. Use this line from the classic movie *Risky Business*: "Sometimes you gotta say, 'What the F**k' and go for it." If you look back on all the actions that you wished you had taken but didn't, you'll find that you stopped yourself with a litany of excuses: it was too hot out, it would take too long, it might make you angry, it might make him angry, it would require too much effort and so on.

If you can learn to say WTF just ten percent more than you currently do, you'll increase your engagement significantly. There may be times when it's impossible or unrealistic to say WTF. At age fifty, you may want to quit your job as a butcher and become an astronaut, but it may not be feasible based on your skills, financial responsibilities, and so on. Many times, however, WTF frees us from our false excuses about why we can't do something. When we aren't concerned about failing, making mistakes, or feeling uncomfortable, we can engage far more often and far more deeply than we currently do, thereby learning and growing to advantage.

LIVE YOUR LIFE AS AN EXPERIMENT. This is the essence of the assignment way of living. This attitudinal shift can foster engagement by getting you out of your routine. Engagement thrives on novelty, and an experimental perspective allows you to test all sorts of new endeavors. Too often, we feel that we have to do certain things and follow certain paths. We create all sorts of boundaries that prevent us from venturing into uncharted territory where we could engage in ways that we don't when we are following well-trod paths.

You may recall a world-class Transformer, R. Buckminster Fuller, who is perhaps best known as the inventor of the geodesic dome. However, Fuller was also a philosopher, engineer, poet, educator, and Renaissance man. He talked about living his life as an experiment designed to discover how he might benefit humankind. He formalized this experiment by referring to himself as Guinea Pig B. With this life-changing approach, Fuller was able to engage deeply in myriad endeavors. He filled his life with novelty and fostered in himself wide-ranging intellectual and emotional involvement. His ideas and inventions did indeed benefit humankind, thus fulfilling his experiment's mission.

Be like Bucky Fuller and live your life as an experiment, engaging in all you do and harvesting more of the infinite possibilities available to you. When we engage in our life project as our personal experiment, we make discoveries—a key element of the next phase of the *Transformed!* process: We revelate.

CHAPTER FIVE

REVELATE:
DISCOVER YOUR PROGRAM,
UNLEASH YOUR POTENTIAL

*When any individual takes the significant step beyond the self-limiting structures
of personal history and cultural conditioning, awakening to a deeper and higher
sense of Self, it is a profound event.*
—ANDREW COHEN

TRANSFORMERS ARE EXPLORERS, continually discovering themselves
and their world anew. Engaging, they take risks, step outside their
comfort zone, and start to perceive themselves, their lives, and their
world in new, expanded ways. They revelate—they become aware of
enlightening truths about themselves and the world and also reveal
more of themselves with others. Breakthroughs in their thinking and
beliefs pave the way for transformational breakthroughs in their lives.
They realize that they have too narrowly defined themselves and their
lives—and previously unthinkable possibilities become commonplace.

In earlier chapters, you began tapping into your deeper yearning
and engaging. Yet there's much more to discover. Even for those of you
who are practiced at connecting to these deeper realities, with increased
sensitivity to your yearning, there is a great deal more waiting for
you. As you engage ever more deeply and widely, you begin to realize
there are possibilities beyond your former imagining—as did this
Transformer: "Growing up, I felt I had to perform to be loved, and that
is what I became, a performance machine. Love always felt conditional.
If I was pretty enough, perfect enough, or smart enough, then maybe

I'd be loved. I lived in fear that people would see I was never enough, and this fear colored every aspect of my life. Despite abundance, I lived my life in survival and fear of abandonment. Now, I realize that it isn't true—I don't have to be perfect to be loved! To know that I am loved just because of who I am, and that I don't have to earn it, is almost beyond belief. And the idea that I deserve this love . . . wow! Underneath it all is a program that I am changing—changing my beliefs about myself and my world. It is like a map to redraw as I change what I do every day, creating my new self as I go."

Transformers develop a lifestyle of revelating. Revelating isn't just one "aha" moment but an ongoing process of discovery—challenging your beliefs and expectations, developing new perspectives, and becoming more conscious, real, and revealed. Small epiphanies lead to larger ones—altering your beliefs, assumptions, and worldview—bringing about paradigm shifts that, when you act on them, open up the possibility of amazing transformation.

This isn't just about insight—it's more all-encompassing and ongoing than that. It involves discovering and revealing more of who you are. You begin to ask, "How do I become more of who I genuinely am? How am I programmed to limit who I am? How do I share and reveal myself to others so they can help me expand my knowledge of myself and help me discover my unrecognized potential?" Answering these questions is revelatory.

Here are some examples of realizations emerging at this phase:

Things are not as I think they are. I am programmed—my unconscious mind is running the show.

I operate from beliefs that are just that—beliefs. They are not necessarily true and they limit me and my possibilities.

Things can be different. In fact, what I thought was impossible is possible.

I create my reality, and my programming will prevail if I don't act consciously.

DISCOVERING YOUR MATRIX

Revelating is an actionable process of cognitive discovery, helping you recognize the unconscious programming that determines your behavior. By engaging in actions in response to your yearning, you glimpse parts of yourself that have always resided beneath the surface. Revelating is a catalyst that helps you grasp what you yearn for. But it can also be scary.

Be prepared to see a reality about yourself that you never knew existed—no matter how much insight you have had to date. Revelating helps you recognize why you do or don't do things—things you do that you know you shouldn't do and things you think you should do that you never seem to get around to. Most of us like to think of ourselves as free agents, making decisions and taking action consciously and independently. Yet each of us operates to a significant extent from our unconscious programming. Revelating exposes that programming so we can study it and consciously change it with consistent, strategic effort.

No doubt you're familiar with the concept of the unconscious mind—how we're influenced to say or do things based on thoughts and feelings we're not aware of. The Freudian slip is the classic example. We say to our nitpicking boss, "Hi, Mrs. Sanders, you're looking mighty *petty* today." Our unconscious is causing us to say something we really believe—that she is petty—even though we intended to say she looked good or pretty. Our conscious mind censors these true feelings in normal conversation out of fear, politeness, and so on, but Freud, the original modern neuroscientist, viewed the slip as a window into our unconscious programming. Of course, we excuse ourselves and say, "I meant to say pretty." But if we are really intent on fulfilling our potential, we need to look deeper and not rationalize our slip away.

But when we refer to our programming, we're referring to much more than a single unconscious thought. We're talking about a complex network of experiences, feelings, and perceptions encoded in our neural pathways that form our unconscious minds—what we call our matrix. Once aware of this network, Transformers can look forward to a lifelong journey of exploring and what we call rematrixing which, as the name applies, suggests we're capable of changing this matrix (we'll cover this more fully in Chapter 7). Our programming is like a Tinker Toy maze of sticks connecting hubs; only in our case, they are neurons firing and wiring together and forming hubs that are intersections of numerous neurons encoded with earlier experiences. Many of these connections formed long before we had language.

Most Transformers in our programs develop a visual idea of their matrix. Many of them think of it as a three-dimensional grid of thick horizontal and vertical layers of neural "stuff," largely formed shortly after birth based on their relationships and experiences with primary caregivers. The matrix is solidified in early childhood through thousands of repeated interactions that establish the biological, neurological, and biochemical basis for who we are and how we think the world is. These perceptions are both conscious and unconscious, the latter often being the opposite of what we profess. When we're born, our brains are a collection of neurons, not yet fully developed with all the adult functions online. Many of our neurons are dependent on experience for their development—what neuroscientists call "experience-dependent neurogenesis."

Life Filters Through Our Matrix

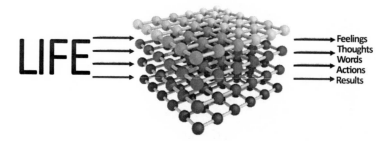

Our matrix defines how we see the world, how we feel about ourselves, and what we believe. For now, though, we need to learn more about how this matrix concept works within the revelating phase.

Our matrix isn't a bad thing; it makes us the unique, talented, compassionate individuals that we are. It also provides us with insight into our strengths and limitations. We use the matrix as a metaphor to talk about how our wiring gets laid down. It also gives us a visual representation that facilitates future strategizing to unleash our full potential, no matter how much growth work we have done.

Regardless of our level of development and success, the primary problem we all face is that the limiting beliefs and unconscious programming of our matrix operate without our conscious awareness or choice. We accept these limitations as reality—the reality of who we are and what the world is.

This takes us to a fundamental truth of revelating:

We discover that our beliefs are just beliefs, not reality.

In fact, what we believe limits our reality and keeps us from realizing our potential. We think, *This is how it is, this is who I am,* rather than *This is how I am programmed, this is what I believe, but it is not necessarily the full truth.* It causes us to believe, *I can't be assertive like that* or *I'm kind and thoughtful; I can't be angry.* In the former instance, it prevents us from speaking our mind and from being as successful as we might be in our career or in relationships. In the latter instance, it stops us from expressing our anger, causing us to become repressed and frustrated. Recognizing these thoughts as reflections of limiting beliefs can be a starting point for an expanded sense of self. And as eye-opening and even mind-blowing as these insights are for your own relationship with yourself, it's just as important to reveal and share more of yourself and your discovery of your programming with others. Revelating is about both discovering *and* uncovering ourselves—revealing ourselves to others who can then help us see what is happening in our blind spots.

But before we see how this works, let's get a better sense of what the matrix is and the science that provides a basis for understanding it.

NEUROSCIENTISTS, PSYCHOLOGISTS, AND EXISTENTIALISTS AGREE

As this section title suggests, a diverse group of experts agree that we are programmed. This isn't just semantics, and it's not just the conclusion of a few fringe scientists. The research is filled with studies and examples confirming that we possess a matrix (our term) of core beliefs about ourselves and the world—neural pathways and neuronal nets that form from neurons firing together and wiring together in early childhood.

Neuroscientists have performed numerous experiments that demonstrate how, when we think we're doing something for a conscious reason, it's the unconscious programming that's directing our behaviors. For the most part we think we make rational, conscious decisions and take purposeful and conscious action, but we most often act unconsciously, making up a post-facto reason for why we did what we did, and actually believing that it is the reason we did those things. As Robert A. Heinlein said, "Man is not a rational animal, he is a rationalizing animal."

Understanding the power of the unconscious is a beginning level of revelating. This leads to deeper levels of revelating that give us greater control over our lives. An experiment cited in *Sway: The Irresistible Pull of Irrational Behavior* took place at MIT and demonstrates how our unconscious determines our experience of the world. The experiment took place in an economics class in which each student received a neutral profile of a visiting professor. Unbeknownst to the class, the otherwise identical profiles had one difference: one profile noted that the professor was a very warm person and the other profile said he was a rather cold person. Sitting in the same class, hearing the same lecture at the same time, the group that received the profile containing the word "cold" disliked the lecturing professor, finding him to be self-centered, formal, unsociable, unpopular, irritable, humorless, and ruthless, while the group that received the profile with the word "warm" loved him, finding him to be good-natured, considerate, informal, popular, humane, and humorous.

Another one of our favorite examples of the power of the

unconscious mind is the fact that, if your name is Dennis or Denise, you are disproportionately likely to become a dentist, and if your name is Lawrence . . . you can guess what you are likely to be, because we unconsciously gravitate to things which are familiar.

But it's not just the neuroscientists who offer evidence of our unconscious programming. Pioneering psychiatrists and psychologists such as Freud and Adler and their followers believe that the unconscious drives behaviors; that what the unconscious mind accepts as true, even though it often is not, creates our reality. Personality psychologist Otto Rank posited that our self-concept is shaped by unconscious conditioning and that to escape its hold we need to "break frame"—let go of assumptions and beliefs and separate from cultural conditioning. And cognitive psychologists such as Aaron Beck and Albert Ellis focus on how our core unconscious beliefs distort our thinking, and as a result, our actions.

The existential philosophers—Heidegger, Kierkegaard, Nietzsche, and Sartre among them—emphasize the need to extricate ourselves from cultural conditioning, positing that we can only be free if we determine our own beliefs and values independent of what has been inculcated by our parents and society. Kierkegaard, for instance, believed that free choice is the key to defining our own existence and that being aware of our own beliefs, versus those imposed upon us, is essential to free choice. Heidegger was even more assertive about how we've been programmed, noting that "We are born in the 'they,' into a fully-scripted, well-organized on-going social structure. And we will remain absorbed in the 'they' for our whole lives unless we discover how to become more Authentic."

Experts in other fields from education to filmmaking to spiritual development agree with Heidegger about the need to free ourselves from the "they." Jack Mezirow, the originator of Transformative Learning Theory, proposes that the purpose of childhood is formation, but that the purpose of adulthood is transformation. And part of transforming is awakening to limiting beliefs and acting from our own purposes, values, and meanings, rather than acting from purposes that we have undiscerningly assimilated from others. To do this, he asserts that we must change our frames of reference—what he calls perspective transformation—and shift from automatic thinking to autonomous thinking. The movie *The Matrix* highlighted the prison of living in illusion—a false reality—and the importance of breaking out to reclaim our own authentic reality. Throughout time, religious and spiritual teachers have taught the importance of awareness and breaking free from limiting perspectives on a path toward enlightenment. Hindu followers speak of breaking free of Maya, the world of illusion.

Recognize, then, that our notion of a controlling matrix is backed by research, experts, and leaders in a whole host of fields. But you don't have to rely on any of these to verify the existence of this matrix. Just ask yourself the following questions:

> *Have I ever eaten when I was not hungry, procrastinated with good excuses, or done anything else my better self told me not to do?*
>
> *Have I ever told myself or others that I can't do something because, "That's not me," or "It's not done that way"?*
>
> *Have I ever regretted turning down an opportunity, from a relationship to a job, saying at the time, "It's not right for me"?*
>
> *Do I ever make decisions "instinctively" that seem right at the time but keep me locked in the same routines and behaviors?*

The reason we act in ways that are detrimental to our growth or fail to take action that would support our growth is our matrix, as the following examples illustrate.

SHARED INSIGHTS PROVIDE REVELATING SPARK

Cassandra was a beautiful woman who was working on her fourth marriage. She had grown up in extreme poverty, with parents who fought and frequently lied—to Cassandra, to each other, to creditors.

Cassandra not only lacked the toys and creature comforts that most kids had, but her childhood was also very painful and lonely, as her parents had little energy or attention for her—they were constantly stressed out, fighting about money, and engaged in ethically dubious behaviors. In an attempt to escape the pain, Cassandra promised herself that when she grew up, she would never be poor.

When Cassandra was a young woman, she realized that her beauty provided her with a way to obtain the influence and affluence she'd lacked as a child. Her yearning was to love and be loved, but Cassandra misread this yearning and felt that what she wanted and needed was wealth. It was only when she began to sense her true yearning and engaged in growth activities and life coaching that she revelated on this pattern, which eventually yielded an "aha" moment.

The first man Cassandra married seemed very wealthy—he drove a fancy car, lived in an expensive house, and wore fine clothes. They had one child, and then Cassandra discovered that their income was dependent on her husband's mother, who had inherited a great deal of money. Her husband had not been honest with her about the source of his money or the fact that his mother controlled him by controlling the flow of money into his household. Shortly after making this discovery, Cassandra got a divorce.

The second husband was also wealthy, and Cassandra knew that the source of the income was not his mother since she had died years ago. He talked a good game—he made it sound like his money came from his investing. But Cassandra noticed that her new husband spent a lot of time visiting and talking on the phone with his late wife's mother (she had died two years before Cassandra met him). It turned out that he curried favor with her because she was wealthy and sent him regular checks for sizable amounts. Disgusted with his pandering, Cassandra divorced him.

The third husband was a corporate executive who had held a series of impressive-sounding titles with well-known companies. He also owned a great deal of real estate. Cassandra was sure that this was the relationship that would provide her with the lifestyle and sense of security she longed for. Unfortunately, she found out that her husband jumped from important job to important job because of various work improprieties; she also learned that his extensive real estate holdings were highly leveraged. Again, she got a divorce.

Because of the emotional trauma of these failed marriages, Cassandra sought feedback and support in a growth group and coaching and eventually she saw the programming behind her behaviors. She had thought that she'd married each man because they were wealthy. Her miswanting for wealth, rather than yearning for love, came from her misdiagnosis of the cause of her pain. She'd believed that her family's poverty was responsible for her pain, when in fact, it was the lying, deceit, and lack of real contact that had caused her suffering. For Cassandra, her early programming and experiences of love meant that people lied and were dishonest. She had been programmed to fall in love with men who were dishonest—this was the lesson that had been burned into her neural pathways as a small child and it influenced her behavior in relationships for years. It was only when she revelated— when she had this moment of clarity about why she was attracted to and fell in love with these "worthless" men—that she was able to loosen the hold this programming had on her.

Again, this isn't a one-time event. For Cassandra to make progress toward satisfying her true yearning, she's going to have to revelate continuously and keep working at understanding her programming so she can break free of it and rematrix. And again, it's not easy. Our unconscious mind senses danger when we approach awareness of what resides beneath the conscious surface, because that awareness threatens our matrix. It prefers to operate unimpeded by our awareness and probing questions. It doesn't want to be unmasked. To paraphrase Thoreau and Sartre, most of us prefer to live lives of quiet desperation rather than noisy exploration. When we start exposing our programming for what it is, things get messy. We have to confront the fact that we've been at the mercy of experiences that happened long ago. This can be especially challenging for those who feel they've already done a lot of growth work.

But it's worth it. It's actually more than worth it, especially when you consider what happens in our brains during this revelating stage. Returning to our neuroscience research for a moment, here is what happens when we gain an insight about our programming. As the insight occurs, our brain forms a fresh but fragile neural connection or pathway. A flurry of activity occurs neurologically, what we call a neuronal "happy dance." We feel an adrenaline rush, recognizing all the life possibilities that are opening up before us. In turn, this rush motivates us to act, to reveal our insights to others, and to engage in behaviors consistent with our yearning. For years, we've been operating on automatic pilot, and revelating starts exposing us to this truth and tears down the barriers to new ways of being.

Consider Dana and Loren, a young married couple. Both are highly intelligent professionals—she's an Oxford-trained economist, he's a graduate of a top business school. As a child of public servants, Dana was expected to do well academically and she never disappointed. Despite the universal health care of her native England, her younger brother, who was ill quite a bit as a child, had received the bulk of the family's resources including Dana's parents' attention. Dana's parents assumed that she could handle just about anything that came her way without assistance, and they were right—Dana was a highly self-sufficient perfectionist. More than that, she never gave her parents any problems—she never got in trouble and displayed a high degree of responsibility from a young age.

Loren, on the other hand, was raised by a father who was a charming con man who made book on any horse race or athletic event where his "followers" would wager. Early on, he instructed Loren in the way he conducted business. He explained the need to keep three sets of books: one for yourself, one for your partners, and one for the government. Loren's parents were tremendously manipulative and deceitful—both had affairs and eventually divorced.

Dana's perfectionism and fear of letting others down caused her significant anxiety, which she brought home. At times, Loren was able to calm her, but in other instances he withdrew, and they would eventually end up fighting. Similarly, when Dana and Loren worked on anything together—a home repair project, a business they wanted to start, planning a vacation—they found themselves having a variety of problems. Dana became increasingly tense, Loren became increasingly withdrawn, and eventually the conflict would begin. Yet when they started the program in which they were introduced to the process of transformation, they began to change. As they engaged in new behaviors, had insights, and shared those insights with each other and their coaches, they became acutely aware of their programming. Dana's revelating led her to understand that she had gone about life in a way that assumed her needs would never be met. This had been deeply programmed into her in a thousand ways from the time she'd begun to crawl. Loren's revelating showed him that he had operated under the assumption that others would use him—that people would manipulate him for their own purposes.

These discoveries shocked and energized them both. Dana had been completely oblivious to how this conviction about her unmet needs would cause her to have trouble setting limits at work, be overly histrionic toward Loren, avoid situations in which she might be less than perfect, and finally, to avoid failure at all costs. Loren, too, had no idea that he'd reflexively withdrawn from relationships over the years when it felt like people were manipulating him, a response from early childhood that would be activated with the slightest hint of manipulation, sending him scurrying deep into his shell and making him remote and difficult to communicate with.

By revelating, Dana and Loren are changing the nature of their relationship—they are becoming much more communicative and intimate. Dana learned to identify her needs earlier on in a relationship or interaction and to ask in a more balanced way for more than she'd ever previously thought anyone would give her. Loren learned to challenge Dana and others and even begin pressing for needs of his own to be met—even identifying when he felt he was being used, forcing himself to talk about this fear whenever it surfaces.

MORE THAN JUST NEW INSIGHTS OR PERSPECTIVES

As we noted earlier, revelating is a tool for Transformers, not just an insight. While it's great to engage and revelate, recognize your programming, glimpse fresh possibilities for yourself, and see how you might become someone with greater authenticity than your current self, this phase also has a "reveal" component. If you limit yourself to the "aha" component, you won't reap the full benefits. Therefore, don't go through revelating only within the confines of your head. As you grasp your programming and learn about your matrix, don't keep all this amazing stuff bottled up inside. Instead, disclose to others what you are thinking, how you are feeling, and what you're discovering. Ask questions of those you trust about what you've found. Respond to what you've learned by acting in more genuine ways—testing your new assumptions by doing things your programming told you that you could not do.

Let's say that through your engaging, you start to revelate that you've been programmed to believe that you're a "nice girl." You've always tried to be kind and understanding, and you rarely if ever criticize others or confront them, even if you feel they've done something wrong. As you engage and see the falseness of this belief, you tell your best friend about your revelation and ask her how she sees you. You talk to your life coach and challenge him to tell you if he thinks you've been too nice in your career, in your family, in your romantic relationships. You test some not-so-nice behaviors. At work, for instance, you're known as a nice boss, a people person who always supports direct reports no matter what they say or do. At a meeting, though, when one direct report gives a report that clearly shows a lack of effort, you challenge him about how sketchy his report seems and how you expect him to invest more time and commitment the next time he prepares a report.

Doing these things reveals a part of you that you previously didn't even think existed. As you do them, though, it may foster yet another revelation—that you can deviate from your "nice" modus operandi and people won't automatically hate you. In fact, you may find that contrary to your expectations, they appreciate your honesty.

The point, though, is that revelating goes both ways—it's an inner recognition and consciousness shift as well as an outer response to what's happening inside of you.

THE FIVE THINGS YOU MUST DO

To help you revelate, it's important to understand the five different phases of revelating. In this way, you will understand when you have fully revelated and when you haven't.

1. **CREATING "AHA" MOMENTS.** Transformers have lots of these moments. The "aha" is a moment of insight or epiphany—the glimpse you get of your programming, and your realization that it is programming rather than part of who you inherently are, or of who you could become. These can include significant insights, deeper joy, disturbing discoveries, and life-altering epiphanies.
2. **REVEALING YOURSELF.** As we discussed, this is where you share your insights in the form of discussion, confession, question, or behavior, but more important, you share more of yourself, becoming more transparent and real. You share your "aha's" as well as newly discovered unconscious fears, hurts, anger, sadness, and joy.
3. **CHALLENGING YOUR LIMITING BELIEFS.** As part of your "aha" and your revealing, you stop being a blind adherent to what you always believed, allowing yourself to recognize the limits of your current beliefs and beginning to consider new beliefs.
4. **ESTABLISHING A BIGGER VISION.** These new beliefs help you see fresh possibilities for yourself; the new revelation is that you can achieve a lot more in any and every area of your life project.
5. **GETTING AND EMBRACING THE GAME.** This is where you have a jump in understanding how your matrix influences your thoughts, feelings, and actions. You see how you've been limiting yourself and deeply understand that you can break free of these limitations—and how to do so. You gain a specific understanding of the way life can really work—and what it takes to have a spectacular life project.

TOOLS FOR REVELATING

As you go through revelating, you need to keep reminding yourself that you can't revelate in a vacuum. Yes, some of the work you need to do will be done alone through reflection. But without engaging along with your yearning, all you're going to get are some brief insights that will be as impactful and long-lasting as a soap bubble.

So you need to engage, and you need to be aware as you do so. Focus on and be honest about what your beliefs and behaviors have always been. To facilitate this awareness, here are some tools you can use:

- **ROLE MODELS.** Daniel Coyle speaks about ignition, and translated to our terms, this is the revelating that happens when we are inspired and challenged by others performing at a high level. For many years, the sub-four-minute mile seemed like an insurmountable barrier in track and field. Then Roger Bannister did it. Within six weeks, a number of other runners had also run sub-four-minute miles. Why? Because these other runners were aware of what could be achieved. Role models open our minds to possibilities that we previously didn't see.

  Find a role model for the type of programming-breaking behavior or life you want to have. It can be someone you read about or, even better, someone you know. This may require a bit of research and interacting with others, but when you see someone who has undergone significant change, or even transformation, in the direction in which you want to grow, it will provide you with an image and mindset conducive to revelating. If you're a shy person who avoids social interactions and believes you're always going to be shy and you find someone who also once felt that way and transcended her self-imposed barriers, then you'll gain the impetus to follow the same path yourself. If you are a go-getter who wants to conquer the world, find heroes who have gone before you.

- **FEEDBACK AND DISCLOSURE.** We all have our blind spots. Yours might be that you believe you can't have it all, or that all bosses are jerks, or that all men are jerks. You might be absolutely certain that your success as an entrepreneur demands such devotion that you can't be equally successful in marriage and family life; you may have decided that you're not the sort of person who marries and raises children. You might be a manager who believes you have to do it all yourself, or you might be unwilling to take risks because you think that you can't handle any activities outside of your comfort zone. Or you may see yourself as a loner, or as the life of the party, or even as the guy who always finishes second.

    These are all blind spots because they're created by your programming—embedded in and emanating from your matrix. You've ruled these out as ways you can be, thereby preventing yourself from becoming all of who you can become. When you reveal yourself to others and ask them for their reactions and advice, however, you invite the type of feedback that leads to revelating—recognizing the limiting areas of your programming. It's tremendously empowering to be told that you're capable of doing or being a way you've always assumed to be beyond you. And while it can be threatening when someone points out the fallacy of your assumptions, it can also open up new possibilities. We know that it may be difficult to ask a boss if he sees you as forever being a mid-level functionary or to ask a close friend if she thinks you're capable of being a good parent—consciously or not, you're afraid of having your programming exposed. But you need to demand feedback from people you trust—a friend, a family member, a coach—since this creates an environment where revelating happens.

    The Johari window is a good tool to put your revealing disclosures and the feedback you receive into a revelating context.

Johari Window

	KNOWN TO SELF	UNKNOWN TO SELF
UNKNOWN TO OTHERS	**PRIVATE SELF** **Known to Self** **Unknown to Others**	**HIDDEN ZONE** **Unknown to Self** **& Others**
KNOWN TO OTHERS	**PUBLIC SELF** **Known to Self** **& Others**	**BLIND SPOT** **Unknown to Self** **Known to Others**

Through these four frames of awareness, the Johari window helps Transformers "see" things they would otherwise miss. As you share what is known to you and unknown to others (private self) and as others share with you what is known to them but unknown to you (your blind spot), you expand your public self and learn new things that had previously been in the hidden zone. In this way, you expand your awareness and revelating—both in discovery and sharing. If you consider that knowledge is power, then expanding your self-knowledge is expanding your personal power.

When others point out data in your blind spot—data that is unacceptable or challenging to you—this feedback can shake you to your core, but in a good way that expands your self-knowledge. In other instances, you may find that others respect you in an area where you feel vulnerable and it's as if you are the ugly duckling finding out that you are a swan. No matter how accomplished you are, you will still possess limiting feelings and beliefs to be explored.

Feedback can make you think, dig deep, and challenge tightly-held beliefs. In other words, it makes you revelate.

DO YOU WANT US TO DRAW YOU A MAP?

To facilitate revelating, draw a map of your matrix. This may sound like a formidable task, but it's actually relatively easy to do. Before showing you what a Matrix Map looks like, recall that the matrix is a complex web of neural connections formed in early childhood—early experience patterns, and some traumas. This is the wiring through which your neuronal impulses flow and that determines your beliefs about yourself and the world, how you limit yourself, and the self-fulfilling prophecy you call yourself.

To help you draw your map, let's examine the rules and beliefs in this representation of one area of the matrix with an example of a core mistaken belief represented in black.

One Segment of a Matrix Mapped

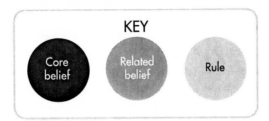

KEY

Core belief · Related belief · Rule

Suck it up

Act like I have it all together

I must give more than I get

Always focus on others' needs first

I need to look to others' needs

Work harder to earn just enough

I am not attractive

The opposite sex won't like me for who I am

I'm not good enough

There is never enough

Money is in short supply

I work harder to earn more

Work like a dog

I need too much attention

My fear is proof I'm not good enough

My feelings don't matter

I shouldn't be afraid

Be tough

I need to push myself

I need to push myself

Damn the torpedoes

Using the tools and techniques of the previous section should provide you with a great deal of information about your matrix. You will be developing this map for the rest of your life as well as rematrixing from the new map indicated by your deeper yearning. You see, the matrix wipes out many of your genuine deep yearnings. As you engage, receive feedback, and employ role models, you'll move through the revelating phases repeatedly. In this way, the matrix that was formed when you were small starts becoming apparent to you. When this happens, map it in a way that resembles this graphic. And as you map it, you'll revelate even more—regardless of how far you have come on your journey of transformation.

Matrix Mapping is just a fancy way of saying we want you to draw a picture of what you revelate. Graphics are good. They provide a visual reminder of all the beliefs and assumptions that have guided your life up to this point. You can put your map next to your desk at work and on the refrigerator at home, a handy way to maintain your revelating awareness.

Transformers are continually developing their Matrix Maps—on the alert for limiting beliefs and rules. To map your matrix, bring to the surface the assumptions and beliefs that unconsciously govern your behavior. You can do this in a number of ways—in fact, you should try to do it in multiple ways, as each method will bring forth different aspects of your matrix:

- *Identify Your Self-fulfilling Prophecies.* To describe what a self-fulfilling prophecy is and how it reveals your matrix, let's look at an example of the "illogical flow" of this prophecy:

  - My unconscious belief is: *I don't matter* (B^1 - my own belief).

  - As a result of this belief, I'm self-effacing and don't assert myself; I think, *That's just who I am.* Then a situation occurs in which I fail to ask for something that I think is important or I am timid while others assert their opinions and make requests (A^1 - my own action or inaction).

- This leads others to believe they do not need to pay attention to me (B^2 - others' beliefs).

- This other person responds to those who are assertive and I am overlooked (A^2 - others' actions). This confirms my limiting belief and I am now in the familiar territory of the self-fulfilling prophecy I call myself.

Self-Fulfilling Prophecy

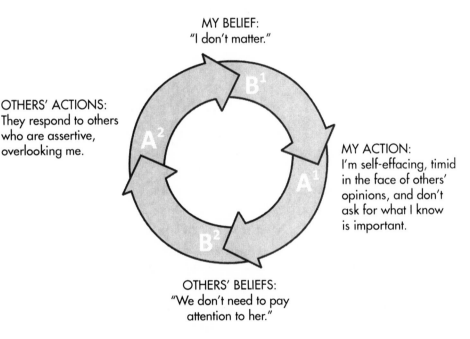

MY BELIEF:
"I don't matter."

OTHERS' ACTIONS:
They respond to others who are assertive, overlooking me.

MY ACTION:
I'm self-effacing, timid in the face of others' opinions, and don't ask for what I know is important.

OTHERS' BELIEFS:
"We don't need to pay attention to her."

UNEARTHING YOUR UNCONSCIOUS MISTAKEN BELIEFS

By finding the pattern of self-fulfilling prophecy in your life, you can sneak a peek at how your unconscious beliefs create your reality. Think about things you do not readily do: ask for help, take risks, and so on. For instance, you tell yourself, *I cannot do that because* . . . Or think about risks you did take that didn't work out—then you said to yourself *I-told-you-so—I told you that risk wouldn't work.* Or look at how you believe things are going to turn out: *See, I knew it wouldn't work because it never does for you.* Think about how you filled in the blanks. For instance: *I told you so—you just aren't creative enough to handle that type of assignment.* Or: *I told you so—you are never going to have a relationship because you're unlovable.* Or: *See, I knew I didn't matter. This is just more proof.*

This pattern doesn't happen in just one area of your life. Whether your unconscious belief is that you're unlovable, you don't matter, you're not creative, you're a pleaser, or anything else, it will manifest itself at work, at home, at play, and in every other life situation. Spot the belief that starts the prophecy and concludes it, and you'll have something to revelate about.

■ **WATCH FOR REACTIONS THAT ARE OUT OF PROPORTION TO A SITUATION.** This will provide another clue as to the unconscious beliefs that govern your life. Do you find yourself unreasonably angry when your spouse asks you to do a small chore? Do you find yourself terribly sad when you hear that a neighbor you didn't even know well has moved? Do you become agitated and upset when someone asks you an innocuous question about work?

These overreactions or disconnected reactions (disconnected from the event that, on the surface, evoked them) can help you track down an unconscious belief. Your job is to identify that specific underlying belief. Again, watch for patterns. For instance, you become unusually angry and lose your temper whenever your spouse tries to help you—he slices the turkey when you're having trouble with it or he tells you to let him take a look at the computer when you're struggling with a function. Force yourself to dig beneath your surface explanation ("I'm in a bad mood," for instance) and think about why these seemingly helpful gestures from your spouse make you furious. Perhaps it's because your unconscious belief is that you're helpless—perhaps your mom was overprotective of you from the time you were born and you remember her not letting you do things yourself.

▪ **SPOTLIGHT COMMON CORE MISTAKEN BELIEFS.** All of us have mistaken or limiting beliefs, as Alfred Adler observed many years ago. These limiting beliefs about ourselves and the world are formed very early in our development and operate unconsciously throughout our lives, and often, these include imagining that everybody else feels great about themselves and has it all together! No matter how successful we are or how magnificent our relationships, our leadership, or our talents; no matter how much work we have done on ourselves, to some extent we all harbor unconscious self-doubt. We may not consciously believe these things, and in fact, may even consciously think the opposite of them, but we still act based on these mistaken beliefs.

Look at this list of the most common core mistaken beliefs that our research has uncovered and see which ones resonate with you. Even if you don't "feel" it, look to evidence in your life to see which mistaken belief might be closest to your core limiting belief. Not getting paid what you are worth? The belief of *I'm not worthy* might be the reason. Always feeling like you don't measure up or you don't have enough time, money, energy . . . or frequently have a sense of scarcity? Then the mistaken belief of *I'm not enough* and *there's not enough* may be the culprit.

Core Mistaken Beliefs About Myself

I'm not enough	*I have to earn love*
I'm too much	*I'm not OK as I am*
I'm no good	*I am insignificant*
I'm not good enough	*There's something wrong with me*

I'm not lovable

I'm not worthy

I'm not OK

I'm alone and on my own

I'm a burden

My feelings are bad

My needs are bad

I don't matter

Core Mistaken Beliefs About The World

There aren't enough:

- *resources*

- *time*

- *money*

The world is hostile

The world is out to get me

People want the worst for me

The world is dangerous

There isn't enough love to go around

- **CREATE A CAN'T DO/CAN'T BE LIST.** Another way to get at the unconscious beliefs that form your matrix involves searching for the things you've told yourself that you can't do or be. Maybe you've long insisted to yourself that you can never get up and speak in front of an audience the way others can. Maybe you've always harbored the fear that you can never be truly happy. You may have ruled out being rich, attractive, or beloved. Whatever it is, you're convinced that you can't be or do something because you're lacking in some way.

  The truth, of course, is that this is an artificially imposed limitation. While not everyone can be an astrophysicist or a professional football player because of their skill set and physical limitations, most of us create barriers to all sorts of life's truly available possibilities because of our unconscious beliefs. To reveal the belief, make a list of all the things you can't do or be. If it helps, break this list into categories: careers, relationships, hobbies, travel, sports, behaviors, feelings.

Once you've completed your list, look for the one overarching belief that prevents you from doing or being all the things you've listed. For instance, you may feel that you can't run a marathon, have a great marriage, form close friendships, or progress much beyond middle management in your company. While these are all very different "can'ts," they're united by one driving belief such as: *You don't matter . . . You're not enough . . .* or *You're lacking in some significant way.*

This belief limits you today from developing the drive to succeed at fulfilling your dreams at work, the trust and openness required of intimacy in a great marriage, the stamina necessary to complete a marathon, the high level of empathy and communication that close friendships require, and the durability and ambition that can take you into top management positions.

DON'T UNDERESTIMATE THE POWER OF THE MATRIX

Expect to be revved up as you revelate, but also expect for the matrix to make its presence felt as you experience slips and frustrations that cause you to want to give up and make excuses, even after you start mapping your matrix.

Your matrix isn't going to like it when you start exposing it. It's going to assert itself when you think, *I have special gifts; I can go further than I ever thought; I'm not inherently unlovable; I am desirable and there's someone out there for me,* or *Maybe I'm a lot more spiritual than I think; I can try to find a connection with a higher power.* This is why stating positive affirmations alone doesn't work—in your conscious mind you say to yourself, *I am lovable,* and your matrix reacts and fights it with an unconscious response of disbelief that if translated might sound something like, *Yeah, right. That's why you're sitting home watching reruns on a Saturday night instead of being out on a date.*

Your matrix will reflexively attempt to restore its version of reality when it hears these positive thoughts. It will be especially assertive when you try to do something that breaks from your programming and it doesn't work out. It may even resort to trickery, lying low until it can subtly reassert itself. For instance, you've been programmed to believe your limitations, such as that you're unlovable, but you revelate and you start a relationship that you think might turn into a long-term one. Then the other person breaks up with you, and your matrix says, *See, you are unlovable.*

At that moment, you're vulnerable to lapsing back into your old way of thinking about yourself. Your rising expectations that come with revelating are dashed in an instant. You become discouraged and disheartened. It's at this point you have to rally emotionally. Recall what you yearn for. Resolve to pursue it despite the setbacks you might encounter. Above all else, keep revelating in a positive emotional state.

IN THE MOOD TO REVELATE?

It is very difficult to gain and maintain the insights that revelating provides when you're down. When you feel defeated or unhappy, you find that all sorts of distorted imaginings—what we call stinking thinking—get in the way of your insights. You'll tell yourself you're being naïve or that you're just wasting your time. Being down is your matrix's way of reasserting itself.

Therefore, reveal to others that you are stuck and have them help you create a more objective, more positive sense of yourself. If you are optimistic about yourself and your future, you'll keep these distracting thoughts at bay and actually be rematrixing. We all need support to be emotionally focused and hopeful as we gain insights about our matrix. We are not talking about mindless Suzie Sunshine ways of being, but instead genuinely engaged ways of living life.

Get back to deeper yearning and engage to rev yourself up with the possibilities that are opening in your life. You will rediscover a sense of excitement about the growth that you're going to experience. Take comfort in the fact that setbacks are part of the process and that your yearning is more powerful than your programming; that you can continue to reach a series of ever more ambitious goals despite these setbacks as long as you trust in what you yearn for.

Remember, too, that revelating is a continuous back-and-forth dynamic involving having insights and revealing these insights. Each feeds the other. Make a conscious effort to share your *aha* moments as well as your challenges—but be careful that you don't listen to naysayers and dream busters. By acknowledging your revelating, claiming it, and sharing your insights with others who support you, you'll gain reinforcement for these insights, reminding yourself both of how you've been wired and the fact that you don't have to be bound by that wiring.

THE REWARDS OF REVELATING

As revelating uncovers your limiting beliefs and opens up possibilities, you will discover the rewards that are unique to you. Similarly, as you share hidden aspects of yourself with others, they will see you in new ways and point out aspects of your behavior to which you were blind. Acting on these discoveries, you will reap unanticipated rewards as Jonas did:

Jonas was at one of his lowest points as he sat in his attorney's office. The vacation house had been sold, they had moved out of the house in which his children had been raised, and he was staring blankly into a future without his wife. Firstborn in his family, Jonas was raised to be a caretaker. He protected his mother from his abusive father and, as a sergeant in the military, prided himself on taking care of his men. It was natural for him to become a cop and eventually, chief of police. He not only cared for his men, but the whole town. Everyone felt good about Jonas and his diligent service to the community—everyone except his wife.

Jonas's attorney was putting the finishing touches on his divorce. There was tension in their relationship and issues about money, and there had been verbal fights. His wife had finally said she couldn't take it anymore and so the divorce process had begun. Jonas moved into a one-bedroom apartment that he found to be cold and oppressive. He worked even harder. But no matter what he did, he could not get himself out of the funk and see his way to moving on with his life.

He met with Judith, and she suggested he attend one of our weekend workshops. Though Jonas's down mood prevented him from showing much enthusiasm about attending, he agreed.

His revelating at the workshop was more than eye-opening. Sure, Jonas knew all that stuff about being a firstborn caretaker and protecting his mother, but he did not know the power and depth of the feelings associated with this history and how they impacted his behaviors. He was chagrined to see how these feelings caused him to be overly tough on their oldest child and to throw his tough life in the face of all of his children. Until then, he hadn't realized how jealous he was of them and how much he wanted to have the freedom and security they had.

His revelating continued to present him with one of his biggest surprises—under it all, he was really hurt and afraid. Hard to believe, but the tough guy really wasn't so tough after all. He was saddened as he realized how much of his kids' childhood experiences he had not understood because he had numbed himself to his own feelings. Like a light switch going on in his brain, Jonas realized what his wife had been so mad about. She felt abandoned. The regret and remorse that flooded Jonas's thoughts were overwhelming as he drove to his wife's new home to talk that first weekend. He and his wife talked all night as he shared and they cried together.

"That was the man I thought I had married," his wife reported after attending the seminar a few months later. For the next year, the two of them worked together on weekly assignments, sharing their discoveries and experiencing the intimacy they had feared would never be theirs.

The work was not easy or fast, but they persisted and today, they are back together, not only living under the same roof, but also working together. No, Jonas did not quit the force, but his wife is now running the consulting business that they started together, along with other staff and Jonas's guidance.

Jonas discovered what so many others do who revelate: *how I see the world is a result of my matrix, my beliefs, and my programming.* And like so many others, he also discovered the joy and possibilities of making new choices. That's the beauty of revelating. By waking up to our unconscious programming, we can literally re-choose and begin anew. And our first step is to take action on that revelation through liberating.

CHAPTER SIX

LIBERATE:
BREAK FREE AND LAUNCH
YOUR SPECTACULAR LIFE

When I let go of what I am, I become what I might be. . . .
—LAO TZU

LIBERATING IS THE SOMETIMES THRILLING, sometimes terrifying process of stepping into the unknown, doing the undoable, saying the unsayable, acting on the unimaginable. This is where you unleash your personal power. Flowing from your revelating, you act on your insights to break free of your limiting programming. Like engaging, liberating requires you to take action, but now your actions are both more strategic and more revolutionary—it's like engaging on steroids.

Liberating is a process of adventure and discovery—not just practicing what you've already done. Even if you've been on a long journey of personal discovery, there is always the next action to take you out of your comfort zone, always the opportunity to explore new possibilities. Liberating isn't just doing new things for the sake of doing new things—it is acting on deeper yearnings and putting revelating into practice. Only when we take action to break free from limiting beliefs and norms do we become free to create our best life.

FREEDOM! THE THRILL AND PROMISE OF LIBERATING

The word "liberate" evokes an exhilarating sense of freedom—we yearn to be free, to bust loose from shackles that have been holding us back and live the life we dream of. Freedom inspires poets, philosophers, revolutionaries, spiritual leaders, and all of us. It is the exciting promise of freedom that we need to keep in front of us in order to liberate.

With liberating you can define and create life on your own terms, according to your own values and principles. Rather than doing things solely to please others, or from a sense of duty or social convention, you experiment with ways of being that lead to becoming a Transformer.

Liberating goes well beyond traditional insight into the development of new modes of behavior. Choice by choice, you become more authentic and transparent. Governed by your own internal values, rather than the opinions and approval of others, you become more fully alive. You experience heightened awareness, sensations, and emotions, and you operate more in the here and now. Your personal power increases—your influence, your ability to assert your will, your productivity, and your sense of self expand. You are in a continual process of unleashing yourself and discovering your potential—to become who you could become. Nietzsche viewed freedom and the responsibility it holds as your true power—the power to take charge of your own life.

THERE BE DRAGONS HERE

Like the hero of a mythic journey, with liberating you leave home and venture into uncharted territory. But like a hero's exciting quest with its trials and tribulations, this phase can also be scary—free from that programming even for a moment, you also experience the anxiety of being authentic. You're acting differently, and people notice and may respond negatively. More to the point, you notice, and it may initially feel uncomfortable and worrisome.

We don't mean to scare you, but we do want to prepare you.

Putting it in a philosophical context may be the best preparation. If you listen to the existentialists (which we do), then liberating represents a crucial trade-off: you accept a certain amount of anxiety in exchange for getting rid of the ontological guilt that's plagued you. What the existentialists mean by "ontological guilt" is that gnawing sense of missed opportunities. In your gut, your heart, or your soul, you sense that you're missing out on what you should be doing—what would really make you, you.

Yes, the anxiety of pure free will can be intense, but facing this anxiety brings the possibility of experiencing existential freedom and joy as you become who you could be—more your authentic self. Authenticity is a key component of liberating, so let's take a moment to understand what it is . . . and what it isn't.

THE ILLUSION OF BEING ME

We like to think of ourselves as being authentic. But in fact, our matrix provides us with a very limited perspective on what authenticity is. It tells us who we are and what we can and can't do. It filters what it perceives as our unacceptable impulses and keeps reminding us when we consider trying something new or different: *That's not me.*

Yet, the existential philosophers tell us that authenticity isn't being true to who you've been—it's being true to who you could become. Authenticity isn't something in the past. There are people who maintain, "Well, I've always been shy," or "I knew from the time I was little that I should be in sales—everyone told me that's what I was good at." What they're really communicating is that they must adhere to this extremely narrow view of themselves, a perspective often developed before they had language, created for them by their family interactions and societal programming.

Disturbingly, who we wound up being from our early life experiences and programming, our matrix, is not our authentic self.

Try this exercise:

> Describe yourself by making lists of *I am* _____ and *I am*
> *not* _____ statements—both what you are proud of, like
> *I am clever; I am not a pushover,* and things you try to hide or
> avoid, like *I am shy; I am competitive; I am not creative.*
>
> Now rewrite the same list starting with *I wound up being* or *I*
> *wound up not being—I wound up being clever; I wound up not*
> *being creative.* Feel the difference? Who you wound up being is
> not the essence of who you are or who you could be.

In every moment, we have the choice between doing what we have always done or doing something new and stepping into the unknown. People think they're being genuine when they tell you that they can't and won't do something because it "just isn't them." In fact, they can't do what is being discussed because their programming prevents them from considering options outside of a narrow range. Rather than being genuine, they're adhering to childhood brainwashing that they're this way and not that.

Authenticity, though, means that you keep trying to recreate yourself anew in line with your yearning. Your authentic self keeps evolving during this liberating phase—you free yourself from your limited—and often fake—self to become what you yearn to be—what we refer to as your *next most radiant self.* This is a concept we'll return to later, but for now, let that bright image wash over you. Imagine stepping into an elevated self and realizing possibilities you never imagined.

Let's root this discussion of authenticity in an example. Joe was convinced that he was a tight-lipped, hard-charging, driven business guy down to his wing-tip shoes. He was sure he wasn't, and would never be, someone who could or would waste time on what he considered "secondary" activities—family, pets, yoga, going to the theater. It wasn't that he disliked these activities, but being obsessive and ambitious was just who he was, and since he was earning a mid-six-figure salary with a top firm at age thirty-five, he figured this was his "destiny."

Nonetheless, Joe understood that something was missing from his life so he came to Wright for coaching and even attended a seminar, and eventually a peer development group. He couldn't believe that he was doing this "touchy-feely stuff." To his surprise, though, other highly accomplished individuals attended the seminar and participated in his group. Initially, he asked us for help in his climb to the top of his company because he had been given feedback that his financial firm was questioning his appropriateness for a VP-level position. As he began doing assignments geared to tap into his yearning, he found himself engaging in new ways that he had considered weak and "not him." He began noticing emotions he had previously blocked. His tight-lipped ways began to loosen. Perhaps the most amazing moment for him occurred one day at work when he told the CEO of a consulting firm that he was hurt by something he had said. This moment of revelating, to his amazement, showed him that what he had really wanted all along was deeper contact with himself and others—to satisfy his yearnings. As he eased into the process and became a Transformer, the program led him through the steps to consistently and strategically liberate.

It was astonishing to see how he began changing after this and other experiences, until he began liberating in earnest. His main insight: What he had thought was directness and authenticity was really nothing more than pushing for results as the driven son of high-achieving parents who pushed him to be even more high-achieving than they were. Once he had this insight, he began applying it in all areas of his life. He found himself creating deep friendships with people who previously had only been acquaintances. He began enjoying conversations with everyone from the doorman to the CEO of his firm. His capacity to be one of the guys increased, and he discovered that the way to the executive suite was through integrity, excellence, and, surprise of surprises, friendship.

He began dating women who he previously would have said weren't his type. Eventually, he married, had children, and became very involved in community service. Liberating introduced him to the adventure of authenticity and became a way of life that keeps him achieving in new ways—light-years from what he originally thought was the genuine Joe.

We don't want to make it sound like authenticity is easy for Joe—or for anyone else. To be authentic, you have to step squarely into your existential anxiety—the everyday worries that simmer beneath conscious awareness. This can mean a lot of things, depending on your yearning and the engaging that follows: refusing to conform (or, if you identify yourself as a rebel, conforming), saying something that doesn't sound anything like you, making a decision that goes against every decision you've made your entire life, or even just blurting out the next thing that comes to mind. It can mean taking a risk based on your revelating, or engaging past your personal limits, based on a deeper yearning. It could be a small thing like challenging an older sibling who you never challenged before, or a big thing like changing careers and moving halfway across the world.

Søren Kierkegaard, the existential Christian minister and philosopher, called for us to consciously and intentionally author our lives instead of remaining well-adjusted conformists. Abraham Maslow, the father of humanistic psychology, puts the challenge another way: will we make safe choices or growth choices? Within the context of liberating, the message is that you can't free yourself without embracing this definition of authenticity. Now let's look at liberating in a more linear way, focusing on the phases people go through as they liberate.

THE POLES OF LIBERATING

There are two aspects of liberating: breaking free *from,* and becoming free *to.* The first is reactive—you free yourself from an old behavior, attitude, routine, and so on. The second is expressive. It refers to the freedom to do things, to go toward, to become. It is creative—it's about being or expressing something you've never been or expressed before. A typical reactive liberating action might be to question authority when you have previously submitted without reflection. Expressive freedom often includes becoming more free and spontaneous, expressing thoughts and feelings you previously weren't consciously aware of, revealing deeper truths. In revelating, you become aware of your limiting beliefs and the ways you have restricted yourself. In liberating, you take action to break free from those limiting beliefs and behaviors and become free to define life by new empowering beliefs and actions.

Let's look at the five phases, from uncaged to free exploration and voyaging into ourselves:

1. **OPENING THE CAGE DOOR.** As you revelate and gain insights about your matrix, you recognize that you've been in a figurative cage all your life. This awareness is crucial. As you think about it and grasp the implications, you realize that the bars have been your unconscious limits on who you are. This realization provides the impetus to swing open that door. Your first instinct is to get out of the cage. You are revelating and considering other possibilities, other ways of being in the world. You're beginning to liberate as you open your mind to consider new options—possible new aspects of yourself. As one Transformer said about this phase: "It is like, wow! I was in these chains and the chains were made by me. I am really starting to shed them."

2. **STEPPING OUT OF THE DOOR.** You've taken that first step toward freeing yourself from your programming. Rather than just recognizing that you can escape your cage, you're actually doing something about it. This may not be a big first step to free yourself, but you're thinking, feeling, and doing things differently— anything to get out of the cage and give you a taste of freedom. One Transformer described the evening in which she decided to test socializing without drinking:

   "I was so scared, but I felt more alive at that party than any other before and had just as much fun. I relied on conversations to stay engaged, and although people were uncomfortable with me, I didn't care because I was taking care of myself. It felt like a small miracle."

3. **EXPLORING THE UNKNOWN.** This is where you experiment with new, more expressive, ways of thinking, feeling, and acting. You're going back and forth from the cage to the unknown territory outside of it. Outside, you are trying new ways of being, often in reaction to your programming. For example, you realize how scared you've been to meet new people and so now you're going to various venues where you have an excellent chance of forming new relationships. But you don't practice these behaviors consistently. Part of you still retreats to the cage, and your experimenting is somewhat tentative and still in reaction to your past. In this phase the Transformer who didn't drink in social situations was confronted with yearnings that were previously unconscious. She began talking about subjects she would normally have avoided and was surprised to find out how many people responded positively to her and even reached out in friendship.

4. **RE-HABITATING.** Now you're out of the cage and creating a new life. You need to commit to setting up a new, more conscious lifestyle to make sure you keep transitioning from reactive to proactive liberating. Your yearnings will dictate the new lifestyle and the new lifestyle will support the continual emergence of your yearnings. You're making an effort to pursue activities and people that help you feel loved, that show you that you matter, that create connections with a higher power. But it's called re-habitating for a reason—you're out of your old cage, but you have to be cautious about constructing a new one. While re-habitating is an essential task, recognize that if you allow this to be your permanent residence, it will prevent you from achieving the sort of transformative experience you desire. In order to be sure she does not revert, the non-drinking Transformer now needed to re-habitat in order to keep moving in her new direction, moving away from her caged self. Rather than just experimenting with not drinking, she is forming a new, conscious lifestyle of healthy habits, engaging friends, and stimulating experiences.

5. **RE-LIBERATING.** Liberate yourself again and again and again. As

soon as you stop, you'll find your possibilities limited and the matrix starting to reassert its hold on you. Therefore, make a conscious effort to keep trying to break free of whatever new situations and behaviors you adopt. This may sound exhausting—and it does take effort— but it's also exhilarating. The effort you put forth to free yourself from whatever new cage you create comes back to you threefold, providing you with a natural energy boost to liberate again and again. The non-drinking Transformer was amazed to discover how many other unconscious limits became obvious. She experimented with hitherto forbidden assertiveness, began asking questions that would previously have been forbidden because they would have indicated a weakness, and even forged connections with interesting people whom she previously would have been too intimidated to approach—all moves that were significant in her Transformation.

LIBERATING BODY AND BRAIN

When you take the five uncaging steps, you're taking steps to freedom with a variety of new behaviors. But as you act, these behaviors are also affecting your mind. As you'll see, when you liberate your body, you also liberate your brain.

Neural plasticity is a critical scientific concept for liberating. For many years, the conventional wisdom was that our brains stop developing relatively early in life and there's not much we can do to stimulate development later on. In fact, a vast amount of more recent neuroscience research says the opposite. Dr. Michael Merzenich, a well-respected University of California professor and neuroscience expert pioneered much of the work on brain plasticity. He states that "plasticity exists from cradle to the grave, and that radical improvements in cognitive functioning—how we learn, think, perceive, and remember are possible even in the elderly," emphasizing, "this is a way underutilized and underappreciated resource that we all have."

Brain plasticity is activated by doing something new and different, stretching just past the edge of our comfort zone. This stimulates new patterns of neural firing to create fresh synaptic linkages, changing the structure of the brain. With focused attention and repetition—the requirements for liberating—it leads to new patterns of thinking, feeling, and doing! Our brain learns better when challenged to form novel habits. In fact, neuroeconomics professor Gregory Berns has done research that shows how our brains thrive on challenge and novelty. We're hardwired for novelty, and liberating is the phase where we embrace novelty for all it's worth. Finding new adventures to experience and new challenges to overcome is where we get truly satisfied.

You may also recall our earlier discussion of the work of Stanford psychologist Carol Dweck, who focuses on why some people achieve their potential while others don't. She has found that a growth mindset is essential for learning and developing and a fixed mindset ensures stasis. Take two equally bright, talented people, but one with a growth mindset and one with a fixed mindset, and you'll see a huge disparity between the two people in everything from achievement to happiness to influence. As you know by now, liberating requires a growth mindset. You need it to deal effectively with setbacks when you try new things, to learn from critical feedback, and to master challenging new skills.

At this point, at least some of you are saying to yourself, *But I've always been shy . . . thoughtful . . . angry . . .* or *aggressive . . .* or *unassertive . . .* or *a perfectionist . . .* or *fearful . . .* or *neurotically worried.* To liberate successfully and continuously, you need to understand that this self-image has been programmed into you. But if we can't convince you, here's some compelling scientific research that might make a difference.

Dr. Philip Zimbardo runs the Shyness Clinic at Stanford University, and he finds that many shy people assume they were born this way, have always been this way, and will always be this way. Yet Dr. Zimbardo has trained many people to overcome shyness, demonstrating that this "disorder" is simply a behavioral pattern representing a lack of skills. In other words, shy people need to practice the social skills that will break them free of their habitual thinking. Their programming loses its power in the face of actions that demonstrate it to be a fiction.

Perhaps most instructive of all is the research regarding our brain chemistry, showing that we seek the neurochemical states associated with different moods. Let's say we believe ourselves to be cranky. We're convinced we were born that way, and our behavior for the last thirty-five years confirms it because we've been consistently cranky. In reality, we're addicted to the wash of peptides that floods our system when we are in a cranky mood and label ourselves as "cranky." Our neural network remembers the chemical high we felt when we scowled at our co-workers, snapped at our kids, or stewed in dissatisfaction. We become habituated to this cranky state, and we intentionally think thoughts that evoke it, triggering that neurochemical wash. It becomes, essentially, a habit of mind.

LIBERATING FACILITATORS

More than any of the previous phases of Transformation, liberating requires facilitation. Some of you may find yourselves taking the five uncaging steps instinctively and reflexively, relying on the information conveyed about how liberating progresses and applying it to your own life. It's likely, though, that most of you will need some assistance both with learning how to liberate as well as with maintaining a liberating mindset and behaviors. That's what the following five facilitators are for:

- **MAKE AND CELEBRATE MISTAKES.** When we do things we've never done before, mistakes are inevitable. Screwing up is an essential part of liberating, because liberating is experimenting with possibilities! Our minds, however, don't like the uncomfortable feelings triggered by our matrix when we try new things and make mistakes, and tries to steer us away from putting ourselves in risky situations. Our matrix sees mistakes as an indictment, a sign that something is wrong with us. So we need to learn from

Transformers and high performers who learn to celebrate mistakes and see them as learning opportunities.

When we screw up, we're in good company! Walt Disney was once fired from a job because he "lacked imagination" and Michael Jordan was cut from the varsity basketball team as a sophomore. It is said that Thomas Edison claimed, "I didn't fail 1000 times. The lightbulb was an invention with 1000 steps."

Neuroscience research backs up the power of making mistakes—we actually learn and remember things better by trying and failing first. Our neurons must repeatedly fail before they can succeed. And if we get our undies in a twist worrying about making mistakes, rather than just going for it, we actually drain our precious prefrontal cortex resources, which makes us more likely to choke and make even more mistakes.

So, give yourself assignments to make mistakes, and celebrate your mistakes as a sign of liberating. Instead of beating yourself up, blaming, or shaming yourself, respond with "Yay, I made a mistake! I'm risking and learning," rather than, "I'm such an idiot." Let others in on what you are doing and enroll them to congratulate and encourage you when you screw up.

Have fun making mistakes and even purposely doing the wrong thing—say the wrong thing, go the wrong way. Make mistakes big and small, public and private—bring home yogurt when your husband asked for milk, tally the column of figures wrong on your report, push the wrong elevator button, pull the push door, wear stripes with plaid, tell your wife you don't like the dinner she made, deliberately get someone's name wrong. Remember to laugh and celebrate.

▪ **NAME IT TO TAME IT.** Liberating, while thrilling, also stirs up a lot of other feelings. Going into the unknown, trying new things, and breaking old rules all threaten our matrix, and our limbic system responds with a fight-flight-or-freeze reaction that clouds our complex thinking. This means we revert to our default matrix routines and lose our liberating momentum.

But there's a simple yet powerful technique we can use to calm the aroused amygdala in our limbic system and bring our higher level thinking back on board. Neurologist Matthew Lieberman's studies have shown that by naming what we are feeling, simply saying "I'm scared" calms the amygdala and brings the conscious, visionary thinking of the prefrontal cortex back online. We become calmer and can think more clearly, and we're able to keep liberating without falling back into old matrix routines.

Your assignment? Learn to name the emotion that is coursing through you. While the assignment is simple, the execution of it may not be. You may be afraid or hurt or angry, but for many reasons, you may have difficulty admitting this to yourself or others—you don't want to acknowledge you're angry, for instance, because your programming has convinced you that you're not an angry person. When these feelings arise, try saying to yourself *I'm angry*, or, *I'm hurt*.

Be sure to share what you are feeling with others, too. Verbalizing the feeling engages the speech centers of your brain as well, which adds to the effect. Writing down the feeling, or even composing a poem, especially longhand, helps to tame your feelings and brings more resources to your prefrontal cortex to support you in liberating.

- **USE LIBERATORS AS INSPIRATION.** Just as you used role models as a tool for revelating, Liberators can keep you focused and inspired as you move through this phase. Liberators are outliers, iconoclasts, innovators. Essentially, they are rule-breakers; they do things that others say can't be done. Some of the most famous Liberators are Gandhi, Martin Luther King, Jr., Buddha, and Abraham Lincoln.

  These individuals didn't emerge from the womb as Liberators. Gandhi was an attorney and Buddha was a wealthy prince. But they revelated in their own ways, freed themselves from the conventions of their professions and the thinking of their times, and became free to create something entirely new.

Look for Liberators. Learn about their lives and draw inspiration from them. It doesn't have to be someone famous. Our students turn to fellow Transformers who are further along on the journey. Also, if your brother-in-law broke free of his matrix and became an innovator and an iconoclast, that's a fine model to use. The key is for you to find those whose lives resonate with your yearning. You may choose someone who traveled a path that seems similar to the one you yearn to travel—if not in the particulars, then in the larger themes. For example, your Liberator created a new paradigm in the business world and that's an area where you feel driven to matter. True Liberators, however, will generally be transforming all areas of their lives, becoming Transformers.

■ **ENLIST MKOs, SPARRING PARTNERS, AND PLAYMATES.** While Liberators can inspire you and help you to see possibilities you wouldn't have seen on your own, it helps to have people who will also directly engage in the transforming journey with you. Understand that your attempts at liberating may initially be awkward, ineffective, or even hurtful to you or others. Think of it like learning a new language—initially your vocabulary is limited and you speak in primitive phrases, sometimes to your embarrassment or to the embarrassment of others. While attempting liberating moves, you may lack finesse or effectiveness in your early efforts to break free of your programming. Liberating requires skill and practice, and a little help from our friends, especially what Russian psychologist and educator Lev Vygotsky calls MKOs—More Knowledgeable Others.

Even if you don't know others who have more experience than you, enlist people to be your sparring partners, providing target practice for each other. Just like boxers who improve their skills with sparring partners, look for liberating growth partners with whom you can practice being more authentic, share more in-the-moment truths, role-play, and improve your skills.

Challenge the mistaken beliefs you discovered in revelating, and you may find that behaviors that break internal rules don't have the negative consequences you had predicted. Find growth playmates who are willing to play with you. Invite friends to growth parties to have fun while practicing liberating behaviors.

* **ADOPT THE ASSIGNMENT WAY OF LIVING.** Most of us don't awaken every morning planning how we are going to act on our revelating with our liberating moves for the day. Still, consistent experimenting with ways of being, acting, and feeling in keeping with our new discoveries are a critical part of transforming. We developed the assignment way of living to help with this and every phase of the process. Our students have step-by-step daily life assignments that emerge from their revelating to help them develop their liberating skills. Skills in thinking, feeling, and behaving increase in developmental level over time.

   Use your Matrix Map (from the Revelating chapter) to help you plan assignments for yourself. Look at the limiting beliefs you're discovering through revelating and the corresponding rules you've been operating from. Plan assignments to break those rules. For example you may have discovered that you operate from a belief that being strong and independent is critical; or that, underneath it all, you feel like you are a burden, so you have to meet your needs and not lean on others. Related to those beliefs are rules like: *Do everything yourself. Don't ask for help—people will think you are weak. Don't be a burden—help other people but don't get support yourself.*

   Now challenge those beliefs and break those rules! Create assignments for yourself to liberate from those limiting rules and free yourself to live by empowering beliefs. One technique to try: ask for things—big or small, tangible or intangible, outrageous or innocuous. Ask as many people as many things as you can—request people to hold the door for you, push the elevator button for your floor, give you an upgrade on your room. Ask your loved ones for hugs, kisses, and special treatment. Request extensions on deadlines, support for a project, decorating tips, vacations, favors—the sky is the limit. Chances are you'll be shocked at what you can create and the liberating—and new revelating—that results. Here's what two Transformers reported after just a few days of this assignment:

> Historically I was raised never to ask for anything at all. My mistaken belief is no one cares about what I want. I went out there and I asked people for what I wanted and I got lots of things. I learned that it is good to ask and that I become closer to other people—what I was taught growing up about asking for things is not the truth and my family did this to shut me down as a kid as opposed to them telling me the truth that they couldn't afford it or didn't have the money for it. They let me think as a child that it was me who was at fault for asking and that's a bad thing to do. I'm over that period now; as an adult I will ask for what I want with a great intention of getting it.
>
> —*Deborah*

> What fun it is to ask for things! It's been also very interesting to note all the tiny little asks such as my wife to massage my legs and aching feet, bring me a cup of tea or coffee, or make a certain dish for dinner. I've asked people I haven't spoken to in years to see if they'd have a lunch or dinner with me. I've also asked others to help me win new business—and it works!
>
> —*Sam*

THREE COMMON TRAPS . . . AND HOW TO GET AROUND THEM

You may be tired of this warning but we cannot issue it too many times: beware of your matrix. As you move through the liberating steps, your matrix is going to try and assert itself. You may tell yourself that you get it—that you know the power of the matrix—and you're not going to let it sway you from your course. Yet the matrix is not only powerful, it's also clever. It can come up with a number of approaches that can stop your liberating in its tracks.

You can avoid being stopped if you know the specific obstacles your matrix is likely to place between you and your yearning. We're going to focus on three of them—the first is relatively simple to address, the second requires more of a discussion and tools to overcome, and the third is all about attitude:

1. **THE ILLUSION OF ONE BIG MOVE.** It's a powerful illusion. You make major changes in one area of your life based on your revelating but stop after that. For example, Sally asserts herself at work, gains a great performance review and a promotion, and then relaxes, becoming complacent and less effective in her job. And Dara overcomes the way she was wired—she was convinced she was too selfish to ever have a serious, sustained relationship or spouse—and marries a great guy, has children, and feels loved for the first time in her life, only to begin feeling inferior and undeserving later on.

   We're not discounting these big moves, but we're also telling you that they can be obstacles to further liberating. People free themselves from their programming in one grand step, and they do it in a showstopping way. It feels like they've broken out of the cage once and forevermore. What they don't realize is that another cage forms without them being aware of it. In fact, the big move they made hides this cage from view—their defenses are down, their awareness is low. Sally failed to integrate her new assertive behavior into her new persona and returned to her quiescent ways. Dara had a relatively short honeymoon period of bliss and then became jealous of the time her new husband spent away from home on business assignments; she also resented the way her children required so much of her attention and was angry with them all the time.

   You need to plan your liberating moves in advance, continuously and variously. It's not just liberating in your career, but at home, at work, in the community, with friends, with family, in your free time. Remind yourself that if you were able to achieve total and complete liberation in one big move, you'd fry your brain. You can't just rip the matrix from your mind and throw it away—you'd throw away a lot of brain matter in the process. Instead, removing its influence is a continuous, incremental process.

2. **FEAR.** Transformers face their fear in order to liberate. Fear rears its head during all phases of the *Transformed!* process, but it's especially insidious as an obstacle during liberating. As you begin to embrace novelty and implement your strategy of change in this phase, you may encounter rejection, uncertainty, ambiguity, isolation, and ridicule. Whew! Even a list of those unpleasant reactions might foster a sense of foreboding. But of course, this is an incomplete list, since we left out all the positives—the euphoric rush of freedom, the quantum leaps in achievement, and so on. Still, our focus here is on fear as an obstacle to liberation, and it's a formidable one.

    When you seek the type of authenticity that we described in our story of Joe earlier in the chapter, you're going to evoke some unpleasant reactions among the people you know and care about. One of our students, in the process of liberating, began to be much more assertive in his relationships and at work. At one point, he found himself vehemently raising his voice at a colleague during a meeting. This guy had always been afraid of his own anger and he had always spoken to people at work in a calm, soft voice. After the meeting, the colleague was upset and told our student, "You've changed. You were always such a nice guy before."

    This is the sort of comment that gives anyone pause. Who doesn't want to be a nice guy? *This liberating stuff is turning me into a monster!* you might be thinking during this phase. But it's not. This may be your fear, but the truth is, liberating is just allowing you to be more authentic in that moment and situation. You're no longer constrained from acting in a different sort of way from your norm. It can take time to integrate new behaviors with the same grace you exhibited before engaging in your own transformation.

The fear, though, can be so powerful that you don't look at how liberating is freeing you to be a bigger, better person. Instead, you say to yourself, *This isn't working,* or, *This isn't worth it,* and give up and go back to how you were programmed to be.

Perhaps the biggest obstacle fear raises, though, is one that you might not even recognize. The brain is a predictive organ, but when you liberate, your actions and their consequences are unpredictable. You break away from the patterns with which your brain is familiar, and the uncertainty and ambiguity that becomes part of your life creates foreboding. Your mind wants you to return to your patterns, and it will try and convince you to give up this silly liberating stuff.

This is what we refer to as *ambiguity aversion,* and you need to be prepared for it as you liberate. Fortunately, we've found a number of effective ways to deal with it.

First, use the name-it-to-tame-it facilitator in the previous section—it's great at calming this particular fear.

Second, prepare yourself for a "tolerable unpleasantness." People stop liberating when they're unprepared for the fear of ostracism, ambiguity, ridicule, and other dreads; they're blindsided by these fears and tell themselves the unpleasantness isn't worth it. But not only is it worth it, it's essential. If you don't feel occasional discomfort, then you're not liberating effectively. Have an internal dialogue about anticipated reactions from people. Tell yourself that Jan may be surprised and concerned by how you act that evening or Tim may be nonplussed by the way you deliver his performance review at work. Explain to yourself that though you may not like the reactions of others, they can be tolerated and dealt with, that you need to push through these reactions and keep liberating. You can also lessen the shock of your liberating by explaining to others the journey you are on.

Third, extinguish the fear response. This may seem impossible at a given moment of fear—when you're seriously afraid of something, the fear feels excruciatingly endless. Only it's not. Face your fear. Force yourself to do the same thing again and again. Relatively quickly, you habituate yourself to this fear—it loses it power over you and you can keep liberating. Your prefrontal cortex will inhibit your fear with repeated exposure to it. Each time you repeat a fear-inducing experience, you become less fearful.

Fourth, employ cognitive reappraisal. Many times, we have a primitive reaction to fear rather than taking a step back and analyzing its cause and impact. What we're suggesting is that when your liberating actions cause you to fear something, focus on reality-testing rather than reacting. More specifically, ask yourself these questions:

What exactly am I afraid of here?

What is the worst that could happen?

If the worst happens, could I live with that?

By sorting through your fear, you give your prefrontal cortex another opportunity to exert its influence and calm your primitive reaction. This part of your brain is your ally in liberating, helping you analyze that first rush of fear and deal with it consciously (rather than through your unconscious programming).

Fifth, reach out for reassurance, encouragement, and support from other Liberating Transformers. Yes, we've offered this advice before, but it's especially useful with this obstacle. Reach out to people who are living according to the new rules you aspire to—seek their advice and reassurance, rather than that of people who are bound by the same mistaken beliefs and rules that you are trying to change. And don't neglect the power of touch and simple human contact to help calm your fear and encourage you. Neuroscience studies show that eye contact, physical touch, the reassurance of a soothing voice (the very things that calmed us when we were babies) can calm our adult selves, too.

3. **A DEFEATIST ATTITUDE.** Philosopher and writer Colin Wilson said, "Human beings do not realize the extent to which their own

sense of defeat prevents them from doing things that they could do perfectly well." If you believe you can't break free from your programming, that you can't be powerful, assertive, insightful, or overcome your shyness, that you will never be loved, that you are not and never will be a spiritual person, then liberating isn't possible, at least as an ongoing regimen. At the first sign of trouble, you'll fold up your liberating tent.

What it comes down to is a choice between taking the safe path out of fear or taking risks for the sake of learning and growth. While you may not experience serious discomfort or failure in the former, you'll also sentence yourself to a life of severely limited possibilities.

When you are in the liberating phase, you will fail. Things aren't always going to go smoothly. You're going to find yourself on the receiving end of criticism; you may even be ostracized. To deal with it, recall our discussion of a fixed versus a growth mindset. A fixed mindset will respond with gloom and doom. With a fixed mindset, your matrix will seize upon criticisms and defeats to justify a return to your old routines. A growth mindset, on the other hand, will see criticisms and defeats as opportunities to learn . . . and to grow. Liberators are intensely curious about the why behind negative reactions, using that information as guidance for further exploration.

So, to overcome this obstacle, resolve to treat setbacks and other negative responses as opportunities for learning. Rather than let these events get you down, use them as motivation to figure out what they mean in terms of who you are and who you're becoming. We're all human, and no one likes to be rejected or embarrassed. But with a growth mindset, you can get past the emotional hurt quickly and use it to fuel your liberating efforts.

BE PREPARED FOR THINGS TO CHANGE

If you're having difficulty picturing what liberating looks like—how this phase will manifest itself in your work, your relationships, your spiritual side, your family—we'd like to bring this picture into focus. That's because when you are liberating fully and continuously, your life will look different. While most of us like to think we make changes along the way, what we really do is stick with a basic pattern inside and make superficial changes on the exterior—we change jobs, move to a new city, find a new hobby. We are very much creatures of habit. Our programming dictates our beliefs, and our beliefs determine our actions.

In liberating, we intentionally choose activities and ways of being that take us out of our habitual state. By choosing activities that are new and different, we end up choosing a life of infinite possibility. Logically, this life is going to be a lot different from the life you've known for years. One of our students discovered this truth relatively late in life:

At age seventy-seven, Deena was known to everyone as a good, kind person, and she rarely spoke up or against anyone or anything—she felt it wasn't her place to cause trouble. As she shared, "I was raised to be a good girl and not complain." After engaging and revelating that her obedient wife, mother, churchgoer, good-girl routine was not the only one available to her, she reached the liberating phase.

Her next revelating was, "My widowhood is just another phase in my life . . . there are thousands of us and how I live the rest of my life is in my own hands." From that, she started engaging more fully and doing things that were out of character for the woman she had been. She stopped romanticizing her marriage and began acting in ways that were, as one of her brothers put it, "very un-Deena-like." As Deena realized, "One of the obstacles to my growth was the romanticized memory of my marriage. To express the truth of our relationship I shouted at my husband's gravesite so loud he could hear wherever he is: 'You should have stopped smoking!' Later at dinner I recounted to my family the times I left him, if only for a few hours. We were not Antony and Cleopatra, more like Ralph and Alice Kramden."

In her volunteer work, she found herself to be much more assertive and influential than she had anticipated. And she really shocked family and friends when she joined an environmental group that was active in protesting a corporation in her community that the group felt was polluting a nearby waterway. She captured her liberating journey in her own words:

> I grew to be spontaneous and follow my urges: enjoying Chicago's beaches and skyline; struggled to overcome my fears of driving in the rain and at night; to stop interrupting and listen to conversations; to explore the basis of my angry outbursts and negative thinking; to stop procrastinating.
>
> I had procrastinated on my goal to volunteer, I set my "do or die" date. I beat that date by applying for a volunteer position.
>
> I asked myself: "Do I intend to be a small link in the chain of humanity that goes back to Eve and continues on or do I intend to break that chain of conformity that binds, walking lockstep with the zombies of routine?" I freed myself to be ME by eliminating self-pity and negativity.
>
> I am now living a life of adventure. I'm dancing instead of sitting out, playing Mozart as well as listening, making decisions on my own instead of waiting for someone else's suggestions, making my requests known. I am sharing my talents by singing in my church choir, crocheting scarves for veterans, writing an essay to encourage other seniors to enroll in the coaching program, and engaging with others at my volunteer satellite center. I'm transplanting a prize rosebush—not sure of the outcome—but joyful at its exuberant adaptation to a sunnier location. I'm beginning each day by placing myself in the presence of the Lord, asking the Spirit for guidance during the day, knowing He has given me a brain to decide what path to take and the will.

Deena had grown up adhering to a certain set of rules that had been drummed into her from an early age. Consciously, they might not have seemed like rules to her at the time, but that's exactly what they were. In revelating, you will learn to see many of your rules as bars on the cage, just as Deena did. In liberating, you break the rules and step out of the cage just as Deena did.

In the liberating phase, however, you regularly break your limiting rules—not just once or twice, but consistently and with focus. This means that if you come up with a great idea for a new project as part of your job, you make it clear that it was your suggestion. It means that you speak up to your spouse and others when you don't agree with their point of view and take strong stands when you feel your way of doing things is better than his. As you break your unwritten rules, people will tell you that you're acting strangely; some may even be upset by this new you and say they wish you would "act more like your old self."

As you can see, from Deena's example of just a few months applying the principles of *Transformed!*, your life changes dramatically. But we want to emphasize that these changes are worth it. No matter how much resistance you receive from friends, family, and work colleagues, you derive benefits beyond anything you might have imagined before you got in touch with your yearning and liberated.

Maslow talked about "peak experiences" as a trait of a self-actualized person. These are experiences in which your creative energies are released, you realize your sense of purpose, you feel the meaning of your existence affirmed. These experiences are a preview of who you can be if you sustain the freedom that liberating grants.

But one word of caution: you have to keep liberating, and you must rematrix to make liberating and its exhilarating freedom your way of life.

CHAPTER SEVEN

REMATRIX:
REPROGRAM YOUR MIND,
TRANSFORM YOUR LIFE

As a single footstep will not make a path on the earth, so a single thought will not make a pathway in the mind. To make a deep physical path, we walk again and again. To make a deep mental path, we must think over and over the kind of thoughts we wish to dominate our lives.
—Henry David Thoreau

LEAP FROM A GOOD LIFE to a great one with rematrixing. This powerful phase makes all the difference between growing and transforming, between doing a few good things and having a great life, between who you've been or becoming who you can become and fulfilling your potential. Rematrixing is where true transformation takes place—where you become a whole new you and live a whole new life.

The exhilarating moves of liberating will fade to fond memories if you don't rematrix. While liberating is thrilling, it isn't enough to transform. Our research continually demonstrated that no matter how many liberating moves you make, courses you take, books you read, good things you try, or good thoughts you think—unless you rematrix, you won't transform. While you may learn and grow, unless you solidify these new ways of thinking and acting through rematrixing, you will revert back to the way you have always lived. As you consolidate your gains in rematrixing, you reap the benefits of all the other phases.

Rematrixing uses the plasticity of our brains to rewire patterns of thought, feeling, and action. You literally change your mind—building neural pathways to align with your yearning, capture the empowering discoveries of your revelating, and realize the possibilities unleashed in liberating. Through rematrixing, you design your life, building the circuits to consciously reprogram your matrix of beliefs, behaviors, and habits to empower you to fulfill your potential. You become the architect of your life, actively designing your transformation. The focused work of rematrixing activates your neuroplasticity to not just change your mind, but to change your brain. We alter the unconscious beliefs that drive us and make structural changes to our lifestyles, relationships, and values in alignment with our new empowering beliefs.

BUILD YOUR DREAM LIFE: TRANSFORMATION IS A CONSTRUCTION JOB

Think about rematrixing as the construction job of your transformation. You are constructing your life project, an organic, ever-evolving manifestation of your yearning, engaging, revelating, and liberating. Rather than a physical construction job of building a dream home, you are building a dream life with all the pathways or roads as well as the house. In the home, you are rewiring and adding on to all the other systems that will empower you to live your dreams. Just like an architect who starts with a vision for a dream home, you've been creating a vision for your dream life through yearning, engaging, revelating, and liberating. But vision needs to be actualized, and now it's time to translate it into a beautiful, enduring edifice—one that also continues to evolve into a most magnificent life project. A designer home starts with a vision and requires a blueprint, a strong foundation, wiring, and step-by-step construction—and so does your great life project.

That vision is formulated in your frontal lobe, the aspect of your brain that serves as the architect and the contractor—envisioning possibilities for your life, designing it to reflect that vision, and then pulling together all of your abilities as you draw from and apply the expertise of the trades (coaches, mentors, teachers, disciplines, tools, technologies). It oversees the construction project of your transformation, keeping you focused and on track.

Like a construction project, detailed planning is required, with meticulous craftsmanship, brick by brick, stone by stone—or, in the case of our lives, conscious act by conscious act. Don't forget that construction sites are messy and noisy, with a lot of debris—expect delays, upsets, mistakes, and frustrations. But also be prepared for the immense satisfaction of being the creator of your life, where *you* are the architect, designer, and builder— the Transformer, living the life you create. You can gain an appreciation for the job from Bari's story of her construction project:

> It's like I am building a new self, over and over. It has sure taken a lot of work—never-ending vigilance. But, if I had known then (when reading self-help books and taking diverse courses) what I know now—that I have the capacity to continually design my life moment-by-moment in a way that allows me to continually discover new gifts and possibilities within myself while deeply connecting with other human beings—I would have started a long time ago, and I would have gone a lot faster. Today, I feel like I am finally living in my own skin. All my parts seem to fit in a vibrant, ever-changing way. It's like I'm building a new foundation of me—affecting me as a wife, mother, friend, my career, my leadership. I can accept the dynamic variations because my life has deep meaning and purpose that carries me through the uncertainties of continual change. Every day I feel like I am on the threshold of a whole new possibility I get to create. With my understanding of personal development, these changes aren't random; they fit into a coherent strategy to develop myself. My vision of myself going forward is like a plan that informs what I am doing in my day-to-day, exciting, unpredictable world.

Bari's life looked like a well-constructed creation before she became a Transformer. It was a nice world of growth and development, but not a transformational project of maximizing her potential. She had not yet engaged the internal architect of her frontal lobe—engaging, yearning, revelating, liberating, and strategically rematrixing. A top performer in high school and college, Bari was a highly recruited student and then professional who was launched into a meteoric marketing career. Winning cutting-edge positions at prominent companies she advanced rapidly, successfully working on emerging technologies. Still this was not enough. She devoured self-help books and even took a widely respected two-week personal transformation course. It was not until she learned to tap her yearning in the here and now that she took risks to make the mistakes indicated by engaging. Her learning and growing accelerated. She discovered herself in totally new ways beyond what she would have called her personality. It was the engaging, revelating, and liberating that led her into her new, increasingly authentic self. Liberating consistently and strategically, she began experiencing the fulfillment she yearned for that had led her to read personal development books before. Now she was becoming the book she was studying. Still, it was not until she understood the need for the consistent, deep practice of rematrixing that she consolidated her gains and actually formed new foundations for future growth and development.

WHY GOOD THINGS DON'T LAST, DIETS DON'T WORK, AND WE DON'T LIVE HAPPILY EVER AFTER

More than any other phase, rematrixing demonstrates why there is no such thing as an easy way or a quick fix. We need to do the work of rematrixing in order to meet the conditions for lasting change—building new mental maps with deep, intentional practice that keeps these fresh neural pathways open and developing.

Ever lost weight only to gain it back, or been inspired by a motivational speaker, determined you'd apply their advice and a week later can't quite remember what it was; or been gung ho on your New Year's resolution only to find it had drifted away by the time February rolled around? Or you may have even invested in a personal development program and seen substantial change while you were in it, but the change didn't seem to last after it was over, aside from having some new philosophical tools for life.

Think about why we have so much difficulty maintaining our resolve and creating lasting behavioral change; why we too often gain that weight back or why the seminars we attend rarely have lasting effects beyond new insights. Our old matrix of beliefs and habits reasserts itself and we are back to where we started if we fail to be vigilant—if we don't do the consistent practice needed to build, and keep, new skills. Consistently learning, growing, practicing, and stretching can prevent our matrix from reasserting itself, but we need to commit to these activities and keep at them through good times and bad.

Without rematrixing, we are bound to be disappointed by whatever self-improvement approach we take. You see, it doesn't matter how brilliant a guru is or how ingenious a program or workshop may seem. If they lack a rematrixing component—and most do—then we're bound to be disappointed. More than that, we actually start to reduce our expectations or feel cheated. We invested time, money, and effort that didn't deliver the promised results. Or, we think there is something wrong with us that we didn't achieve the outcomes we hoped for, because we did not understand the requirements of true transformation. We feel hoodwinked, bamboozled, and swindled by anything that promises a quick fix. Sadly, the promise of these activities is real; it's the method that is missing—when we do not understand or fully tap the magic of rematrixing.

THE MAGIC AND MIRACLE OF REMATRIXING

The magic of rematrixing is that we can literally rewire ourselves—we can change our brains and our minds, and what we believe, and who we are, and how we live. Rather than unconsciously repeat and live out of the directives of our matrixes, we take charge of our destinies.

The miracle is neuroplasticity, the property of the brain that allows rematrixing—the ability to build new neural circuitry, new selves, and new lives. Transformation occurs, guided by our yearning, stimulated by the attention of engaging, informed by the insights of revelating and the novelty and challenges of liberating. In rematrixing, these become new neural pathways guiding new thoughts, feelings, and actions.

The dynamics of our development in childhood are analogous to our transformation in adulthood. Children become more themselves as they grow up, like watching the image of a photograph emerge during processing. Transformation in adulthood is a similar process of emerging, where you become more "you," not just different. The more we transform, the more of ourselves we become. For adults, however, the transformational design requires conscious activation—rematrixing.

Children change naturally; their minds are as flexible as their bodies. Young children learn so easily and effortlessly because they have an advantage that we adults do not. Children's bodies release a lot of brain-derived neurotrophic factor (BDNF) that triggers their brain's ability to absorb and learn at high speed. This keeps their brains constantly stimulated to take in new information by watching, doing, and experimenting.

Adults are designed to transform differently. We must engage consciously and intentionally in order to activate the same development process. Unlike children, for whom the process works automatically, we must deliberately guide our development from our own values, will, and intent.

The magic of rematrixing activates the amazing miracle of our neuroplasticity. Merzenich and other neuroscientists have found that the brain's ability to grow new nerve cells, forge plastic change, and acquire new skills requires certain conditions to be re-opened: highly focused attention, novelty, stretching into new skills a bit outside our comfort zone, and repetition—but not just mindlessly doing the same thing over and over again. We have to pay close attention to the tasks we're engaged in, which is why engaging is so important. We must constantly stretch into new territory, and continue to liberate in order to make changes last.

Neuroscience and high-performance research show that we have to intend to transform, to pay attention, to focus attention on the areas where we want to achieve mastery. We have to stretch and do something we don't already know how to do (liberate), and we have to do so repeatedly. We can take a lesson from researchers who have studied people who have developed mastery in fields as diverse as music, golf, symphony conducting, playing chess, sales, leadership, and so on. If you've read Malcolm Gladwell's *Outliers*, *The Talent Code* by Daniel Coyle, or *Talent Is Overrated* by Geoffrey Colvin, you've run into the work of K. Anders Ericsson. Ericsson studied mastery and found it wasn't so much talent but long, hard work of a certain kind—what some call deep practice and others call deliberate practice—that promotes high levels of performance.

This kind of practice is the stuff of rematrixing. Across disciplines, people needed about 10,000 hours of deliberate practice to develop the neural pathways of mastery. And, once they developed that level of skill, they didn't coast. They kept practicing, growing, and improving. Asked why he practices so much, world-class pianist Vladimir Horowitz purportedly responded, "If I do not practice for one day, I notice it. If I go two days without practicing, my wife notices it, and if I go three days, my audience notices it." This comment demonstrates an inherent understanding of the law of brain plasticity: use it or lose it. The same is true of Transformers who live great lives. They develop mastery of intentional, satisfying, yearning-based living and must continue the disciplines that got them there.

Many hours of deep or deliberate practice of focused attention, novelty, stretching beyond our current skill level, and repetition are required to activate our neuroplasticity. This is very different from strumming familiar tunes on your guitar on a Saturday afternoon, hitting golf balls at the driving range, listening to a motivational speaker, or reading about transformation in a book—even this one!

Colvin details the requirements of deliberate practice: *deliberate practice is designed specifically to improve performance.* Deliberate practice means that we identify defined elements of performance to improve, work intently on them until they improve, and then go on to the next skill. We usually need a teacher or coach to design the activity best suited for our performance, since it is difficult to know how to do a skill we've not learned before. In addition, *the skill has to be repeated a lot and needs to be an activity beyond our current abilities, with continuous feedback* available. Again, this finding makes the case for having a teacher, coach, mentor, or MKO—actually, all of the above. Plus, you need goals, self-observation, and metacognition (thinking about your thinking), and *choosing comparisons* and standards that stretch you just beyond your current limits.

TAPPING THE MAGIC—TRAINING OUR BRAINS

Rather than slipping into comfortable routines, rematrixing means that we seek novelty; we shake things up. We trick our brains into paying selective attention. Our minds want to turn skills into unconscious automatic patterns, and because our minds are sloppy, they will settle for good enough. To rematrix and transform, we need to trick the mind to pay attention and make distinctions to become better and better, to build new pathways. Practicing slowly, breaking skills into tiny parts, and repeating the behavior forces our brain to make better patterns—and having a coach or mentor to design these steps and help push us to better performance—all contribute to our mastery.

Meadowmount School of Music is an intensive program that has produced some of the most skilled musicians and symphony conductors of our time, including Joshua Bell, Itzhak Perlman, Pinchas Zuckerman, and Yo-Yo Ma. They advertise their school as a place where "students can accomplish at Meadowmount in a summer what would ordinarily take a year to accomplish at home." They cut music up into pieces and rearrange it, have students play music backwards, or have one student bow while another fingers the strings—all to break the automatizing process. Their process, when practiced, produces amazing results—an inspiration for us to apply this process in order to rematrixing to create amazing results in our own lives.

CREATURES OF HABIT OR CREATORS OF DESTINY?

Why is intentional practice necessary? Why doesn't normal activity lead to rematrixing? Neuroscience provides some answers—and clues to what makes rematrixing work.

Without rematrixing, we become creatures of habit. While rematrixing is critical at any age, it's especially important over time as the matrix becomes more and more entrenched each year. In fact, by the time we are about 35, we are rarely learning and growing, but are, for the most part, just repeating the habits we've already developed. We think we are active and deceive ourselves that we are learning like we did when we were younger. To be sure, we may be busy doing things and think that we are active, but we rarely bring a youthful, focused attention to learning opportunities. As we age, we mostly replay our already mastered skills—practicing our profession, going through the habits of our lifestyle, doing what we are already good at. This gradual neglect atrophies our brain's attentional systems, which are what we need to engage in order to learn, grow, and transform. And by the time we are 70, we may not have systematically engaged the systems in the brain to trigger neuroplasticity for learning, growing, and transforming for another 50 years!

Our brain circuits work in combinations of sequences and patterns, and if we keep processing the same thoughts every day and doing the same things, those brain circuits strengthen and become hardwired, releasing the same chemistry and forming the same stream of consciousness. Unless we apply the awareness of revelating into liberating and then escape our habits through rematrixing, we won't retrain the circuits in our brain and be free of the neurochemical fix we get from our limiting beliefs.

Having years of "experience" doesn't give us mastery; it is just many years of repeating the same thing. In fact when we are burned out or tired from work, it's not from the intense focus and concentration of rematrixing and mastery. Burnout is from long hours spent cranking out what we already know how to do or doing the same routines repeatedly—that is what's exhausting! Most of what we do in our lives or at work is not designed to make us better—in fact it's usually not designed at all—but instead is unconsciously guided by our matrix.

When we rematrix, though there is some discomfort in stretching, we have the greater satisfaction of knowing we are participating in our own transformational construction project. We're operating at the edge of our competence—that somewhat uncomfortable place that Daniel Coyle calls the "razor edge of our ability." On this edge, we acquire what researchers term learning velocity—the rate at which you can learn increases greatly. Trying, reaching, failing, trying, and reaching again bears neural transformative fruit. And the repetition and persistence of rematrixing builds these neural circuits and literally wraps those circuits in myelin, which increases the speed of the electrical signals—from ten times faster to thousands of times faster. As Coyle says, "It's literally like installing broadband in your brain."

TRANSFORMERS DO IT LONGER, HARDER, AND DEEPER

Rematrixing, with its repetition and persistence, takes advantage of deliberate or deep practice to build new neural pathways, a new matrix. This may result in small changes, but Transformers don't stop with small change. In *The Talent Code*, Daniel Coyle points out that for the highest performers, "small successes were not stopping points, but stepping stones." In other words, small change provided them with the impetus and path for big change. Instead of being content with reaching a goal, they pushed beyond it to the next goal and then the one after that.

A phenomenon occurs when human beings achieve goals: they are finally able to get that plum job or establish a meaningful relationship or lose fifty pounds and they become content. We're not disparaging these achievements. It's terrific when our students are able to break the hold their programming has on them and grow and change, but we found that those who rematrixed were always looking beyond to higher levels of possibility. The joy for them was in developing mastery and improving their skills, not just the accomplishment of a goal. They were literally looking over the current goal, eager to complete it, and move on to the next one. Small steps were wonderful, but they were after great leaps—vaulting from a good life to a great life.

These Transformers literally achieved what would have been unimaginable if their old matrixes had remained in place. They capitalized on their neuroplasticity and created a new matrix, shattering the barriers that held them back from their most heartfelt dreams and desires.

All this may seem challenging, but we want to assure you that it is within your reach and we'll give you tools and advice to facilitate rematrixing later in the chapter.

FEELING YOUR WAY TO TRANSFORMATION AND REMATRIXING

With all this talk about changing your brain and rewiring your mental maps, you may be thinking that rematrixing is just some sort of cognitive exercise. Transformation doesn't take place only in your thoughts. While cognition is part of it, the real fuel is your yearning, rooted in your emotions. Rematrixing requires us to broaden the scope of our transformational focus, bringing feelings more completely into the process.

Your emotions are an amazing, often overlooked, part of the process—providing information and direction. More than that, you must feel your transformation as well as think and act. Intense joy is a catalyst for change, and fear, when harnessed, also drives a great deal of change. While Chapter 9 will discuss the emotional aspects of transformation in detail, here we need to describe the role feelings play in rematrixing.

Transformation produces an acute tension between hope and fear. On the one side there are the thrill and excitement of possibilities of change and on the other side the fear of change and the unknown. Joy and the hope of possibilities fuels transformation; turning your fear into dread fuels resistance.

Expect these seemingly contradictory emotions. They are explained in part by the battle between our old and new matrixes. Recognize that this happens to everyone.

Your frontal lobe, the more recently evolved part of your brain, is at its best when helping you maintain awareness of these forces. It keeps you focused on transformation. It loves questions like: *Who can I become? What are the possibilities for me? The world? Humanity?* As you focus on the possibilities of transformation, your frontal lobe is stimulated by all the inspiring and optimistic feelings about your transformation. Focusing on transformation activates your frontal lobe and helps to calm your amygdala, your fear center, which the old matrix is using to make you fearful about changing.

USE IT OR LOSE IT

And the old matrix will rise up against any change with all its power. Remember, your old matrix is never going to disappear. It will always look for an opening to reassert itself. This, again, is why rematrixing demands such intense strategy and focus. Triggering our neuroplasticity to make the initial changes in our neural pathways isn't enough because our brains also have *competitive plasticity*—if we don't keep up the work, the brain relegates that neural real estate to something else. We have to use it or lose it—literally.

Don't believe us? Think about that foreign language you learned in high school but haven't used since. Still fluent? That mental real estate has been relegated to holding whatever you've been concentrating on lately—the last ten winners of *American Idol*, your team's sports stats, or the latest sale prices on designer shoes, for example. The brain is constantly assessing how important it is to allocate space to certain skills and functions. The more we demand of a certain skill the more space and brain power it gets. The less we use a certain function or skill, the more it loses its brain real estate to other functions.

It's literally an observable, physical transformation in the brain itself, as shown by neurological studies of people who have radically changed their behavior. In *The Power of Habit,* for instance, author Charles Duhigg cites a study of a woman who had transformed from being overweight and unable to hold a job for more than a few months to a slim, fit, gainfully employed woman. When researchers examined images of her brain, they saw that "[o]ne set of neurological patterns, her old habits, had been overridden by new patterns. They could still see the neural activity of her old behaviors, but those impulses were crowded out by new urges. As [her] habits changed, so had her brain." Yet, the pattern of her old habits will resurface if she doesn't continue to build and strengthen her new habits.

FROM ESCAPING TO GROWING AND BEING FIRED TO TRANSFORMED

As you may recall, we introduced you earlier to Doug, a corporate executive who came to us thinking he needed to change careers or become an outdoor leadership instructor but soon discovered he actually needed to change from the inside out. Working with us, he had made good progress through the transforming phases and achieved success in various areas of his life when he hit the rematrixing wall.

Doug didn't consciously choose to stop stretching or growing. Rather, his matrix asserted itself in insidious, unconscious ways as he started to coast. He rationalized: given all the time and effort he had put into his personal and professional growth, perhaps he could take a break for a while. It would be nice to stop challenging himself all the time, to just enjoy his success. His matrix raised questions that it had asked him years ago before he had become so successful: *Why work so hard?* Even more deeply, his self-doubt resurfaced. He doubted, *Why would anyone want to work for me? Why would anyone want to be my client?* Doug's historic low self-esteem was reasserting itself.

What was happening to Doug happens to many people who begin to transform and satisfy some of their yearnings. As they make major progress in changing their lives, their matrix reasserts itself. Our brains operate under the same principle as our bodies, the principle of homeostasis, and change is threatening to homeostatis. Because the brain is designed to be a predictive device, at its most basic, it scans for danger, and if things change, it can't predict. Our brains register the threat of change as stress and subsequently activate the amygdala. All kinds of resistant thoughts and feelings then arise like, *Oh, no you don't . . . That's too much . . . I sense a change here and I'm not going to let it happen . . . You should just coast . . . Things are good enough.* Each of us has particular coding in our matrix related to danger and the unknown. What causes one of us to be excited, terrifies another. For this reason, rematrixing is a very personal job—universal in process but individual in specifics.

Doug was changing, becoming more powerful. The uncertainty of significant success had Doug on the verge of transformation, activating the warning system of his matrix. It could no longer predict—and even though the changes were all desirable and planned by his conscious mind, his matrix had no code for what it was experiencing and his unconscious defense attempted to get him to return to his old, familiar self. Fortunately, Doug had a lot of supporters who were on their own transformational journeys. They were all dedicated to covering each others' backs, and they recognized that Doug was coasting and resting on his Transformer laurels. Life was "good enough." At this point, his leadership group challenged him as they saw his old matrix reasserting itself. He was no longer responding immediately to emails, his work was getting sloppy, and the senior partner who had recently given him a fantastic review had given him a warning, puzzled by what he saw as a dramatic change in Doug. Doug had not yet learned the lesson of vigilance to the ever-present pressure of the re-emerging old matrix.

Doug ignored his leadership training group, so they let him know that if he did not change and get going again, they would kick him out of the group. He was angry; he considered quitting for two weeks before he woke up and realized that he was starting to settle. His support team had helped him wake up before it was too late. He resumed consciously going about his rematrixing and staying aware of the need to keep stretching and pushing forward. Doug recognized a deeper yearning to dig into his work. He began researching, writing, and publishing. He started his own business, became a thought leader in his field, earned his doctorate, and stretched in ways that would have been unimaginable just two years before. Today, his status as a national thought leader and prominent businessman keeps him on his toes as he continually stretches into corporate governance and other areas of cutting-edge concern. In this way, Doug is constantly faced with new challenges that force him to build new neural networks that override the old networks that formed his matrix.

As natural as it is to want to relax after achieving a goal, enjoy the success. As Dr. Barbara Fredrickson points out in her broaden-and-build theory of positive emotions, it helps you rematrix if you savor victory. But avoid the seduction of complacency and refuse to reside in self-satisfaction, which interrupts the *Transformed!* process. Rematrixing requires vigilance in guarding against neurological backsliding. Rematrixing is an unconscious process that you pursue consciously. In other words, you are acutely aware that in all areas of your life, you need to keep striving, trying new things, taking risks in the service of your yearnings. By taking these actions, you ensure that you're building a new matrix on top of the old one.

REMATRIXING STAGES

So how do you meet this challenge of rematrixing? We're about to share some ways to sustain your effort, but first, remember what we are doing in rematrixing. The purpose of rematrixing is to build a new matrix encoded with empowering beliefs and ways of being that help you transform and develop your potential. You work to shift your beliefs and your behaviors to be in line with your deeper yearning, to implement the discoveries of revelating, and to make the gains of liberating your way of life. Understanding the four Rs will maximize this important work. They are Reorient, Restructure, Reform, and Re-identify—the phases in which rematrixing takes place.

Learn to recognize and strategize these 4 Rs so you can be sure to succeed in your transformational work:

1. **REORIENT.** There are three ways to reorient. First, you are going to be more aware of how your matrix impacts your thoughts and behaviors. This means making a conscious attempt to do more things differently, attuned to the gaps between old matrix behaviors and new ones. Second, reorienting means reweighing your values and considering how they determine your current thoughts and behaviors. A lot of us go through life with unthinking allegiance to a set of values or beliefs—values and beliefs that are spun by our matrix and that drive our thoughts and feelings without our realizing how they limit our experience of the world. Third, you reorient by revisioning. As you discover the new values that lead to rematrixing, you develop new visions of the life you want to live.

    A successful businesswoman, Tricia's reorientation only became possible once she began following her yearning and revelating— which led her to reweigh her values and shift her vision for her life as she began to rematrix:

    > I had been very competitive and stuck in the rat race. I don't regret my striving in that I learned a lot, but deep down, I felt the emptiness and yearned for a change. The change came slowly as I learned to yearn and took it into my work and relationships. I became aware of values driving me that were not what I really cared about. As I engaged and did new things more and more, I learned to orient to what really mattered to me. I really needed to get over my fear of ending up in

the poor house and aim higher. I can't tell when it actually happened, but my aim changed a lot. My values and my view about myself and the world have shifted so much! I no longer see life's value solely attached to things keeping me off the streets and being destitute. My career, relationships, academic achievement, materialistic comfort, my job title and position, and travel are all more fulfilling and fun. I see tremendous value in just being me as a unique individual, being a valuable member of my family, society, and the universe. I'm still successful, traveling, having fun . . . but now I am orienting to being more *me* wherever I am. I see others differently too. They are not all opportunities to get ahead but co-voyagers in this adventure of life.

2. **RESTRUCTURE.** In this step you establish a formal discipline for your reorienting. Specifically, it calls for you to analyze and strategize the structures that will make your new reoriented matrix a reality. When developing your restructuring strategy, you analyze your thoughts, behaviors, and beliefs to see if they align with your new matrix. And if they don't, work to change them. Essentially, you're learning to think differently. If you wanted to run a marathon, you would structure your life differently around food, sleep, exercise, and other key areas, and possibly work with a trainer. Similarly, we must structure our lives even more strategically to rematrix. Tricia needed to put certain activities on her calendar, make sure she journaled, set up weekly sessions with a coach, and join a program that introduced her to new skills.

3. **REFORM.** If the restructure step is the way you redesign your matrix, then this reform step is how you build it. Your analysis and strategy are put into practice here as you re-create your thoughts, beliefs, ways of being and feeling, and lifestyle. Tricia explained that "I changed from using a harsh inner voice to a loving one . . . I can still slip back to that berating voice, but it's no longer the norm.

I am sweeter with staff too—sweeter and tougher, if you can get that. It is like I have been formed into a very different person—both more assertive and more loving. It blows my mind."

4. **RE-IDENTIFY.** Here, you identify with your rematrixed self—you define yourself as your new self. This helps cement the new matrix in place. You can see above how Tricia is re-identifying herself as both demanding and loving—neither would have been how she identified herself historically. The power of re-identifying cannot be underestimated. By redefining how you see yourself, you're reinforcing the cognitive structure you've helped create. You're re-identifying your values, your way of being in the world, your sense of self. In the following chapter, you will be introduced to Gary McPherson's work on the importance of this process.

REMATRIXING IMPERATIVES

Five imperatives drive your rematrixing. These imperatives are ways of being, rules to follow, and commands that will help you keep focused on rematrixing your emerging, transforming self.

JUMP OFF THE OK PLATEAU. Rematrixing is not a task that you can undertake lightly, randomly, or narrowly and expect to be successful. As the previous sections in this chapter suggest, you need to go at it with a comprehensive plan that will help you sustain your rematrixing efforts.

To understand the challenge of rematrixing, you need to be aware and perceptive about a concept we discussed earlier but didn't name, called the "OK Plateau." Joshua Foer, who introduced the term in his book *Moonwalking with Einstein,* describes it as the place where people stop improving at a given endeavor, having reached an unconscious level of acceptable performance. He notes that typing is a typical task that people may do daily but never become much faster typists after a certain point early in their typing lives. The only way to become a faster typist is to stop it from being an automatic task and take conscious control of the activity. Foer says that "you have to push yourself past where you're comfortable."

The danger in rematrixing is settling once you have improved—or arrived at OK. As you make great strides by engaging, revelating, and liberating and start achieving certain objectives, you feel like you've done a lot and that you're entitled to coast. Like Doug in our previous example, you figure life is good now; why not take a break from all that learning and growing and just enjoy what you've achieved?

Two reasons. First, settling allows your old matrix to reassert itself and return you to behaviors, thoughts, and feelings you assumed you had left behind. Second, if you take up residence on the OK Plateau, you will never achieve the greatness of Transformers. Foer's research confirms Jim Collins' assertion, "Good is the enemy of great," and though you may have achieved some good things in your life, settling for them will prevent you from striving for more and better things. Remember Doug's story—he was told we would fire him from his leadership group rather than watch him sink into the habitual existence of OK.

GIVE UP THE QUICK FIX & ADOPT THE 10,000 HOURS PRINCIPLE. As we noted earlier, K. Anders Ericsson's groundbreaking research on expertise revealed that it took a given person 10,000 hours of practice before attaining mastery. That is in any discipline, from chess to music and sports. We believe that it takes an investment of well over 10,000 hours before sustained transformation becomes an everyday reality—and the numbers mount still higher for Transformers, who are always engaged in fulfilling their potential.

If 10,000 hours seems like a lot, understand that these are hours devoted to your own transformation: hours at work, play, in relationship, and worship. While some of these hours may feel uncomfortable, many of them will inspire and excite you. Perhaps more to the point, they are hours invested with the highest return possible in all you do. You'll see the results in the moment and in the long run—in every activity you undertake. You are becoming a Transformer, finding everything you do to be far more meaningful than any time you did that activity in the past; and you'll see it down the road as you begin to achieve goals and dreams that once seemed impossible.

But it is a commitment. You'll never reach 10,000 hours if it's something you do in your spare time. More to the point, you'll never rematrix if you don't consciously and continuously pursue your yearnings. You see, rematrixing isn't something you do outside your regular life. It's not 10,000 hours of extracurricular living. Using the assignment way of living, you intentionally stretch your capacities daily. You take risks, are consciously aware of the beliefs and habits you want to transform, and are actively acting in consonance with the new beliefs you wish to live by.

MAKE STRETCHING AND STRATEGIC NOVELTY A WAY OF LIFE. This is how you should be spending a significant percentage of those 10,000+ hours: yearning in tasks that are new, that push you to your limits, and, at times, beyond. It is impossible to recognize limits if we do not press beyond them. Yet you're going to be tempted to spend your time repeating tasks and using skills in which you've already achieved competency; or you're going to accept a certain level of achievement and convince yourself that you can't go any higher. The truth is, in most cases, you choose not to go higher, and there are certain endeavors in which you will, indeed, maintain. These could be pastimes such as chess, a sport, a musical instrument, or another pursuit. The idea of rematrixing is to strategically apply yourself in challenging new areas. Common areas for successful rematrixing focus are communications, complex tasks, leadership, team building, relating to family, writing, public speaking, parenting, and other more personal pursuits that challenge our very being to increase our capacity for understanding, expressing, and serving.

Think about how often you volunteer for an assignment at work that you know you might not be able to handle as well as your usual tasks. Consider how many times in the last year that you've sought feedback, gotten coaching to improve, taken a class or signed up for a workshop that involved stretching into an area or skill strategically earmarked for improvement. Reflect on how often you've declined opportunities, challenges, even invitations to events or parties, making excuses, while underneath, had you been honest with yourself, you declined because you were afraid. Try and come up with an instance recently when you've taken a significant risk—a risk of being embarrassed in front of others, of trying to do something new or difficult and failing, a risk of speaking your mind no matter what the consequences might be. These are the challenges that Transformers embrace because they stimulate our growth and ultimately, our transformation. This is the way to rematrix, to forge new neural pathways and keep those freshly-forged pathways strong.

Be aware, too, that taking risks, trying challenging new tasks, and looking for novelty are a kind of insurance against falling back into the ways of your old matrix. The legendary cellist Pablo Casals was in his nineties when a student reportedly asked him why he still practiced three or four hours daily. Casals responded, "Because I'm improving." Like Casals, you can't coast or settle if you want to keep improving your life.

MAP YOUR FUTURE MATRIX. The matrix map you made in revelating, which exposed your mistaken beliefs and the actions and thoughts that stem from them, will be an invaluable tool for you in rematrixing. Look at your core mistaken beliefs (or identify them now if you haven't previously done so) like *I'm not good enough, I'm too much, I'm not lovable, I'm not worthy,* and the thoughts and behaviors that come from those beliefs. What do you want to believe instead—perhaps *I am lovable, I'm sufficient, I am worthy, I am a gift?* Now, think about what actions, thoughts, and feelings would reflect the new, empowering beliefs you'd like to live by. Start your rematrixing map by adding your ideal beliefs, actions, feelings, and ways of being onto your matrix map. Even if you have a great system, coach, and support, doing this exercise will facilitate their support and guidance.

CHANGE YOUR SELF-FULFILLING PROPHECY CYCLE.
Remember the self-fulfilling prophecy we discussed in Revelating. We had you identify how beliefs generate actions and how these actions influence the beliefs in others around you. Rematrixing changes this cycle. The more rematrixing moves you make, and the more consistently you make them, the better. Intervene at any aspect of the cycle—change your beliefs or your behavior, or be with others who see you more positively than you do yourself.

For example, you may have a limiting belief that you are not worthy, but instead of acting that way, you choose to go into a situation acting as if you are worthy, behaving with a sense of self-respect and pride. To do this, imagine what someone who felt good about herself would do in this situation. As a result, you'll walk into the meeting holding your head high, making acknowledging contact with the other members, and speaking up when you have a point to share, even if your knees are shaking. As a result, you'll notice that others are responding to you, asking you what you think about different points, or asking you to take initiative on the suggestions you made—they see you as worthy. You fake it until you make it.

WHAT HAPPENS WHEN YOU REMATRIX

You can spot the outward evidence that you're rewiring your matrix when you observe the following thoughts, feelings, and behaviors:

- **CAPTAINING YOUR OWN SHIP.** Win or lose, with rematrixing, you have a clear sense that you are not only captain of your own ship, but that you are able to modify the nature of the ship while under sail. You certainly don't always win at your pursuits, but you have no doubt that they are your pursuits and that, win or lose, you are progressing to your next port of call.

- **DOING THE IMPOSSIBLE.** More specifically, you're saying to yourself and others: *I never thought I'd be able to . . .* and *I used* *to think this was a pipe dream, but now I'm actually doing it.* Transformers often feel this way. They marvel at their ability to do something that they had never done before and that seemed inconceivable at one point in the past. It may be that they never imagined being successful entrepreneurs, writing books, testifying before Congress, or that they were intensely shy and are now on the speaking circuit. It may be that they were convinced they didn't have a spiritual bone in their body, and now they're meditating regularly and transcendently. Inconceivable transformations are a good sign of rematrixing.

- **FEELING CAPABLE OF GREATNESS.** Transformers rematrix and align their actions with their yearnings. This is a tremendously empowering and energizing sensation. When you are doing this, it helps you rise above your doubts and fears and aim for a life that is beyond good and approaching great. You have this sense that you have unlimited capacity for achievement, for connection, for happiness. In the past, you may have dreamed of achieving greatness or fulfillment, but these dreams were quickly shot down by both subtle and not-so-subtle messages from your matrix. Now, you know you can make these dreams come true.

PORTRAIT OF A REMATRIXER: JEAN

Jean hungered for greatness and aimed at what she thought was the impossible. For most of her adult life, Jean was all about making money. She was set financially by 40. She excelled in her career and was well-compensated, but she had resigned herself to living in wealthy isolation. She was a flirt and a man-chaser, dating only the handsomest men, with whom she had the upper hand due to her superior income and education. She had few friends, wasn't married, had no children, and wasn't connected to her community. It is fair to describe her at this point as a high-functioning isolate. No doubt, to an outsider, she seemed as if she would always be this way. Nonetheless, when Jean became a student at Wright, she did so because of her stated desire to "become more social." Over time, Jean figured out that she yearned for connection, to make a difference, to love and be loved. She began to engage, revelate, and liberate in ways that took her out of her self-imposed isolation.

She was diligent at her assignments and especially good at employing our 10,000-plus-hour protocol. Few people we've worked with have been as focused on putting in the time on assignments, risking, and learning to achieve what she yearned for. Jean noticed results immediately. With great diligence, she continued to become more social, forcing herself to ask people out for lunch daily, to attend networking events weekly. She was interacting with many more people and learning that everyone has some degree of vulnerability.

Similarly, she confronted her past and surfaced the messages that she was receiving based on her upbringing. Through revelating and liberating, she created new messages of encouragement and belief that supported her yearning. Jean embraced stretching and novelty as if they were part of a strict workout routine, seeking out challenging people and situations that demanded she develop and use her social skills. Her career took off, and she was recognized as the strategist for global initiatives as she became an increasingly effective team member and leader.

Her relationships with men changed dramatically as she met and engaged with stronger men who challenged her and were more of a match for her. She learned more on her dates—developing skills of mutuality, connection, and intimacy. She eventually met and married a strong man she could not look down on and started a family with him. You could almost see the rematrixing taking place. She became an integral part of a community group. She became chair of a significant charity. While she had been successful before she came to us, Jean's newfound awareness of herself, her desire to have a greater impact, and her need for connection made her a much better developed leader. She became a trusted advisor to many community leaders, not just a skilled technician. She rose to COO with a fast-growing national financial firm. More than that, she now derived much greater meaning and satisfaction from her work, personal life, and public service.

Jean's transformation would have been impossible without her commitment to rematrixing—developing new beliefs and values that provided her with guidance and support as she pursued what she yearned for.

TWO QUESTIONS OF TRANSFORMATION

Geoffrey Colvin states that the answers to two questions are the foundation of all you will ever achieve. The first is: "What do you really want?" Or in the words of transformation, "What do you yearn for?" Yearning is critical because the deliberate practice of rematrixing is an investment and your yearning provides the motivation and the fuel to fulfill your potential.

His second question is: "What do you believe?" Do you believe that you can transform and live a great life? If you do, this can become the foundation of all you will ever achieve. If you think a great life is only for special people, or only happens under special circumstances, or through raw talent, then you will remain a dreamer and won't dedicate yourself to creating the great life you could be living. But if you do, transformation is possible—if you dedicate.

CHAPTER EIGHT

DEDICATE:
CHANGE FOR THE BETTER FOREVER

The moment one definitely commits oneself, then providence moves too. All sorts of things occur to help one that would never otherwise have occurred. A whole stream of events issues from the decision raising in one's favor all manner of unforeseen events, meetings and material assistance which no one could have dreamed would have come their way.
—W. H. MURRAY

GRIT. GUMPTION. COMMITMENT. Devotion. Dedicating. Yeah, we know, these words aren't as mind-blowing as rematrixing or as energizing as liberating, but you won't transform without dedicating. Dedicating may sound like little more than a simple promise or pledge, but that is only because we haven't explained its power. This is where the long-term fuel for transformation comes from. This is the story of the little engine that could. This is how your character is developed, how you guide your life by your deepest values, and how the thread of transformation and greatness weaves its way throughout all aspects of your life—your relationships, career, sense of self, well-being, service, and leadership. Through dedicating you guide the choices that create your life project—to live spectacularly.

Between a good life and a great life, there stands a choice, a commitment, a decision. While many people add good things to their lives—they get new jobs, upgrade houses, read self-improvement books, participate in workshops, do yoga, do career training—their good lives don't transform into great ones. Our research demonstrates a marked difference between those who merely add good things, and those who pursue greatness in every area. Those who dedicate themselves to the *Transformed!* process discover an ever-expanding landscape of possibilities for themselves, experience a deeper sense of richness each and every day, and live ever-greatening lives.

Sometimes the Transformers we studied seemed like regular folk, not necessarily those from whom you would have predicted greatness. More Frodo than Indiana Jones at the beginning of their journeys, they were often the ones who made the most progress over the long haul. Those who dedicated developed a courageous lifestyle of putting themselves in uncertain and demanding situations that forced them to change and transform.

Dedicating is the stuff of heroes, not necessarily in the public sense, but in being heroes of our own lives. Real, everyday heroes aren't only those who save lives—but also those who make significant contributions to our world in many different ways. Heroes don't just dabble. They don't just fantasize about being discovered or becoming famous. They don't brag about their great touchdown/big sale/mystical experience of twenty years ago or rest on the laurels of some other past success. They never stop risking, stretching, learning, growing, and transforming. They are dedicated to doing these things—not just once or twice but at every opportunity—and their persistence is heroic. Their fierce determination to take risks, to embrace novelty, to contribute— this is the stuff of heroism, the stuff we can all aspire to.

Dedicating reinforces our rematrixing and then provides us with the impetus to return to the other phases and redouble our efforts. Without dedicating, we will be conscientious seekers but fall short of transformation. As we'll discover, it takes an act of will to cross over to transformation, and dedication is all about will.

THE POWER OF DEDICATING—DON'T UNDERESTIMATE IT

Perhaps you're thinking: *I've read this far in the book, haven't I, doesn't that prove I am dedicated?* And if you are on the journey, haven't you already demonstrated your commitment to transformation by expending great energy and effort to become aware of and satisfy your deepest yearnings? You've worked tremendously hard at stretching yourself, at taking risks, at confronting your fears. Your life has changed in wondrous ways, and you've managed to rewire your mind to support these positive changes. If all this hasn't demonstrated how dedicated you are, what else can you do?

We don't doubt that you're serious about and committed to the *Transformed!* process. But that's not enough. Never underestimate the power of your matrix to assert itself beneath the level of consciousness and return you to old habits and patterns. Never settle for small, positive change rather than going for a magnificent metamorphosis.

When you settle for small change, you fall short of your potential. When you work so assiduously to change just one part of yourself, you are more vulnerable to all the forces that threaten to return you to a mediocre existence. In Hamlet, Shakespeare gives us an example of a gifted man of high accomplishment who wavers. His flaw is the failure to dedicate to his purpose. He fails to be focused and steadfast, wavering in philosophical questions rather than developing himself, and his lack of perseverance prevents him from achieving greatness.

You, too, can fall short if you do not dedicate and fulfill your potential. To be or not to be *is* the question that we have to answer definitively. Will we truly live, be, and become our best selves, or will we choose to coast, get by, and just let life happen to us? Will we dabble or dedicate?

Dedicating can be a somewhat elusive concept, so we need to begin by defining how it works, what it is, what it does, what it takes, and how it translates into attitude and action.

HOW LONG ARE YOU IN FOR?

Dedicating helps you harness the intent, flow, and excitement of yearning into engaging, revelating, and liberating. The burning passion of dedicating is what keeps you going in tough times and accelerates your growth in good times. Don't wait, however, to dedicate until you feel passionate about something. It is when you dedicate that you unleash the passion!

It all starts with you changing your definition of who you are—you are a Transformer who dedicates, not just a dabbler in growth. As Daniel Coyle found in his study of top performers, when we link our identity to a skill or outcome, or in our case, transformation, "when we envision ourselves doing it far into the future, we are tapping into a massive evolutionary energy source."

A fascinating study by Gary McPherson demonstrates how this works. McPherson studied several hundred children and their musical progress, beginning from before they started playing and then following them for a dozen years. As the children began playing their instruments, they fell into predictable patterns—a few of the them progressed really rapidly, a few made little progress, and most were somewhere in the middle. McPherson wanted to know why some took off and some just plodded along. Was it the ability to identify a tone or keep rhythm, or practice time, or math ability, or socioeconomic status, income, or parental influence . . . ? It turns out it was none of these things. The only factor that determined their progress was their answer to a question that he had asked them *before* they ever started playing an instrument.

The question was: How long do you think you're going to play this instrument? The children who said, "I'm going to play for a year or so," didn't make much progress. The kids that said, "I'm going to play through grade school," were in the middle. And the kids who said, "I'm going to play this my whole life," zoomed off. They progressed 400 percent faster than the other children! The moment when the children claimed, *"I'm going to be a musician,"* determined their future excellence.

This doesn't mean that they didn't work hard. They did the deep practice that is the hallmark of rematrixing and building expertise. But what is interesting is that even when these skilled musicians practiced less than the children who did less well, they did better. The long-term commitment group, with a mere twenty minutes of weekly practice, progressed faster than the short-termers who practiced for an hour and a half. Because their music was important to them, a part of who they are, they treated it differently—they tended to practice in the morning when they were fresh, were more likely to engage in more demanding deliberate practice, sought great teachers, and participated in demanding and rewarding programs. And when the children with long-term commitment practiced an hour and a half a week, their skills skyrocketed!

This same phenomenon occurs in dedicating. Identifying yourself as a Transformer helps you tap into all kinds of energy to put into transforming and building a great life. Not just practicing in the right way, or being motivated in the right way, but having transformation be part of your identity is where you tap its power. It is the identification that makes the change, not the words.

By identifying ourselves as Transformers, we become more conscious that we *are* changing in many magnificent ways. Our focus on these major changes and our experience of them triggers more transformational moves. By dedicating, we tap into this powerful energy and motivational force to do the work of transforming.

FULL-FRONTAL . . . LOBE, THAT IS

Dedicating and living with intent activates the most highly evolved part of our brain—our frontal lobe. By dedicating, you unleash a superpower for transformation that can help you dream big and live those dreams. Ever read comic books about superheroes? Often as children they discover they have a superpower—they find they can leap tall buildings with a single bound, or see through walls, or turn things to ice. Of course, in the beginning it is a big surprise to them that they have had this power within them all along. And, to use this power, they have to engage in deliberate practice. But the metaphor holds—we have amazing powers within us, but we have to be dedicated to practicing and using them to reap their benefits.

When fully activated, the frontal lobe, particularly the prefrontal cortex, gives us the capability to be in control of who we want to become. This powerful part of the brain is the seat of creativity, intention, and purposeful action. Using it is like conducting a vast orchestra of all the other parts of our brain, controlling how the rest of the brain operates, directing attention, keeping us from being distracted from our purpose, helping us to break out of the unthinking routines and reactions of our matrix and acting intentionally.

How do we activate it? We dedicate! When we dedicate we have made a conscious choice and commitment. When we resolve to transform, to be our best self, regardless of how long it will take, we spark this part of the brain into action.

Unfortunately we are more likely to live from what has been referred to as our mammalian brain, the more primal limbic system structure of our brain, and not from our frontal lobe. The limbic system is designed primarily for survival, it focuses on the Four "Fs": fear, feeding, fighting, and f—, uh, well, fornicating. The questions the limbic system is concerned with are related to comfort and stasis like: *When's lunch? Is it too hot in here? Is my butt going to hurt if I sit here any longer on this chair? When will this meeting or lecture or chapter be over? How long till I can leave work?* Safety is its primary function and it seeks comfort, sameness, routines—because any time it can't predict what is going to happen, it responds to those circumstances as a threat. So, if it can keep the same ol', same ol', then it is happy and secure. But same ol', same ol' isn't transformation!

SELF-INDUCED LOBOTOMY, ANYONE?

How many times have you chosen the comfort of your familiar routines over making courageous moves? How often have you felt blah and uninspired, or not followed through on projects, or slipped into repetitive routines (and been upset when your regular routine gets interrupted), and gotten offtrack? While these routines are part of the human condition, they can also be signs that we haven't dedicated.

Signs of Not Dedicating

- Lethargy

- Lack of inspiration

- A desire for sameness

- Falling into routines

- Difficulty maintaining single-minded focus

- Failure to follow through on projects or commitments

- Failure to learn from situations

- Emotional outbursts when routine is threatened or interrupted

- Inability to plan for the future

How many of these sound familiar? Chances are you can relate to most, if not all of them. We hate to break this to you, but, while these are signs of a failure to dedicate, they also are symptoms of someone who has had a frontal lobotomy! Lobotomies involved surgical removal of this part of the brain to "cure" people of violent tendencies or undesirable behavior. Fortunately, this operation, which was popular many years ago, isn't performed by surgeons today.

Unfortunately, many of us perform it on ourselves. We figuratively lobotomize ourselves when we go through life entrenched in limiting routines and soft addictions such as too much television, texting, overeating, procrastinating, workaholism—we rely on our limbic system, and fall into the familiar routines of our matrix. We fail to activate our prefrontal cortex. These routine activities from our matrix require little creativity or intention. Novelty and challenge, however, demand more than our limbic systems can give us.

The science clearly indicates that we are what we focus on—or dedicate ourselves to. Where we put our awareness is key. Beginner or old hand, if you start coasting at any point in the transformative process, you cease to use your frontal lobe and begin relying on your limbic system. That's why it's crucial that you use your frontal lobe to develop "attention density"—a laser-like focus on challenging objectives in all areas of your life. This is where neurological magic happens.

In the famous Stanford University marshmallow experiment in the 1960s, Walter Mischel's researchers told children they could have one marshmallow immediately or, if they waited awhile, they could have two later. Through follow-up studies years later, the researchers learned that the children who were able to delay gratification and focus on the more challenging goal achieved more in their lives than the kids who opted for the immediate satisfaction of one marshmallow. They were more competent, scored an average of 210 points higher on the SAT, had much higher college completion rates, and higher incomes, while the kids who ate the marshmallow had much higher drug and alcohol addiction problems and much higher incarceration rates. So if you can keep from going to the kitchen to get a marshmallow right now and finish reading this chapter before you indulge your marshmallow craving, you are on the right track!

Translated into dedicating terms, this means that if you can resist the easy tasks and mindless activities that provide small gratifications, you can focus your mind and energies on the more meaningful stretch goals that are necessary for transformation.

When we dedicate and activate our frontal lobe, we experience hunger to learn and grow, develop perseverance, and discover inspiration for the future. We are energized and motivated. We experience the attributes of frontal lobe living, which are also the signs of dedicating.

Signs of Dedicating

* Energized

* Motivated by mission and purpose

* Embracing the new and unusual

* Varying routines constantly

* Stick-to-itiveness

* Zealous pursuit of activities to their conclusions

* Resilient—bouncing back from failure and disappointments

* A hunger to learn

* Ability to adapt to changing circumstances

* A vision for the future

The frontal lobe is the place of our dreams and possibilities—where we ask questions like: *How can I become my best self? What am I capable of? What is possible for humanity?* It's where we plan and answer those questions with intentional activity. This intentional, dedicated living is what we most admire in our heroes, whether they be Martin Luther King, Amelia Earhart, Nelson Mandela, Marie Curie, Mahatma Gandhi, Mother Teresa, Benjamin Franklin, or Abraham Lincoln. They kept focus on their intention, and principles like freedom, honor, love, and service, and overcame obstacles, distractions, and attacks in order to live their ideals.

THE POWER OF A DEDICATED LIFE

The impact of Benjamin Franklin's life really hit us when we wrote this section. We had just lit a fire in our Franklin stove, switched on the electric lamps, walked past our library chair, put on our bifocals, and plugged our laptops into the electric outlet and realized that all of these things were invented or facilitated by Benjamin Franklin! Not to mention that we are living in a country founded in large part through his influence, dedication, and ideas. Now if we put on swim fins, drive our car with its odometer, and go to the library during daylight savings time, we'll be experiencing even more of his innovations.

The list of this dedicated Transformer's achievements and interests are staggering—one of the Founding Fathers of the United States, author, printer, politician, political theorist, diplomat, scientist, musician, inventor, and statesman—and this is not even an exhaustive list! Biographer Walter Isaacson called Franklin "the most accomplished

American of his age" and the most influential in inventing the type of society America would become, while another biographer called him "the harmonious human multitude."

Franklin followed his yearning and his urges and engaged in the adventure of life. His revelations in the arenas of science and politics as well as in ways of living are legion, and we are all beneficiaries of his belief in liberating. Though he lived just a bit before we opened Wright, he was clearly dedicated to his rematrixed view of the world. We can see the results through his amazing accomplishments, his constant learning and growing, his passion for discovery, experimentation, and public service, and his leadership and impact.

Ben Franklin was a dedicated Transformer who designed his life with structures, strategies, and support for his continual success. While there was no neuroscience research at the time to back up what he was doing, and he obviously didn't call it rematrixing, Franklin developed a system to "refine his character"—his term for rematrixing. Early in his life Franklin put together a list of thirteen virtues and related principles by which to lead his life (such as temperance, sincerity, and justice). But then he did what dedicated Transformers do—he set up structures and disciplines to support him in living these principles.

He listed each virtue on a page of his notebook and picked one to focus on each week. Reviewing his progress every night, he'd see where he'd been successful and where he'd fallen short, think about what he could do differently, and make a plan for the following day to live the principle more fully. While he wasn't always successful (nor is that the point), he crafted his life more consciously with this system. He wrote, "on the whole, tho' I never arrived at the perfection I had been so ambitious of obtaining, but fell short of it, yet I was, by the endeavor, a better and a happier man than I otherwise should have been if I had not attempted it."

As a Transformer, Franklin sought novelty and discovery—as we know from his many inventions and from the fact that he was an Enlightenment thinker, scientist, scholar, and traveler. At forty-two, he turned over his successful printing business to concentrate on science and develop technological innovations, saying, "I would rather have it said 'He lived usefully,' than 'He died rich.'"

Franklin knew about the importance of always learning and growing and never stopping, one of the characteristics of dedicated Transformers, as seen in his statement: "Without continual growth and progress, such words as improvement, achievement, and success have no meaning." Ben Franklin kept learning, growing, and making progress. He invented bifocals at the age of seventy-eight! His life demonstrates all of the aspects of the *Transformed!* process, and particularly, the aspects of the dedicating phase.

A MATTER OF HEART, MIND, AND SOUL

The purpose of sharing Franklin's story isn't to intimidate you, but to show you what's possible when you dedicate yourself to following the *Transformed!* process. Franklin's dedication may have sparked your own yearning to transform, to explore life more deeply, and increase your contribution to our world. And by now, we've demonstrated the power of dedicating and hopefully you are hungry to know even more about how you can harness its gifts. So let's look more closely at dedicating— to discover its components and the structures and strategies you need for success.

We're sure by now you understand that dedicating is much more than a simple statement like, "From now on, I'm going to do everything I can to transform who I am." Such a statement is fine, but in the face of all the daily turmoil and travails that life presents us with, we too easily become distracted or stressed and fail to follow through.

In fact, your matrix *loves* declarations, because they 'buy off' the brain and distract you so that you don't realize that you really aren't committed to changing! You are just getting high on the idea, with the burst of a dopamine rush. But it is an empty promise without the depth, rigor, and implementation strategies of rematrixing and dedicating to back it up.

When we talk about dedicating, then, we are describing a more substantive commitment to transformation. To help communicate this substance, let's examine the six components of this phase:

1. **DEVOTE YOURSELF TO TRANSFORMING.** Devoting reflects the all-encompassing commitment that Transformers make to fulfilling their potential and transforming. It is not a commitment to *either* career or relationship alone—true devotion has no exceptions. You can't devote yourself to change in your career and ignore your personal life. You can't be devoted to rematrixing during one particular time frame—a summer off or a sabbatical— and then not be devoted to it when you fall back into your routines. When you devote yourself, then, you prioritize having a great, transformed life above everything else.

2. **DEMAND MORE OF YOURSELF WITH "CHOICING."** Choicing generates opportunities that will force transformational changes. Choose challenging situations in which you will be forced to transform—accept a new job that you know will require you to develop new skills and shift your ways of interacting; join a group of people who are known for their excellence and won't tolerate anything less from you; take the job in another country to shake you out of your provincialism and stretch you; or apply for that scary promotion. Make choices that create more choices, options, and possibilities for your transformation. Don't miss moment-by-moment opportunities to choose—as Maslow recommends—the growth choices over the safe choices.

3. **PERSEVERE.** Be committed to keep engaging in the process no matter what—both when it's going well and you want to coast, and when it's difficult and you want to quit. You can't be naïve about what it takes to transform if you want to live a great life. It would be nice if the transformative steps became increasingly easy as you focused on them and if eventually nothing could stand in your way. Unfortunately, life isn't like that. You're going to encounter people and events that threaten to halt your progress: a friend who tells

you she doesn't like how you're changing or a family problem that saps a lot of your energy. Whatever the obstacles might be, regroup and resolve to fight through them.

How? First, you need discipline and support. This means you don't wing it—create a system of support and accountability that increases the odds you'll stay on your transformative path. Break your moves down into smaller steps and keep taking them. If you find yourself faltering, you have people you can call to set you straight.

Second, overcome blocks. Obstacles gain power when they seem to come out of nowhere and when you're not prepared to deal with them. To persevere, anticipate the barriers that may emerge as you pursue new opportunities. For instance, if you're engaging in a new project and fail, you may need to overcome devastation and feelings of humiliation, or if you are shy and trying to be more social, you can anticipate that if someone rejects your offer of friendship, you may be deeply hurt and this will give your matrix a chance to try to throw you back into your old way of interacting with others.

Third, develop a resilient mindset. According to Robert Brooks, a Harvard Medical School psychologist who has studied resilience for decades, the keys to bouncing back are: avoid self-defeating assumptions, don't allow rejection to derail your dreams, and see mistakes as just a problem to solve. Remember, your vision is important and a great life is worth fighting for.

4. **INVEST IN YOURSELF, YOUR TRANSFORMATION, YOUR LIFE.** Transformers never stop investing, and investing requires paying a price. While you've put in a lot of work up to this point, you may have had periods when you underestimated the amount of energy you needed to invest in transformation; or you may have opted for magical or simple solutions to the issues you faced. At the dedicating stage, you must make a full commitment of your resources—your time, money, energy, attention, and intention. Dedicated Transformers invest in training, hire excellent coaches who provide sequenced skill practices and feedback, develop

and implement structures and disciplines, investigate learning opportunities, and devote their time and energy toward becoming their best.

We've said it before and we'll say it again: You have to pay the price. No doubt you've sacrificed to reach this stage in your transformation. But the price to be paid in dedicating can be more than just spending more time on your personal growth and less on watching television. The price may be the loss of a lifelong friend; mockery from your peers; giving up a high-paying job; moving from a familiar to an unfamiliar location.

To grasp this investment, here is what one of our dedicating students had to say about investing and paying the price: "I gave up a full tuition scholarship for my master's degree, subsidized housing, and favorite-daughter status in my family and church when I realized that I would not have been in integrity to follow that path. There was a different and more difficult path that would give me more of what I really wanted."

Remember, there is no better investment than the investment in you and your potential—and the rewards far outweigh the costs.

5. **FLIP ON THE UP.** For many people, this aspect of dedicating feels counterintuitive. Most of us are willing to make significant changes in our life when we're in trouble. We go to counseling when our marriage is falling apart or start an exercise program when the doctor warns us we need to lose weight and get in shape or risk serious disease. What we are often loathe to do, however, is make changes when things are going well. We operate under the mistaken belief that if it ain't broke, don't fix it. But this is exactly when we need to push ourselves.

    True dedication means being willing to try something new or embark on a challenging or difficult task when things are going well and it would be easier to coast. Simplistically, flipping on the up refers to Kahneman and Tversky's Nobel prize-winning research revealing loss aversion, namely that most people try new things in desperation, when they have nothing to lose, but fail to try new things in the face of success. When you flip on the up, you don't wait for problems to act. Think of it as doubling down in the face of success. You proactively seek, choose, strategize, and embrace the new, the ambitious, the uncomfortable. Instead of staying with a job that has become easy for you, you request a transfer to one that will provide new learning and experiences. Instead of staying comfortable in a relationship that is pleasant but stagnant, you insist that you both get coaching or join a program that will help you work to grow the relationship. Essentially, flipping on the up is a way to maintain your momentum, ignite your transformation, and move you off the OK Plateau.

6. **LIVE PURPOSEFULLY.** Transformers live purposefully and with intent. They don't meander through their days; they are on purpose—to follow and fulfill their yearning to learn, grow, love and be loved, to matter, to make a difference. Transformers care so deeply about living with intent and pursuing their purpose that they can persevere through extreme hardship. Their yearning is so powerful that they feel compelled to engage, and in engaging, they revelate, liberate, and rematrix. To develop this sense of mission and purpose, dedicate yourself to following your deeper yearning—substantial, real, here-and-now yearning—and your purpose will emerge. Purpose is not an escape, and rarely is it a charity or cause alone—it's a way of living. It is something that is a unique expression of you.

Your yearning and purposeful living can be expressed in many individual and personal ways. For you it could be serving or being awake and conscious. Maybe it's being determined to fulfill your potential and help others to see and develop their potential. Maybe it's work-related: helping the young people in your company grow as people and professionals. Maybe it's spiritual: maintaining a relationship with a higher power and helping others do the same. Whatever your mission might be, it keeps you dedicated to your own continuous transformation and often to the transformation of others, as one of our students discovered:

Until recently, I never had the support I saw others getting in life. I guess that is one of my yearnings—to get and give support. One way I engage in my mission to be a "developer" is by hiring young workers in my company and cross-training them to be excellent not only in all areas of the business, but also in all areas of life. I encourage them to face fears, express their truths, and be genuine in their lives. It brings me great joy to see them develop their talents and themselves. At the same time, I am developing myself along with them.

Serving and leading become a natural part of living purposefully for Transformers. Everyone in our study was a leader. They didn't necessarily start that way, but by dedicating and living the *Transformed!* process, they naturally began to serve and to lead. They engage in deeply meaningful conversations with others, support others in being their best, hold visions of possibilities for their family members, friends, staff, and employees, and support them in achieving them. They contribute. They serve. They lead. By their dedication, living with purpose, they become greater people with greater influence.

DEDICATING IS A SHARED RESPONSIBILITY—MENTORS, MENSCH, AND MKOs

Think about all the myths, stories, and movies about heroes on a quest. They don't pursue their quests alone. Han Solo wasn't solo. The Lone Ranger wasn't alone. King Arthur had the Knights of the Round Table, Frodo had Sam and the rest of the Fellowship of the Ring. Even Thomas Edison had a laboratory full of fellow researchers. And think about high performers, whether Olympic champions, prize boxers, or the best tennis players: they practice and work out with sparring partners, they train with coaches, they run with the best.

You can't dedicate in a vacuum. Transformers immerse themselves in cultures of allies, whether fellow Transformers, talented coaches, teachers, inspiring role models, truth-sharing friends, or high-performing teammates. They hang out with people who share their values, who speak truth, who are living large in their own lives.

These relationships are critical for transformation. Just like at the talent hotbeds across the world—Meadowmount for musicians, Spartak for tennis players, etc.—Transformers not only receive excellent training and coaching, but they are also exposed to other highly skilled, risk-taking individuals who inspire them to greatness: *If they can do it, I can do it . . . I want to be like them, so I'd better get busy . . . I need to do what they do so I can be like they are.*

There's a tremendous motivational boost that occurs when we identify with a group, when we belong or see ourselves belonging in the future. University of Colorado's Dr. Geoff Cohen's research shows that motivation explodes when we identify with others who are performing: "When we get a cue that we ought to connect our identity with a group, it's like a hair trigger, like turning on a light switch. The ability to achieve is already there, but the energy put into that ability goes through the roof." It now becomes "us" not "me," and since, as Cohen says, "We're the most social creatures on the planet," this stimulates our built-in motivational triggers and funnels our energy and attention.

Not only do we need to be inspired by other Transformers and to identify with them, we also need to be with people who challenge us. People who dedicate successfully surround themselves with people who don't put up with their crap. Excuse our bluntness, but that's the best way to communicate the point. If you only surround yourself with people who offer you unconditional love and approve of everything you do, then you're going to struggle with this stage of the process. When Bob coaches musicians, for instance, he doesn't tolerate behaviors that allow them to lose their edge. He knows enough about their art and their profession to figure out when they're coasting or settling—when they offer an excuse about how now isn't the right time. By pushing them to stretch and learn, Bob helps them remain dedicated to becoming great. Even one of the best musicians in the world can still learn, even if that means traveling to Europe for lessons, for instance. You need "pushers" on your side, especially at those times when you hate and resent the idea of being pushed.

Look at this list of dedicated Transformers throughout history who formed mutually empowering relationships, benefitting from the inspiration, support, mentoring, and training of other skilled and talented people:

- J.R.R. Tolkien, C. S. Lewis, and G. K. Chesterton were among the regular members of the Inklings, who met for more than two decades to read and discuss each other's unfinished work—with robust criticism.

- Ernest Hemingway, with a letter of introduction from Sherwood Anderson, met and became friends with the elite Parisian writers and artists of his age from Ezra Pound, Gertrude Stein, Sylvia Beach, James Joyce, and Max Eastman, to Miro and Picasso. These friendships were instrumental in his development as a writer.

- Pissarro, known as the dean of Impressionist painters, was mutually inspired by working, teaching, learning, and painting together with Monet, Cézanne, Gauguin, Renoir, Seurat, Signac, Mary Cassatt, Sisley, Manet, Morisot, and Degas.

From The Academy and Lyceum of Athens with Plato and Aristotle to gatherings at the Mermaid Tavern in London during Shakespeare's day, where he, Marlowe, Jonson, Donne, and Raleigh met to talk and match wits, people committed to being their best band together.

Malcolm Gladwell cites the powerful team who supported Paul Cézanne to develop his gifts and become a famed Post-Impressionist painter late in his life, from his childhood friend Emile Zola who coached him into the artist's life in Paris to a long list of amazing people:

"But for Zola, Cézanne would have remained an unhappy banker's son in Provence; but for Pissarro, he would never have learned how to paint; but for Vollard (at the urging of Pissarro, Renoir, Degas, and Monet), his canvases would have rotted away in some attic; and, but for his father, Cézanne's long apprenticeship would have been a financial impossibility. That is an extraordinary list of patrons . . . Cézanne didn't just have help. He had a dream team in his corner."

Our students are part of a transformational learning community who hold vision for one another and support, expect, empower, challenge, and inspire each other. But they don't stop there. They assemble life teams of mutual empowerment, sometimes global teams, who play different roles in their lives—truth-telling friends, career mentors, and so on.

NO EXIT

Dedicating is the point in the process when the door closes behind you and there's no going back. This is scary stuff. When you invest so heavily in change and become singularly focused on fulfilling your potential and living with purpose, you move away from who you've been for most of your life. As you approach greatness, you may fear the responsibility that comes with it. People's expectations of you rise and you wonder if you can meet them. Similarly, people look at you differently. They may tell you that you're getting too big for your britches, that they hardly know you anymore, that they liked the old you better, that there's no way you'll achieve what you're trying to achieve.

Notice the threat you represent to them. Acknowledge the fear you feel in these circumstances. Articulate it. Recognize it for what it is. Imagine taking off on a rocket ship, zooming upward without an end in sight. It's natural to be afraid given the speed and uncertainty of this experience. At the same time, you also feel exhilarated, especially when you have More Knowledgeable Others around to guide you, because they have been there before or have at least been on similar voyages, so they know it can be done. By both drawing on the positive feeling and acknowledging the fear, you will increase the odds of dedicating yourself to your transformation.

DEDICATED TO LOVING BY BECOMING A NATIONAL LEADER

Riley is a Christian counselor and Wright leadership trainee who exemplifies a dedicated life. His dedication took him through a great deal of fear to the point where his faith became so solid that he wrote a book on the subject: the importance of challenging faith to strengthen ourselves and our capacity to trust God. It took him quite awhile to reach this point, but when he did, he demonstrated an unusually high sense of purpose and mission, of principled living, and of investing. Let's examine one aspect of his dedicating behavior—we'll draw and paraphrase from a written description he provided so you can understand the extent of his dedicating.

After years of personal development and challenge, Riley realized that running a successful business was not enough. He needed a greater undertaking so he began to pursue his goal of becoming a nationally recognized therapist, author, and thought leader in the Christian community. As part of this goal, he began a six-year odyssey to complete his book. As we know from our own experiences, writing a book is a challenge. It's not just that it takes an enormous amount of time and energy, but there are also all sorts of internal obstacles, self-doubt, and frustrations along the way.

Riley soon encountered these obstacles and frustrations. His leadership group kept asking for progress. At first, he required a great deal of prodding to get an editor to look at his writing and help him whip it into shape. Then he got one agent who wanted it redone—at each juncture, he would stall until his leadership group would once again challenge him to overcome his fear. He initially feared that he was not smart enough but got over that hurdle and came up with another draft, only to have his agent take another job so he was once again adrift. He required another push, which he received, and he began sending his rewritten book along with a proposal to publishers, only to receive one rejection after another. As Riley wrote, "I would then feel hurt, angry, and sad. I was unaccustomed to failure . . . I would withdraw to lick my wounds . . . Eventually, with the support of Bob Wright and the men in my leadership group, I would get the encouragement I needed to resume writing yet another version of my book."

Riley was a dedicator. He persevered. More than that, he was able to move past the sting of rejection and learn and grow from it. He recognized that as nice as it would be to have a big-name publisher give him a contract, his book project was an ongoing journey rather than a single destination. He needed to be dedicated to the process rather than just the end result. As Riley wrote, "What appeared to be a rejection was actually an injection of personal growth hormone. With each rejection I was deepening the roots of myself and strengthening my core . . . (I was) reframing failure as the measure of my willingness to risk enough to actually learn something."

Riley has now written and is publishing his book, which in itself is a tremendous accomplishment, but his dedication to transformation extends in other directions. He has become an ordained minister, begun doctoral studies, is deepening his already successful marriage, and has begun an international ministry to aid other ministers and ministries. He leads a minister's growth and support group, and is developing sermons to go with his book along with a curriculum and workbook for deepening of faith. For instance, he has embraced the idea that he must deliver sermons widely in order to fulfill his mission and promote the book—a possibility that he admits would have terrified him before. He also no longer avoids being hurt and failing but is dedicated to making choices so that hurt and failure are part of his purpose, giving him a rich, productive life experience. He knows that this is a small price to pay for learning, growth, and transformation.

WHAT HAPPENS WHEN YOU DEDICATE YOURSELF

Dedicating isn't easy, but the reward for making the effort is nothing less than a dramatically changed, tremendously fulfilling, and high-achieving life. When you are dedicating, you're on a direct path to transformation, since you've moved past your resistance to growth. You can create who you are within the image of your highest self. You determine your reality.

Dedicating also facilitates rematrixing. If that statement is confusing, because dedicating comes after rematrixing in this book, remember that in real life all the stages can actually occur simultaneously or in any order. So dedicating is a kind of insurance against your old matrix reasserting itself. It provides you with a framework for thinking and doing that keeps you moving forward instead of slipping backward.

From devoting to purposeful living, this stage gives you a way to apply everything you've learned thus far. It keeps you aware of and responding to your yearning. It motivates your engaging in behaviors that are consistent with your yearning. It encourages the type of reflection and self-analysis that produces revelating epiphanies. It facilitates liberating actions that push the boundaries of what you thought was possible for yourself. And, as we noted, it reinforces the rematrixing that emerges from your liberating moves. In a very real way, then, dedicating makes the whole process work.

But how do you know if you're dedicating? To determine whether or not you're truly dedicating, you have to observe yourself closely—what you're thinking, feeling, and doing. One of the best indications that you're dedicating effectively is the following: a resolve to do something no matter what. Even if the task before you is difficult or it makes you uncomfortable, you do it anyway. You don't let the concern about something being scary or time-consuming stop you. When you have doubts, feel overwhelmed, or are up against it, you know it is part of the process—you reach out for support, strategize how to overcome your blocks, reorient to your purpose, and keep going. When you're dedicating, you're burning with a need to fulfill your vision, and everything else drops by the wayside. You cease to be distracted from your purpose. You fasten onto the things you need to do and nothing stops you from doing them.

Another key is the *The Black Page Paradigm*. The late Frank Zappa wrote a jazz solo for drums that is among the most challenging pieces ever written for that instrument. It's called "The Black Page" because the solo pages are so filled with black notes that they almost obliterate the white space. One of our student leaders, a gifted, internationally recognized percussionist, played it in concert and said he had to practice more for that performance than any other in his thirty years of playing.

What does this story have to do with dedicating? It's relevant because in this stage, you need to relentlessly seek out difficult challenges such as this one. No matter how much you've accomplished or changed, you can always take it to a higher level. Seeking the Black Page in different areas of your life is a sure sign of dedicating.

Another key sign is that dedicating becomes a way of life. Up until this point, you may have thought of this transformative process as something to complete, running in tandem with your "real life." You practiced engaging, revelating, and the other phases with great seriousness, yet you saw it as something you would "get done" or an activity you did in addition to your career, your relationships, your religion. With dedicating, everything merges. Everything becomes connected to a larger purpose, whether it's going for a walk in the woods or volunteering to head a community organization. Dedicating widens the swath you cut through the world, and your extraordinary commitment to transformation impacts every area of your life. It is never-ending.

Transformers make a sincere and irrevocable commitment to living a great life. For instance, as Muhammad began awakening to his yearning, he realized that he had chosen to become an academic because his family expected him to continue its long tradition of scholars, not because it met his deeper yearning. Stepping out of the family mold, he began what seemed to him to be the adventure of being a consultant and businessman. This led him to ask yet deeper questions about how to satisfy both his immediate day-to-day yearnings as well as his life direction. His dedication to following his yearning led to transforming many aspects of his life—from becoming a technician to a practice leader in one of Chicago's most desirable, fast-growing consulting firms; from being shy and self-effacing to becoming a humble, yet assertive and potent contributor and leader; from being someone who had cultivated only his mind to becoming a virile, fit man who is currently taking up boxing; from being a loser in love to having a fantastic marriage and partner.

Asking himself what he wanted to say about his life on his deathbed (an exercise—Muhammad is in good health as of this writing), Muhammad realized that he also yearned to help others transform and to ease the pain of people in his homeland, Bangladesh. Driven by this inspirational motivation, Muhammad began growing even more rapidly, contributing to others as a mentor and role model. His progress was enhanced even more when he and his wife began a not-for-profit to contribute to the future generations of Bangladesh, her homeland as well. Following their collective yearning has led Muhammad and his wife to significant levels of dedicating, making life an adventure beyond anything either of them could have imagined.

Dedicating works for people of any faith: Buddhist, Muslim, Jew, Christian, and Hindu alike. It works equally well for atheists and agnostics. It works in all areas of life, from career to parenting. But faith is a good prism through which to view dedicating since dedication and transformation are the essence of what is good and right in every faith, in every people—leading naturally, rarely easily, through infinite pathways to what is highest and best in each of us—learning, growing, stretching into becoming the most radiant, fulfilled, service-oriented, loving beings, fully celebrating the life we are given.

CHAPTER NINE

THE HEART OF TRANSFORMATION

There can be no knowledge without emotion. We may be aware of a truth, yet until we have felt its force, it is not ours. To the cognition of the brain must be added the experience of the soul.
—ARNOLD BENNETT

AN AMAZING FORCE AWAITS YOUR DISCOVERY —the transformative power of your emotions. We're referring to those often pesky, demanding, embarrassing, exhilarating, and overwhelming feelings of joy, sadness, anger, hurt, and fear—all of your emotions are powerful agents of transformation. Yes, we mean all of them, not just joy or happiness. Those uncomfortable waves of emotions that we so often numb, hide, or push down are actually amazingly powerful tools of transformation! And, when we numb them, we deprive ourselves of their transformational force.

Mounting research demonstrates that you need them all to be your best. You won't transform to your fullest without facility in the whole range of emotions. You may improve, learn, grow, or even master a skill, but you won't be a Transformer without them all. You may become an expert skier, software engineer, or scientist, but you won't lead a spectacular life without maximal access to your emotions.

And, you'll miss out on the remarkable benefits that research shows we derive from emotional intelligence: making more money, being more productive, becoming a top performer, achieving more satisfying relationships, enjoying better health—even a longer life!

No matter how much work you have done to get in touch with and master your emotions, or how high your EQ, there is always more you can do to unleash your unlimited transformational power. And for you rational logic-lovers and *Star Trek* Spock aficionados of the world who are relentlessly factual and analytical, you'll soon see that Spock's lack of emotion would have made him the least functional crew member on the Starship Enterprise! Not to mention the least likely being or life form on the ship to transform and live a spectacular life.

Without access to the power of your emotions, you'll lack not only the motivation to change in spectacular ways but also the information and transformative magic that emotions unlock. And without a positive relationship with your emotions and the emotional facility to sense, express, and use their wisdom, you are likely to be sidetracked from your yearning path. We'll show you the astonishing roles they play in learning, growing, changing, and transforming. We will then show you how to "be with them" so you don't let your discomfort and mistaken beliefs about feelings derail your transformation process.

NEUROSCIENCE IS MORE THAN YOU THINK . . . IT'S ALSO WHAT YOU FEEL

Since we've emphasized the neuroscience of transformation throughout the book, you may think that neuroscience is about cognition, thoughts, and your rational mind. But it's not like that. Your brain isn't a place of orderly, rational thought and your body a place where some disruptive, irrational volcano is waiting to erupt without notice (although it can certainly seem that way sometimes!). Your mind and body, your thoughts and feelings are all intricately linked. Neuroscience is the study of the nervous system and that doesn't just apply to what you think. It pertains to what you think *and* feel. This includes how your thoughts and feelings influence one another and you. In fact a field of neuroscience is dedicated to the study of emotions—affective neuroscience. Emotions are related to areas of the brain that direct attention, motivate our behavior, and determine the significance of what is going on around us.

So you see, the mind alone is insufficient to create the life changes you seek. If you are not in touch with your feelings, you won't be able to sense your yearning or the nudges of your urges. You won't be able to engage meaningfully with heart, or revelate effectively by accessing creative thought, facing the fears of busting your beliefs, and experiencing the joyous space that fosters insight. You won't venture beyond the fear-based boundaries that form the bars of the cage of your limiting beliefs. You will miss out on liberating and feeling the joy and freedom of stepping into your next most radiant self. You'll miss the intense emotions that are the ripest moments for rematrixing, and you'll be unable to weather the frustrations of the deliberate practice that rematrixing requires. You won't harness your passion or experience the immense satisfaction of dedicating—and you will miss out on the great life you could be living.

As you yearn, engage, and take the other steps in the process, you must learn to ride—and enjoy—an emotional rollercoaster. This may sound scary, but as some of you know, rollercoaster rides can also be exhilarating. It is all in your perspective. The climb to the top is great, but it's not possible without the plunge to the bottom. We're going to help you appreciate, draw energy from, and use the transformative power of those stomach-churning, twisting dives at 100 miles per hour, and the way to start is by understanding what your feelings are all about.

AN EMOTIONAL EDUCATION

Let's start with a primary education—primary feelings, that is. Primary emotions are fear, anger, hurt, sadness, and joy—and we all have them whether we are conscious of them, in touch with them, experience them, like them, or actually "feel" them. These primary emotions are hardwired into all of us. So often, because of our ambivalence or judgments about what we erroneously refer to as negative emotions, we deny them, numb them, distract ourselves from them, or suppress them. And as you'll soon learn, by doing so, you've diminished a transformational urge—even negated it in many cases.

Secondary emotions are combinations of primary feelings, like guilt—a combination of fear, hurt, and often, anger. Your guilt may not look like fear, hurt, or anger at first glance, but it usually contains these big three in some proportion. Remember, we are discussing unconscious levels, not the public relations spin your conscious mind broadcasts. Secondary emotions are based on our own unique internal experience base and are therefore experienced differently by different people. We'll keep to the primary feelings—and you should too—because they are the most foundational emotions with the clearest encoded actions in them. They are more precise and more powerful. Remember, though, that they are in the unconscious mind, hidden underneath blankets and facades of denial based on our core limiting beliefs about ourselves and our world.

When you can recognize an emotional blaze—whether it's joy or red-hot anger—it's a clue to what really matters in your life. Similarly, when you are feeling down, or what some people call depressed, it is really hurt, sadness, or even repressed anger. If you misidentify these feelings, you will not take the effective action they indicate. That's why we've encouraged you to recognize and express powerful feelings in every phase of the process. They can help you differentiate surface wants from your deeper yearning—wanting to check your Facebook page or to shop doesn't stir up powerful emotions—needing to be loved does.

Your feelings will spur the action of engaging. Flowing emotions, freely expressed, more readily lead to revelating. When you are more in the here and now, expressing what you feel, you often blurt out truths you weren't consciously aware of until they come out of your mouth. Your feelings will guide you in breaking free from the bonds of what constrains you in liberating, and guide you toward what you desire. It's liberating to be spontaneous, expressing how you feel, and flowing with your emotional truth. Moments of intense feelings are some of the most potent elements in rematrixing—where we can re-encode beliefs, experiences, and memories with compassion, acceptance, and new interpretations. Recognizing and harnessing the passion of dedicating helps you carry on in the face of the world's challenges and your own inner barriers. It yields a new you.

At the same time, when powerful emotions overcome you, you'll need the skills to interpret and express them effectively. These skills may include comforting yourself, using anger to get rid of pain, or engaging in a whole host of other responses such as allowing the full process of loss in sadness and risking to reach out and share with others in joy. You'll also need to develop the skills of comforting yourself since you will be hurt more as you transform. We all need to seek comfort and allies for the unpredictable emotional changes of transformation—not the surface solace of soft addictions like mindless gossiping or over-indulging in "comfort foods," but the deeper succor of self-soothing, a skill we will discuss later in this chapter.

SCIENCE UNMASKS SPOCK AS THE LEAST FUNCTIONAL CREW MEMBER ON THE STARSHIP ENTERPRISE

Without access to his emotions, chances are Spock would never even have made it to Star Fleet Academy, much less up to the bridge of the Starship Enterprise. With his Vulcan logic and lack of emotions, it would have taken him five or six hours just to decide what color underwear to wear that day. And all that energy he used suppressing his emotions? He would have drained his cognitive resources, and degraded his ability to recall, leaving himself less capable of productive action. He wouldn't have the ability to learn, make distinctions for decision-making, recall memories, or direct his attention appropriately, because these are the powers of emotion. He wouldn't be rational at all—because emotions are actually necessary for rational thought!

Given how neuroscience has definitively demonstrated the function of emotions with overwhelming evidence of their role in everything we do, it is hard to believe that we once thought that logical, emotionless people were superior and that emotions were irrational impulses that got in our way or led us astray. It has really been our lack of skill in dealing with emotions and our lack of understanding of their true power that were the problems. And when we understand their power and develop the skill to utilize them, transformation is fostered. Our life not only becomes richer, but we also become more effective Transformers—following our emotions intelligently into the realization of our potential.

While you may grasp the richness that your emotions provide in your life, the scientific evidence of their purpose and function is, well, mind-blowing. It's no accident we often say, "I am so moved," when we are touched emotionally. The word emotion comes from a Latin word that means "to set into motion" and shares the root word with motivation. Emotions literally move us to action and motivate us to engage in the phases of the *Transformed!* process.

Rather than being a mistake or leading us offtrack, emotions are designed to keep us *on* track. Each emotion is evolutionarily dedicated to give the resources we need to contend with the very situation that evoked the emotion to begin with. How cool is that?

Neuroscience research shows that our emotions anticipate our needs and prepare us to act. As the arbiters of our pleasure-pain mechanism, emotions are designed to move us toward pleasure and away from unnecessary pain. For instance, fear warns us against the danger of an approaching saber-toothed tiger and triggers the body to respond appropriately—by running away. Anger lets us know that a given situation is violating our values or is wrong in some other way—a painful experience—and causes us to take action that leads to a more pleasurable outcome. And when these emotion-specific resources are unlocked, they are accompanied by a sense of energy and vitality, broader awareness, openness, and a sense of well-being.

Emotions don't "get in the way of" rational thinking—they are essential to rationality. Neuroscientist Antonio Damasio's research shows that emotions are not separate from reason—in fact, they are at the center of our thinking, the foundation of reason—because they tell us what to value. They are vital to the higher reaches of human intelligence. And because of that, David Brooks, the *New York Times* columnist and author of *The Social Animal,* concludes that "reading and educating your emotions is one of the central activities of wisdom."

And it's not just our rational thinking but our decision making that is dependent on emotions. Remember how we said Spock would spend five or six hours trying to decide what color underwear to wear? We weren't kidding. Damasio found that people with a tumor on their emotional centers, leaving them without access to their emotions, would spend five to six hours deciding which pen to use, the blue one or the black. They didn't have the gut instinct to nudge them one way or another.

Emotions also unite our minds and our bodies, our hearts and our minds, helping us achieve wholeness. Daniel Siegel's research shows that, as we develop our facility with them, emotions are integrative. They give us a sense of our self, allowing us to ride the waves of life between "the banks of rigidity and chaos." Emotions direct our attention and our behavior, enhance our memory and our creativity, and tell us what to value. It is through our emotions that we create and experience intimacy, both with ourselves and others. They are how we come to know ourselves and deepen our spiritual connection.

And just what is emotional intelligence? We define it as emotional awareness and emotional facility—knowing what you are feeling and having the skills to read, utilize, manage, and express your emotions. Emotional intelligence isn't just relevant for new-agers or sensitive types. Daniel Goleman's article on emotional intelligence has been the most requested article from the *Harvard Business Review* in the last ten years, leading *HBR* to conclude: "Emotional intelligence isn't a luxury you can dispense with . . . It's a basic tool that, deployed with finesse, is the key to professional success."

TRANSFORMATION . . . OH, THE PLACES UNLEASHED EMOTIONS CAN TAKE YOU

At this point you might be asking yourself, *Why do I have to know so much about emotions; How does all this knowledge help me with transformation?*

Think about olives. Olive oil is contained within the olives but it has to be ex-pressed, or pressed out, in order for you to enjoy the wonders of the oil. The same is true of your feelings. They need to be expressed in order for you to fully experience their transformational power. Think of a reverse transformational process. Ancient plant matter becomes coal, and coal can be expressed in fire or compressed so its essence expresses as diamonds. Just as appropriate pressure and time bring out these changes in olives and coal, recognizing emotions and following yearning bring about our transformation. At the same time, pressure can be misapplied and ruin things. We'll talk about the problems with irresponsible or unregulated emotional expression in a bit, as well as how to develop the skills to deal with your fear of strong emotions. But for now, let's focus on the relationship between emotions and transformation.

Imagine that you embrace, appreciate, and skillfully deal with your emotions. Being in touch with your emotions, you express your yearnings in the present moment. Through your complete emotional expression, these feelings will lead you toward possibilities and new aspects of yourself. In fact, researchers over the last thirty years have found that we are transformed as we shift away from being exclusively in our heads and move toward being fully in the moment, sensing and feeling our emotions within our bodies in conjunction with our cognition.

Transformation follows our emotional expression—when emotions are expressed in a way that causes a new element of ourselves to emerge. For example, when we begin to acknowledge the fear and anger we've habitually held back or repressed, the process begins. Once we identify and responsibly express our fear, we've done something we would previously have defined as "not me." As we continue on the journey of realizing and expressing our anger, we're opening to new zones within ourselves. And we find that fully and responsibly experienced anger often results in a sense of empowerment, inner strength, and assertiveness.

The same can be true of the entire range of primary emotions. Fear, in particular, is a "not me" for many leaders. The awareness of their fear is actually blocked, so strong is their denial. They unconsciously use fear to anticipate problems. We have found, however, that their denial of fear is so strong that they actually think they never or rarely experience it. Fear represents not only a "not me" for them, but an "inferior me," just as anger represents, for many, a "bad me."

All emotions, when allowed to flow in an integrative manner, take us into zones of "not us" where we become something we were not—we are transformed.

A newlywed couple in their first quarter of our Year of Transformation program got into a fight, and their quarrel illustrates emotion taking them from the "not me/not us" zone to a "new me/new us" zone with increased trust and intimacy as a result.

Darren, an affable guy studying for his doctorate at a prestigious university, talked about the fight in this way:

> I'm expressing what I want and what I'm feeling in the moment. It started as a pretty typical fight, but at one point where I might have stewed for a few minutes, I expressed how hurt and angry I was. As I was saying it, more and more emotion came out in my tone, and I realized I was almost numb to how much I had been holding back. At one point I slammed my hand on the countertop, which is totally out of character for me. I realized I hold back my anger sometimes to avoid scaring the other person. But it felt really good to express it and I felt much better almost immediately. When we talked about it later, we both noted how much faster and cleaner we were able to resolve the fight. I know it's always better to express yourself fully, but this helped me see it firsthand.

Lorie, a brilliant professional who was a top student at the best schools, provided her perspective on their fight:

> I am learning that emotion is also a gateway to truth. Darren and I had a fight last night—one of the biggest we have had in some time—that was qualitatively different than fights we have had in the past: Darren was more directly expressive of his anger and hurt than I think he has ever been; and we got to resolution a lot faster than we usually do, even though (and almost certainly because) the emotional expression was so intense. I am not sure if the focus on truth got us to the real emotional expression faster, or if the emotional expression got us to the truths we needed to say faster. But either way, I credit both with the end result. At one point, I stormed off to the bathroom and thought about staying there for a while (passive aggressively), but then I thought of the assignment and consciously told myself that I was going to go back and tell the truth, whatever it was at that moment. Even if I didn't feel like I knew quite what the truth was yet. In the end, I was left with this mix of intense joy and sadness.

Dan Siegel's research shows that when we share emotional experiences like these with another, our interactive experience allows us to "feel felt" and understood, which also may establish new neural network firing patterns that can lead to neural plastic changes—another vote for the transformational power of emotions.

Researchers in the field of interpersonal neurobiology have found that when we complete, or bring to resolution by expression, our experience of intense emotional events, these biologically based and wired-in emotional processes culminate in experiences of "aliveness, hope, faith, clarity, agency, simplicity, compassion, truth, self, and beauty." By learning to responsibly access these processes, we become able to soar to the greatest heights and plumb the greatest depths. And, as neuroscientist Richard Davidson has found, as we continue to build our emotional intelligence, it actually changes our brains, shifting the gene expression in them! Not only do we feel, think, and behave in transformed ways, but our brains are actually transformed.

YOU'RE SO EMOTIONAL—INSULT OR COMPLIMENT?

Take a moment and consider how you treat your feelings. Now, answer these two questions:

Do you act as if any of your emotions are an embarrassment or an enemy you need to fight?

Do you characterize any of them as either "good" (love, joy, bliss) or "bad" (anger, fear, pain)?

We assume that you probably answered yes to one or both questions. We were all raised with messages about which emotions are "okay" and which ones are "bad," and it's not just the latter that we're trained to suppress. We may have also been taught that unbridled joy is undignified or that we are "too much." We may refrain from showing any, or all but the mildest form of, anger because we're convinced that it will be judged negatively. Expressing our aliveness in any form can often feel threatening to others. While there are some families and cultures that have a healthier relationship to feelings than others, Western society, as a whole, tends to view emotions as problematic.

Lessons learned in childhood as well as social norms cause us to be out of touch emotionally and reluctant to express our feelings genuinely—or at all—in certain situations. Most families have rules, implicit as well as explicit, against expressing certain feelings. Business, social, and gender norms discourage men from expressing any authentic feelings, especially hurt, fear, and even sadness, in many situations as doing so will make them seem "weak" or "unprofessional."

We limit our emotional expression to what we feel is appropriate, but limiting *any* feeling limits *all* feelings. To the extent that we suppress our pain, we also suppress our joy.

Now let's consider emotions from a neuroscience perspective. Neuroscientist Candace Pert's research shows that our unexpressed emotions are lodged throughout the body and aren't fully expressed until they reach consciousness. Through the body, up the spinal cord, and into the brain, raw emotion works to be expressed, moving up the neural access through the spinal cord. The cortex, however, often resists this expression. Why? Because when we harbor mistaken beliefs (e.g., *It's not manly to express fear*) and rationalizations (e.g., *If I get angry, people won't like me*) about emotion, we push our feelings down to be repressed rather than up to be expressed. When the cortex responds this way, it is trying to prevent itself from being overloaded. This creates a physiological struggle, since our emotions are trying to be expressed and integrated yet the cortex is not allowing them to reach consciousness. But suppressing emotions is costly—not only does it deprive us of the power and gift of our emotions, but it is a high-intensity task that chews up limited prefrontal cortex energy and resources. It degrades our ability to recall information and limits our cognitive performance.

So pity poor Spock, the emotionless Vulcan. By trying to suppress his emotions, he is using up his cognitive resources, degrading his recall, and limiting his cognition!

When we are aware of our emotional rationalizations and mistaken beliefs and address them, we make it much easier for our cortex to allow our emotions to bubble up into consciousness. Not only is this a healthier way to live, but we also feel more alive, vital, and present in the moment—our emotional energy is available to facilitate transformation.

Think about the negative messages we often hear about emotions, things you've probably thought or said yourself: *Calm down, what's wrong with you? . . . You're such a wuss . . . Get a grip . . . I'll give you something to cry about . . . Cry-baby . . . That time of the month? . . . You're too sensitive . . . Go to your room . . . Calm down . . . Chill . . . You're weak . . . You're so unprofessional . . . Drama queen.*

If you never learn to express your emotions responsibly, they can build up and eventually explode in destructive tirades and hysteria—which may account for some of these epithets. This doesn't mean we need to get rid of our feelings. Instead, we need to recognize our limited emotional skills. Emotions aren't the enemy and there is no such thing as a bad feeling, they are all good. We didn't say they *feel* good, but they *are* good. They have positive functions despite the fact that they often don't *feel* good. That means we need to develop emotional facility and emotional regulation skills, which is what Transformers do.

THE INS AND OUTS AND UPS AND DOWNS
OF EMOTIONAL FACILITY

Now we know that Transformers develop their emotional facility, powering their transformation and enriching their lives, but what exactly are those emotional skills? Too often, people think it is toning feelings down, numbing them, or making them go away. Well, if you are approaching a total meltdown, about to create a toxic spill, or at the edge of a lose-your-job, over-the-top hysterical tirade, then down-regulating is helpful. But other times you need to rev up—increase your emotional idle so that you can engage more quickly, intensify your joy, or activate your anger to get your keister moving.

Because developing emotional facility is essential for Transformers, we'd like to share with you the four core concepts our students need to master to obtain a graduate certificate in Emotional Intelligence at Wright—the Ins and Outs and Ups and Downs of emotional facility:

The Ins, Outs, Ups, Downs of Emotional Facility

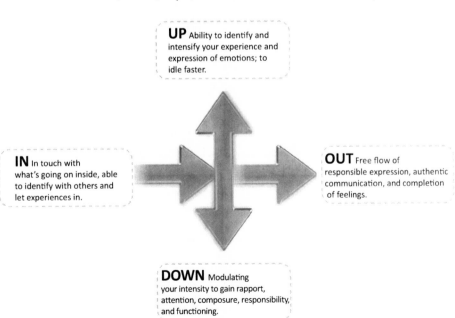

UP Ability to identify and intensify your experience and expression of emotions; to idle faster.

IN In touch with what's going on inside, able to identify with others and let experiences in.

OUT Free flow of responsible expression, authentic communication, and completion of feelings.

DOWN Modulating your intensity to gain rapport, attention, composure, responsibility, and functioning.

- *In.* Means being in touch, knowing what's going on inside of you and what you are feeling. This area has to do with perception and the capacity to feel what is going on consciously in the moment, being able to let experiences in. It's about developing an expanded capacity to understand yourself, and through identifying with others, to understand them. Some call it being sensitive. It means being able to sense, feel, and name your emotions, which helps you experience full aliveness and empathy—and be aware of your yearning.

- *Out.* Refers to the free flow of responsible expression. This is the ability to fully express your feelings and allow them to complete themselves. It is not hysterical dumping, but responsibly communicating and expressing emotions in a way that brings us into greater accord with ourselves as well as with others. It is key to engaging and revelating. It's about authentically expressing your emotions, being fully present, with a full range of responsible feeling available, from crying to belly laughing.

- *Up.* Refers to increasing your affect in expression or reception. It requires awareness of your present state and the ability to increase your awareness and presence. It is about being able to intensify your emotions, experience your feelings deeply, enjoy your joy more fully, engage more quickly. It's key to motivation and taking action, like having a faster idle so you can take off more quickly.

- *Down.* Refers to modulating your intensity, especially when trying to establish rapport and gain attention. It includes the capacity to soothe, calm, or contain your emotions when you are overwhelmed, or when you are prone to being irresponsible about their expression, or when you've "flipped your lid" and lost your higher-level functioning and need to regain your composure.

These four areas of skill are developed over time and are central to your transformation. In the example of Darren and Lorie above, you see the results of Darren up-regulating and Lorie down-regulating—both responsibly, in a way that has brought them closer and that is facilitating their transformation and the emergence of their next most radiant selves. Note how Darren is becoming aware, and his expression is causing further growth in that awareness. They both take the other's expression in, put some out, and demonstrate up- and down-regulating.

DETECT AND EXPRESS

For the Wright emotional curriculum, we've created a number of ways to help people be more in touch with their bodily cues, thoughts, and sensations and express emotions more accurately and effectively. While we can't re-create all these experiential exercises in this book, these two techniques might help you:

- **BECOME AN EMOTIONAL DETECTIVE.** Be on the lookout for clues to feelings you are having. The question is not, "Am I having a feeling?" You always are. Better to ask yourself, "What is my primary emotion right now?" You will begin to recognize the omnipresent emotions that course through you, unrecognized, in the course of a day. Identify the thought patterns and states that indicate emerging emotions that require your attention. Do you become tense, defensive, critical, shy, sarcastic, or even aggressive to cover up emotions? Do you indulge in soft addictions such as overeating, eating sweets, watching too much television, complaining, or procrastinating to mask your feelings? Notice your moods, states, and thought patterns, as well as any soft addictions that indicate the need to pay closer attention to your emotions. Scan your body for emotional clues—a clutch in your gut, an aching back, holding your breath, sweaty palms, rapid heartbeat, shallow breathing, a racing pulse—that indicate feelings.

- **MONITOR A FEELING PER HOUR.** Set a timer to go off every hour. When it goes off, close your eyes, discern the primary feeling you are having at that moment, and then immediately write it down. You may be surprised at how much is going on inside of you!

A top attorney with Ivy League credentials, Benjamin wasn't contemplating a major life change or the fear that accompanies such contemplation. Instead, he wanted more of the qualitative changes he had seen in a friend, one of our graduates who was also a very successful attorney. Benjamin was in the early stages of getting in touch with his feelings, and to help him, we gave him the *Monitor a Feeling Per Hour* assignment. Here is an excerpt of what Benjamin wrote:

> The most interesting thing that I learned is that there is a lot of joy in my life. Almost every time the timer went off, I was enjoying what I was doing. Even if I was anxious, frustrated, under pressure, worrying about a problem or a deadline . . . I was basically happy about being where I was and doing what I was doing.
>
> Historically, when I thought of my feelings, I focused on what I didn't like about (them). I held a mistaken belief that feelings are bad and get in the way, so I thought about my feelings as a synonym for my problems. I focused on things like what I am anxious or angry about and why do I feel like I am not good enough. It was very surprising to me this week to notice how often I am happy.

This discovery provided a firm foundation for Benjamin to follow the full range of his yearnings, stepping out of his comfort zone and stretching himself because he has pushed past his assumptions about his feelings, often inaccurate, and discovered truths about them. This is critical for everyone who aspires to transform, especially when it comes to the emotion that sabotages many aspiring transformers: fear.

Fear is the biggest challenge for many Transformers, but the more they face their fear, the more they are also able to feel their joy. While anger can also be a challenge for Transformers, it's fear of what others will do or our own self-judgments that keep us from using our anger responsibly and effectively. We also fear sadness, afraid we can't handle it or that we'll get stuck in "the blues." By learning to face our fear and unlock the yearning inside of it, we are taking a huge step into transformation.

In fact, Transformers learn to follow their fear. They know that if they're not in conscious relationship with their fear, it can act like the brakes on a car. In conscious relationship with their fear, however, they can ease off the brakes and allow their yearning to propel them forward.

EMOTIONAL EXAMPLES

Here are two stories of Transformers who learned to use their fear to facilitate their growth. They not only confronted powerful emotions along their paths to transformation, but also used fear and other emotions as a transformational force. By telling their stories, we hope to convey not only how fear can cause these emotions to sidetrack you, but also how, by facing the fear, you can use them to make great progress in your personal evolution.

Doug, whose story we shared earlier, had been consciously engaged in his own transformation for some time. As a consultant, he had always felt there was a lack of integrity in his profession that few were willing to address, himself included. He feared even mentioning it to people until he had done a significant amount of transforming. He had never been trained to be a revolutionary and described himself as a shy, number-crunching, green visor kind of guy. As he learned to face his fear, he learned that there was a huge source of energy in it and he was ready for significant transformation. He wanted to face the lack of integrity in his profession, and he feared confronting it would cause many of his clients to abandon him. Facing this fear, however, was not without benefit, because he was betting that he would move higher up the corporate hierarchy to the board level if his challenge of the status quo was successful.

Doug felt that current "best practices" were unethical and that there had to be a better way. Doug not only began working on formulating this better way, he also began working with national standard-setting agencies, risking a great deal to bring about change. The fear he was facing with each move in this direction was palpable, but he also noticed it caused him to think more analytically and strategically. He was more consciously intentional about finding allies in the pursuit of a better way. This motivated him to become friendly with a wider range of highly influential people.

Finally, he was ready to unveil his major strategic move, and he did so by co-sponsoring a conference to correct this lack of integrity, partnered with Nobel laureates and the top national and international standards boards. All the national business publications from the *Wall Street Journal* to *Barron's* and *Fortune* were in attendance. His move was the opening salvo in a national debate on the subject which led to wholesale changes that are still going on today. A major publisher solicited a book from Doug, still another asked him to write what is now the bible for corporations in a particular area of his profession.

His professional transformation was exploding to a new level. He lost none of the clients he'd feared losing, and instead added Fortune 50 boards to his client roster. Doug did not get rid of fear, and he now lives under more professional pressure than he ever faced in the past. But he says, "I feel more—more hurt, sadness, anger, and joy every day than I did in a week before. But, my feelings aren't a barrier; they're a help to me. I face them and use the information they give me to be more in touch and more effective and to get more support in my life."

Now, let's look at a much different example, one that just about everyone can identify with. Kendra, a single, professional woman in Chicago, had gone through years of what we term "cautious" dating. Fear dominated Kendra's behavior—fear of rejection, judgment, or even gossip. As a result, she was always worried about saying or doing the wrong thing—afraid that if guys really knew what she thought or felt or who she really was, they wouldn't like her and worse yet, would judge her. She'd try to gauge what they wanted to hear, what wouldn't upset them, or what would impress them before she spoke. As a result, her dates generally went smoothly, but she rarely expressed herself in ways that felt true and meaningful. Though she went on a lot of dates, they never developed into serious relationships—or at least never relationships that she took seriously.

As she began to note her yearning to really be known and learned to face her fear, she started forcing herself to take risks on her dates. For instance, she began saying exactly what was on her mind—and her heart. If she was uncomfortable with how a guy was treating a waitress at the restaurant, or more importantly, how he was treating her, she shared her feelings. If a guy took a position on politics that she didn't agree with, she expressed her disagreement. If she wanted to go see a movie that she suspected that her date would find to be overly serious or arty, she spoke up and said that she would really like to see this film. She let her dates know when she was angry, or happy, or afraid.

Sure, some men rejected her, but similarly, to her amazement, many men seemed to like her much more! How did she get past her fear of rejection? She took advantage of a skill we already mentioned—she embraced the WTF (What the F***) attitude. Kendra said WTF and found it helpful. As she said, "The worst that could happen is that my date might walk out on me. Actually, the worst that could happen is that I don't speak my mind and I'll end up with a second date by pretending to be someone I'm not."

NOTHING TO FEAR BUT FEAR ITSELF

Expect a wide range of emotional responses to transformation. You may feel guilty when a friend tells you that you're not acting like yourself, that you're not as much fun as you used to be. You may feel ashamed for how joyful you feel, since you've been raised to believe that too much joy is sinful. Yet fear is the most common emotional response to transformation and the most challenging, so let's probe beneath its scary surface.

It helps to understand that our brains are designed for survival, so they prioritize keeping us safe before other higher functions can kick in. When we keep things the same, comfortable, and familiar, then the brain has a predictable outcome and it is not threatened. But when our brain can't predict the outcome, when something new and unpredictable is happening and transformation is afoot, the fear responses of fight, flight, or freeze are triggered.

This made sense in evolutionary terms—we were wired to respond quickly to any life-threatening danger, like monstrous predators. But there is another fear that emerged and became increasingly important to early man's survival—social fear—which is fear of anything that threatens our sense of belonging, our relationships, or our social status (i.e., being ostracized, rejected, losing status, being ridiculed, humiliated, or abandoned). In fact, we feel the social pain of rejection in the same brain area where we feel physical pain! Evolutionary scientists suggest this got wired in because early man was safer with other people around—to help fight off predators and find food. And, in any given group, the more status you had, the more resources you had, which meant that your odds of survival were higher. It's rare in today's time that we would experience such life-threatening circumstances, but our brains still respond to the possibility of rejection, or change, with the same primal mechanism as if the stakes were still life-or-death.

It's not just fear of doing something challenging or new that causes problems—we also become afraid when we're faced with growth opportunities. We think to ourselves: *If I take that promotion, I'll stop being friends with my colleagues since I'll be their boss.* Or: *If I go after what I yearn for, I'll change in ways that will alienate me from my spouse.*

Consider this checklist of potential fears, which is only a partial list:

- Fear of failure

- Fear of success

- Fear of being disliked

- Fear of being humiliated

- Fear of being rejected or ostracized

- Fear of losing friends

- Fear of making a mistake

- Fear of being too pushy/aggressive

- Fear of being overly emotional

- Fear of being angry or experiencing any other primary emotion

- Fear of being inauthentic

In reality, it's the opposite of that last fear on the list that stops people in their transformative tracks. As author Carolyn Myss says: "What we're afraid of isn't success, and it isn't failure. We're afraid of the responsibility to be who we can be." Author Marianne Williamson puts it another way: "Our deepest fear is not that we are inadequate. Our deepest fear is that we are powerful beyond measure . . . We ask ourselves, who am I to be brilliant, gorgeous, talented, and fabulous?"

In other words, we fear becoming our greatest self.

In the process of transformation, the worst thing you can do is ignore or minimize your fear. With Benjamin's, Doug's, and Kendra's stories, you have seen how facing fear can provide direction and motivation. When you admit your fear to yourself and others, you take away some of its limiting power. You've taken the brakes off a little. It's still scary and can block you from making progress, but it's much more manageable when you bring it into the light. You begin to notice the yearning underneath.

When fear is allowed to operate beneath the surface, however, it does the most damage. When people quit things, it is often because they fail to acknowledge and deal with their fears so they rationalize instead. Typically, they approach new activities brimming with confidence and even cockiness—generally a sign of someone not listening to their fear. They communicate that they're ready for anything, be it a new job, new school, or even a marriage—that they have no anxiety about what the process requires of them. As much as their gung-ho attitude provides them with initial positive energy, this energy can easily turn negative. It begins to sound an alarm in their unconscious mind, warning them about taking risks, about trying new activities, about pushing themselves into areas where they aren't skilled or comfortable. They may offer all sorts of excuses about why they're dropping out or quitting—"The program isn't for me . . . The job isn't a good fit . . . The marriage was a mistake . . . I don't have the time . . . I'm under too much stress . . . She isn't who I thought she was"—but the real reason is unacknowledged fear and this leads to quitting rather than facing the fear and developing the skills necessary to persevere and transform.

Ignoring or minimizing fear often follows a common pattern: initial bravado, excitement, and energy followed by a relatively short period of challenge, concluding with exiting or stopping, accompanied by a weak excuse. Some of the best athletes ever drafted into major league baseball don't make it because they cannot deal with the fear. Bob coached one such athlete years after he had unexpectedly quit baseball. Interestingly, he was now in the process of ending his second marriage as well.

TENDING TO YOUR FEAR

If you've ever been swamped by a tidal wave of emotion, then you may think that you're powerless to do anything in the face of such force. We acknowledge the power but not the helplessness. To extend the metaphor, not only can you ride out the wave but, like Doug and Kendra both did, you can use it to take yourself further on your journey. Remember to use all the tools we've given you to deal with your strong emotions. You learned the importance of adopting a WTF (What the F**k) attitude to spur you into motion in the Engaging chapter. And in the Liberating chapter we shared with you these tools to deal with your fear:

- *Name it to tame it*

- *Prepare for "tolerable unpleasantness"*

- *Extinguish your fear response*

- *Use Cognitive Reappraisal*
- *Reach out for Support*

Here is another tool to help you sort through your fear and move forward into right action:

DETERMINE IF IT'S REAL FEAR, IMAGINED FEAR, OR REAL IMAGINED FEAR. Gestalt therapy founder Fritz Perls referred to "three zones of fear." Recognizing the zone of your fear—how "real" it is—can guide you to right action. It really helps with reality testing and your risk/reward assessment. Consider this "visceral" example: Real fear is when someone is about to stab you with a knife. Real imagined fear occurs when days, weeks, or years after being stabbed, whenever you are in a similar place to the stabbing, you start sweating and trembling, and want to run— you fear that it will happen again. And imagined fear is when you worry about being stabbed even though no one has ever stabbed you or even come close to doing so.

When you're afraid, see which of these three fear zones it falls into. As you engage, for instance, you may have the *real fear* that speaking your mind could get you fired if you tell your thin-skinned boss that his plan will never work. You may still choose to speak your mind, but you may want to plan how to best present it, how you'll deal with it if your boss reacts negatively, and what is the best growth move for you to make. You may have *real imagined fear* in this situation if you were fired in the past by a thin-skinned boss, even if your current boss is open-minded and wants you to be honest. Recognize the difference and speak your mind to your open-minded boss. It's *imagined fear* if you know your boss wants you to be honest with him and you've never had a significant problem in the past with an authority figure when you spoke your mind—so again, speak up!

TACTICS FOR THE TOUGH TIMES: COMFORT, TOUCH, AND WATCHERS

We know we keep encouraging you to take risks, challenge your belief systems, and go into the unknown, for this is the path of Transformers. We've been advocating the assignment way of living—the various activities and behaviors that we've recommended throughout these pages—which is designed to bring you face-to-face with your emotions, especially your fears. We have recommended that you place yourself in situations that make you uncomfortable and even fearful because that is the only way you can deal with them effectively and move forward rather than fleeing from the fear and moving backwards or staying stuck.

Earlier in the chapter, we gave you some advice about how to become more emotionally intelligent as you implement these recommendations, such as becoming an emotional detective and expressing your feelings. But what do you do when you're in real emotional turmoil? When your transformational actions make you so angry you could spit or so sad you could cry?

Like all Transformers, you deserve respite and support for your journey and these tactics will help you use your emotions productively:

- **SEEK COMFORT VS. NUMBNESS.** We love the old saw, "God disturbs the comfortable and comforts the disturbed." When we're angry, fearful, or emotionally hurt, we often seek the anesthetic of false comfort in soft addictions—zoning out in front of the computer screen or TV, indulging in a chocolate fest, shopping for shoes. But while these soft addictions may numb our feelings, they don't soothe or tend to them in a way that facilitates our transformation.

  Our capacity for being soothed comes from our early childhood attachment experiences, when soothing helped to regulate our emotions as kids, and it has the ability to do the same thing for us as adults. We never outgrow our need to be held, touched, or reassured.

  Children develop their own self-soothing techniques, like thumb-sucking and rocking back and forth, and you need to, too. We're not suggesting you suck your thumb or rock back and forth—though there are a lot worse ways of dealing with strong emotions—but that you engage in the adult equivalents of these self-soothing behaviors. Nobody needs to know what is going on inside when you take a walk in nature, watch and listen to the waves come in and out in the ocean, pray, brush your hair 100 times, or listen to calming music. Come up with your own list of what activities are soothing for you—and use them. Frequently.

* **REACH OUT AND TOUCH SOMEONE.** Reach out to others and share your concerns. Verbal comfort can be as effective as a warm hug. Hugs have a function—babies who don't receive enough loving hugs fail to thrive and adults who don't receive enough comfort fail to transform. Whether it is verbal or physical, we need our hands held, our backs patted. Being embraced verbally or physically by someone we care about and who cares about us provides the same sense of security (and of attachment) that a parent offered when we were children. It helps us tolerate our sadness; it allows us to deeply experience our joy. Studies have shown that when people experience the anxiety of an MRI (when they are in that dark, noisy metal tube), their anxiety diminishes significantly when a loved one or even a nurse holds their hand.

   Reach out at times of emotional turmoil. When you're liberating, for instance, and you feel like you're making a permanent break from the person you used to be and feel sad, go for a walk with your spouse and hold hands; cuddle with your child as you read her a bedtime story; ask someone you care about to give you a massage.

* **FIND MENTORS, COACHES, AND OTHERS TO WATCH OVER YOU.** Mentors have been where we're going. They know there is another side to the confusions and challenges we face and understand when we're dealing with complex and confusing emotions. While MKOs can provide great assistance by lending an empathetic ear and offering feedback and advice, their main role here is paternal/maternal. In other words, they remind you that someone cares about you and what you do; that there is someone in a position of authority whom you respect watching over you and

also respecting you in return. Their presence alone can provide tremendous reassurance in the face of roiling emotions. They can center you and calm you down so that you can handle your emotional reactions.

When Bob was a little boy, his aunt and uncle took him to a local swimming pool. At the time, Bob, like a lot of children, didn't want to put his head under the water—many kids are scared to be completely submerged. Bob's uncle stood with his legs wide apart and his aunt swam through them and emerged on the other side. They encouraged him to follow suit—his uncle waving him forward, his aunt waiting behind his uncle to pull Bob up after he swam through his legs. Before, nothing could have motivated Bob to do what they were suggesting. But their attentive, loving presence allowed Bob to move past his fear and dive into and under the water.

Find your own MKOs, the adult version of Bob's aunt and uncle. Make sure they understand the feelings you're grappling with and let them know you need them to be there for you if you need to talk, want advice, or just require their company.

EMOTIONS LIGHT THE WAY

As you move through yearning to liberating to dedicating, emotions will provide you with guidance on a path that may at times be twisty and uncertain. They will tell you what you yearn for as you listen to what your fears and joys are telling you.

Besides giving you information about what you yearn for, feelings provide the basis for taking action and the fuel to propel you—to engage, revelate, liberate, rematrix, and dedicate. Remember, attached to each emotion is a transformative urge—certain types of emotions provide you with certain types of action steps to take on your transformational journey.

Learn the skills required to be with your emotions and apply their wisdom. When you venture into the unknown and take risks, you're going to feel anxious, angry, and hurt at times. These can be uncomfortable feelings, but that does not mean they are feelings to avoid. Quite the contrary, a certain degree of discomfort can be energizing. It can provide you with the drive to cycle through the six phases time and again. It can keep you engaged rather than sitting on the sideline with your soft addictions. It can give you the strength to transform.

So take a moment and consider Judith's rhapsody to emotion:

As we open our hearts and feel our feelings, we nourish ourselves. We can feel the relief of releasing, the bubble of joy within, the heart surges of love, the energy of anger, the warning of fear, the tenderness of pain. We are bathed in the deep truth of our experience through our emotions. Be prepared for both the magical energy and the warmth of your emotions. Befriend these emotions, learn their secrets, and unleash their power.

Whole new worlds await your discovery. Use your emotions as the transformative force they are to discover possibilities beyond your imagining. Like the unseen beautiful worlds under the sea, there are gifts, truths, creativity, even whole new you's awaiting to be created—your next most radiant self to be revealed.

CHAPTER TEN

YOUR NEXT MOST RADIANT SELF

There is a vitality, a life force, an energy, a quickening that is translated through you into action, and because there is only one of you in all of time, this expression is unique.
—MARTHA GRAHAM

TRANSFORMATION IS ABOUT THE CONTINUOUS release of your most radiant self; it is not about making a long-cherished dream come true. There is so much more to life—and more to you—than far-off dreams allow. Transformers learn to live their dreams in the here and now, and while they may also have traditional dreams, they go far beyond them.

One of the most misunderstood aspects of personal transformation is that it is about achieving a fixed, known goal:

I've always wanted to live in Bali.

All my life I've hoped that I might quit the rat race and make a living doing what I love, which is being a potter.

I've dreamed of the day when I could stand up to the people in my life and tell them what I truly, honestly thought.

There's nothing wrong with any of these hopes and dreams. In fact, as a byproduct of the transformation process, you may achieve some, or even many, of them. But if you fixate on a particular hope or dream, you do yourself a disservice. These dreams cause you to put up with things, to grin and bear it—in short, they block your transformation. They limit what and who you can become, making your life all about a single, far-off goal. Transformation transcends goal achievement—your goals are a part of your larger life project and oftentimes emerge as right actions rather than good ideas to pursue. In fact, the *Transformed!* process leads to accomplishing an ongoing series of goals of ever-increasing challenge and difficulty that flow from your yearning—possibilities beyond your imagining when you begin the process.

Our yearning pushes us in directions that aren't always initially apparent. They often don't fit our original childhood or family values. To facilitate our emergence, we need to heed what we yearn for, not just at the beginning of the transformative process but for the rest of our lives. It may well be that quitting the rat race and retiring to our cabin in Montana has nothing to do with our yearning. In fact, it may represent an escape from dealing with our deepest desires—better to retreat by ourselves to the isolated woods than confront what really scares us in our own backyard. In most cases, we need to change ourselves, not our surroundings. Our fantasy of an escape from life will never be as satisfying and fulfilling as making the moves to transform in the right places.

When we transform in the right places and the right ways, we release our next most radiant self, continuously and in ever-changing ways. Here, we want to give you a sense of what this shining self looks like, in everything from relationships to careers to spiritual endeavors. In this way, you can develop a vision of where this process will take you, not a fixed point or place but the nature of the journey you will be on and the many rewards it provides.

First, though, we want to share with you an experience Bob had in Paris that will shed some light on the concept of a radiant self.

WAITING FOR JUDITH NEAR MONET'S *IRISES*

One Easter Sunday a few years ago, we were at the Musée d'Orsay, the main museum of Impressionist art in Paris, and the museum was crowded with holiday visitors. Judith's experience of art is unifying and spiritual. She is so moved by the beauty and mystical inspiration of the art, in this museum in particular, that she is often moved to tears. In this state, she is able to stand oblivious to the press of other museum visitors around her, drinking in a single painting for what seems to me to be an eternity while I, on the other hand, become irritated by the jostling people and so I find a place to rest—in this instance, a bench directly across from Monet's *Irises*. I was especially bothered by the mass of people surging before me, since I was getting only the briefest glimpses of this beautiful painting. People were generally dressed poorly, in casual clothing that compared unfavorably with the beauty on the walls.

I don't remember what sparked it, but suddenly, I had an epiphany. I moved from extreme irritation to being deeply moved by what I was seeing in those who, moments before, had been irritants. The beauty had miraculously shifted from Monet's painting to each of the people passing by. Touched by the radiance I perceived in each person, I reflected on references to Impressionist painters as masters of light. I had always assumed that this referred to the light *on* the objects. But as I watched the people passing by, their tattered sweatshirts had disappeared, and I wept at the unique magnificence manifest in each person: nobility, sprightliness, determination, warmth.

I thought back to the paintings I had seen in the other galleries and realized that the people in these paintings were often common-looking, and sometimes singularly unattractive—that is, if I limited my seeing to the surface. Yet if I looked deeper, I found the inner reality of each person that was captured by the artists, and it was not just the light on the subject being painted, but the unique light emanating from *within* the subject that was so radiant and compelling.

The epiphany took form in my mind: the Impressionist mastery was of inner light, the capacity to capture the nascent beauty of each individual. The artists were revealing an essential quality emerging from each subject they painted—their next most radiant self, a self beyond their current manifestation, but real and pulsating nonetheless.

Michelangelo was quoted as saying that he sees a statue contained within every block of marble; in essence, his sculpting released the figure contained within. In the same way, I had always looked at light as external to an object. In fact, what made the Impressionists so brilliant was that they illuminated the people and things they painted with their own internal light. They were pulling out the bright nobility in one person, the mysterious depth in another.

As the museum visitors flowed past where I was seated, I was seeing the radiance of that same inner light—the singular brightness within each person seeking release. And it was this radiant beauty inside of each person that caused me to weep. I became aware that there is, in each one of us, a next most radiant self, seeking to be released.

We offer you this story to help you understand what the rewards of transformation are really about. When you start a personal growth seminar, change careers, or embark on a pilgrimage, you are not aware of that internal radiance. But to transform, you must facilitate its emergence—it is this emergence that yields the gifts of transformation. Your next most radiant self is not a fixed point on the horizon but an ever-changing light within. The challenge for Transformers is to be open to the deeper yearning within—a yearning that will facilitate the emergence of your next most radiant self and lead to paths of increasing fulfillment, challenge, and meaning as you transform.

We know what we're suggesting is counterintuitive. We've been brought up to nurture hopes and dreams; to settle on an ambitious destination and devote ourselves to getting there. Don't get us wrong. We're not anti-dreams, hopes, or goals; it's just that we are pro-transformation, because it offers so much more. We're not suggesting that you throw away all your hopes and dreams but recognize that they may well lock you into thoughts and behaviors that ultimately are limiting. As you yearn and engage, moment-by-moment, you stir up hopes and dreams, both momentary and far-reaching, that exist below or on the edge of consciousness.

You never know how much you yearn to connect and where

these connections will lead you—into deeper conversations, new relationships, previously submerged fears, challenging work roles, new friendships that reshape your idea of what life can be. You're constantly re-cycling through the *Transformed!* process's six phases, and so you are constantly awakening to still more yearning. As you follow these emerging yearnings, you become a different person and what drives you evolves too.

Now let's meet a lawyer who has responded brilliantly to his evolving hopes and dreams.

THE WINDING, SURPRISING TRANSFORMATIONAL PATH

Joe, one of our students, was on the fast track to nowhere. His background—top schools, editor of the law review, federal clerkship, a job at a leading Chicago law firm—seemed to guarantee career success. He certainly was succeeding financially and in status. Yet Joe told us that despite his aptitude for the law, he was bored by it. He insisted that he wanted to be a "poet, novelist, or politician" to unleash his creativity. For Joe, these professions were his dreams, his fixed points on the horizon. If we could help him transform himself into a writer or political figure, he believed he would be able to change his life in dramatic and satisfying ways.

Bob asked him to try an initial tactic in his larger strategy. He requested that Joe prepare thoroughly for his next meeting with his client at the law firm, rather than skating by on ability and marginal preparation. Joe agreed to do so, staying up most of the night doing research before the meeting. The next day after the meeting, Joe arrived at our offices and said to Bob, "I can't believe it. I controlled the meeting! I was able to point out strategic issues and precedents and everyone listened to me despite my junior status." Joe was beginning to experience the emergence of his next most radiant self—he had yearned to be potent and influential, and met this yearning which he had previously relegated to daydreams.

The experience revealed to Joe that, contrary to his expectations, the law could provide him with a way to satisfy his yearning to have an impact and make a difference. Once he engaged in behaviors aligned with his yearning, he began revelating and grasped that certain assumptions that he had always believed to be true were not only false but were restricting his professional growth.

Later, Joe joined a firm owned by one of the largest corporations in the world. It was an organization with many in-house attorneys and Joe came in as low man on the totem pole. At one high-level meeting attended by a head of the parent company, they discussed a global strategy that everyone, including the division CEO, endorsed. As they were speaking, though, Joe knew that it was the wrong strategy and that if it was implemented, it would be a disaster. For him to speak out against this strategy, though, would violate many unwritten rules of protocol. At the same time, he yearned to contribute and to help the firm succeed.

Fortunately, Joe was far enough along in the transformation process that he was able to move out of his comfort zone and take a risk to follow his yearning despite trepidation. He raised his hand and said that the strategy was flawed and doomed to failure. After Joe finished speaking, there was a prolonged period of silence. During that time, the company's general counsel, as well as Joe's immediate boss, looked as if they wanted to strangle him on the spot. The head of the parent company said in an ominous tone, "Please explain yourself." Overcoming still more fear, Joe began explaining why the strategy was ill-conceived and the negative results that he foresaw if it were to be implemented. Another long silence ensued, accompanied by dagger looks directed toward Joe. The head of the parent company, though, was not looking at anyone but instead seemed deep in thought. Breaking the long silence, he said he was tremendously impressed with Joe's analysis and he pointed to Joe, saying, "This is the man I want to run our global defense strategy."

Thus, following a yearning despite rules to the contrary, Joe was given an opportunity that he had never thought was possible—especially at this stage in his career. Parenthetically, he succeeded mightily and made a good deal of money for all concerned in the process.

While we're only looking at one particular area in Joe's life (and the leaps in his relationships, spirituality, and the rest of his life are just as compelling), you can see how real transformation is neither predictable nor logical. When you make the commitment to follow your yearning and go through the process's six stages, you find yourself taking actions of which you never thought yourself capable and achieving goals you never anticipated.

Jack, for instance, came to us searching for something, though he wasn't sure what it was. On the surface, he seemed to have it all. Not only was Jack highly successful in his career and wealthy, but he was also dynamic and influential. He had enjoyed a series of model-beautiful girlfriends. Yet he always suspected something was missing, and he spent years taking courses, attending workshops, and pursuing self-improvement in all its forms in order to find out what he lacked. You name it, he'd read it, done it, ingested it—the newest seminars, self-help books, therapy, prescribed medication, herbs and medicinals, bodywork, trampoline-jumping, energy work, and traveling to India to study with the hottest gurus. When he began consciously responding to his yearning and engaged, he was still suspicious, yet his revelating led him to a fair amount of liberating that pleased some people and displeased others. People Jack respected, however, saw him growing and getting better. Jack finally dedicated and threw himself into the transformation process. He stopped being a change dilettante and became a Transformer.

Following his yearning, he began having more genuine conversations and his relationships deepened. His next most radiant self was emerging and he was inviting the emergence of his partners' next most radiant selves—or not, as the case seemed to be in many cases. He began seeing through the facades of his beautiful girlfriends and noticed values that he did not respect. These conversations led to a new intimacy, one he did not even know he wanted. He was forever engaging and revelating on both himself and the women he dated. He shared more deeply and found that each of these relationships went to emotional levels of contact that felt amazing to him and to them.

Already quite wealthy, he began risking more at work, and his work changed similarly. He was operating at a very high level of finance internationally—way beyond anything he had ever done before.

Jack has quit looking for magical easy solutions, understanding that personal transformation takes time, effort, and persistence—an investment he was finally willing to make in himself. And, the rewards are beyond his former imagining.

While Jack is still a work in progress, as is the case for all Transformers, the strides he has made are nothing short of astonishing. Before, Jack was a narcissist, focused on himself and how his current girlfriend enhanced his stature by her beauty. Now, he is involved in what he calls "the first real relationship in my life." He treats his girlfriend with respect and kindness. As he says with more than a note of surprise in his voice, "We don't even watch television because we have so much to talk about." He said he had never known what love was before he met her, and once, he actually started crying when speaking about her—Jack had never shed a tear over a woman in his life before this.

Like Joe, previously Jack could not imagine himself in this type of relationship. If he had set a relationship goal before doing his transformation work, it probably would have been to have a girlfriend who was a Victoria's Secret model and smart enough to share interesting conversations. He didn't know he had it in him to form a deep, meaningful, mutually caring relationship with a woman.

What these examples demonstrate is that transformation is a process of continuous self-discovery, traveling into unknown territories both internally and externally. That is the challenge and the job of re-creating aspects of yourself time after time.

WHAT TO EXPECT—THE MANIFESTATIONS OF TRANSFORMING

Having a vision will help you build the mindset of where you are going.

It is useful to break down the experience of Transformers so you can build your vision and develop expectations of higher performance in your life. Just as the young basketball player is preparing himself to shoot the winning basket in the final seconds of a tie game or a young musician is practicing Rachmaninoff for the day she'll play in Carnegie Hall, you are preparing yourself for the fullness of the Transformer's life.

The manifestations of transforming are as varied as the individuals themselves. Jack and Joe represent two possible paths, but there is an infinite variety available to you. Your transformation will not resemble your neighbor's, at least not in the particulars. If we take a step back and look at transformational manifestations in a more general sense, however, we can see commonalities.

"What will I become?" is a question on the lips of many people about to embark on a transformational journey. While there's no way we can know the specifics of your journey, we do know that you will become many things. In fact, Transformers have five "Becoming" traits in common: Becoming Great, Becoming Alive, Becoming Your Self, Becoming Your Potential, and Becoming a Catalyst. Let's look at these Becoming traits so you know what you have to look forward to:

- **BECOMING GREATER.** Transformation doesn't have a discrete end point for a great life. It's a very personal journey, an ever-expanding process with ever-expanding impact. The process of becoming, growing, and changing is one of becoming greater—not just better, but transformed. Your life becomes greater in depth, breadth, and quality, enhancing all aspects of your life. While most people have a great moment here and there, it is often not sustained or widened from one area into another, or sometimes we're doing great in one area of our lives, but our life isn't great across the board. You know what it's like—you're doing great at work, but you're putting in long hours, and you don't seem to have time to do your workouts and you're overeating and your health, not to mention your weight, is showing the effects. Or your relationship is suffering. Or maybe your relationship is going great but you're underemployed at work.

Imagine, though, that all areas of your life are improving and getting better—you are learning and growing, facing challenges in all areas—your relationships, work, your personal and spiritual life.

Typically, what happens is that one area of your life, such as work, becomes great as you begin to follow the *Transformed!* process. By yearning and engaging at work, however, you start to revelate in other areas of your life too, and begin to expect, and generate, more fulfillment in these as well. When your career becomes fulfilling, you start realizing what's possible in other areas and are motivated to find that same sense of fulfillment with your kids, your significant other, your religion, and your community.

▪ **BECOMING ALIVE.** Just as some people can cover a longer distance in less time than others by running faster, Transformers live more life—they are enlivened. No doubt you've had this feeling at some point in your life. Some people say they've felt it during a moment of exhilarating adventure, such as parachuting from a plane. Others talk about never feeling so alive as when they hear a beautiful piece of music or during a meditative exercise. In most lives, these instances of enlivening are rare, but they needn't be. When you follow your yearning and find ways to allow your radiant self to emerge, your energy gradually increases as you decrease your resistance to your emotions. You become more sensitized to the moment-by-moment opportunities in life, more aware, alert, and receptive. "I am so present in the moment," said one Transformer, "it's like a fullness of experience I couldn't have imagined."

Abraham Maslow observed that self-actualized people experience things fully and vividly, what we call becoming alive, which leads to them being more likely to have peak experiences, those moments when we become deeply involved in, excited by, and absorbed in the world.

Transformers have an altered perception of time that Maslow describes as an aspect of peak experiences, and that researcher and one of the fathers of positive psychology, Mihály Csíkszentmihályi, describes as a factor of *flow*. Because you are more alive and present, your sense of time is impacted, as expressed by this Transformer:

"The thing about living this more alive lifestyle is that it seems to be moving at hyperspeed! They say time flies when you are having fun so I must be having a really great time. My life feels like it is in high gear, not going too fast and out of control, mind you, just moving quickly in an exciting way." Another described this paradox of becoming alive: "Time flies and since I appreciate every moment, it also seems long and luxurious."

■ **BECOMING YOUR SELF.** More solid, substantial, centered, or secure—these are some of the terms people use when describing their experience as Transformers. They have a more solid sense of self and seem to be gathering more as they go about their lives. This manifestation may not be as obvious as the others, so bear with us as we try to explain what it means to have a greater sense of self. One of our transforming students expressed becoming yourself as the following: "I know so much more about myself . . . I am not wearing a mask; I'm showing who I really am no matter what others think."

The phrase "being full of yourself" has a negative connotation, but the fullness of self we're describing isn't about being egotistic. Instead of being self-centered, it is about being centered in one's self. Self-confidence, self-acceptance, and self-love all grow and emerge as part of the *Transformed!* process. It is tremendously uplifting to feel like you're being who you're supposed to be rather than acting a part. As one of our students said, "I accept myself for who I am; I don't have to hide."

Becoming yourself allows Transformers to shuck off the old poses and disguises they felt they needed to wear to protect themselves—or to protect others. In the past, they believed they had to be calm and hide their feelings because family members would become upset if they lost their cool within the family dynamic. Or they believed they had to be acquiescent at work so they wouldn't offend their boss. They are more focused on the emergence of their next most radiant self and the tasks at hand rather than on pleasing others.

Let's let Lynette tell you about her transformation in Becoming Herself in her own words:

A Tale of Becoming Your Self

From Ghost To Goddess: In Lynette's Own Words

I grew up pretty much as a ghost in my family, the sixth of seven children and the youngest girl of five. I excelled in school, performed in theatre, band, and choir, and yet offstage, when it was just me being myself, I very easily disappeared into the background of my family. I was painfully shy, avoiding talking to people or making eye contact. This has been a pattern that has defined my life since that time. I'd perform well but disappear into the background.

When I started my transformation, I realized there were things I wanted in my life that I wasn't really even prepared to admit to myself, and I realized that what I was doing on my own was not working. It struck me that to get to what I wanted I might need some support and guidance—I began the *Transformed!* process. . . . I learned how to pay attention to my thoughts and feelings with an ear to what is the data and what is the action it is indicating, instead of listening to my own internal critic and believing everything she said. I also had the permission to try new things, new attitudes, new ways of being, and to see what fit me and how each one would serve me. I came out of the closet in a big way through these assignments, and though I felt the pain of having a brand-new pink skin really exposed to the elements for the first time, I also felt the joy of being seen and touched.

Now, it is so amazing to see how far I have come. I am in my seventh year with a full-time salaried position at a company where

I get to support organizations to live their missions more fully and more clearly communicate their vision, mission, and stories to the world. This is something I never had before and never even realized I wanted or could have! I am holding my ground with people both with vulnerability, pain, anger, and upset—I am in it, at work, in my family, and in relationships with friends.

Challenged by her MKOs to put her story to song, here are a few verses she wrote about becoming more "me":

I've opened up my eyes
And started to revise
My whole worldview.
I've set out upon a path
Of self-discovery
A journey to
Become more me.

And from ghost towards Goddess, I've come a long way
Battling limiting beliefs and the nasty self-talk I say.
Revealing strengths and talents that I barely knew—
You better watch out world 'cause I'm comin' for you!

I'm evolating!
Can't stop me now I've got a yearning to be!
I'm dedicating
To the emergence of the next radiant me.
Yeah, I'm dedicated to rematrixing me!

You can witness Lynette's transformation as she performs the song she wrote about her transformational journey at www.wrightliving.com/transformed.

▪ **BECOMING YOUR POTENTIAL.** Lynette was also becoming her potential. You'll recall that we've talked about transformation as saying and doing things you never imagined you would say or do. This takes you into new elements of your potential. No matter how much you have worked to develop yourself, as your transformation unfolds, you will see that there is more potential to pursue. This is especially true for folks who have had development spurts and then feel stuck or as if they are slowing down.

The transformation process is eye-opening. It reveals how much we can achieve, how well we can tolerate the discomfort of the unfamiliar, how far we can stretch ourselves without snapping. When we glimpse our unlimited potential, we start thinking in bigger terms and start doing bigger things. In the words of Abraham Maslow, when we become our potential, we self-actualize—we act on the "desire to become more and more what one is, to become everything that one is capable of becoming."

■ **BECOMING A CATALYST.** You're a change agent. It's not just about recreating yourself but about being a force for change in whatever environment you happen to be in. This doesn't mean that you're going to foment revolution at the drop of a hat (though you may contribute revolutionary ideas frequently). But as you reach the point where your next most radiant self emerges, you'll come to recognize your own power and purpose, and you will begin to notice the next most radiant selves of others around you emerging—you are catalyzing.

It's natural to want to use that power to make things better for friends, family, community, and others. It's natural to want to respond to that purpose—the yearning to have impact, to make a difference—by holding big visions for others and supporting their transformations, starting a new company, implementing a plan to clean up the local environment, creating a collaborative entity designed to help others in need.

Transformers develop naturally into contributors, leaders, and catalysts for change and transformation for those around them. Through their way of being, Transformers positively influence and lead their families, friends, and many others, including those they don't know well—strangers sitting next to them on an airplane, baristas making their coffee, or the doormen in their buildings. As one Transformer student put it: "I reach out constantly to people I don't even know sometimes, just to let them know they can be living a better life. That's my audacious caring, that's my vision for my community."

CONNECT THE DOTS: FROM YEARNING TO RADIANCE

Our yearnings are the province of our next most radiant selves. We yearn to live greater lives, to be truly alive, to be ourselves fully, to realize our potential, to make a difference, which is exactly what those Becoming traits help us do.

Radiance means excelling—in careers, finances, relationships—as leaders. But it's much more than that. It has to do with the quality of life that Transformers lead, the kind of people they become, their ways of being. More the stuff of poetry than prose, the quality of their lives is hard to capture. This credo of Transformers may describe it best:

> Transformers . . .
>
> Love fully
>
> Laugh loudly
>
> Pray often
>
> Feel deeply
>
> Express fearlessly
>
> Play hard
>
> Work joyously
>
> Commit totally
>
> Touch tenderly
>
> Live consciously

You can tell when you are with a Transformer because Transformers radiate. Their energy is palpable; their curiosity and the depth and range of their interests are inspiring. They are aware, conscious, awake. When they walk into a room, you can feel their presence. They have deep concern for others, the world situation, possibilities for humanity. They are value added in any situation in which they find themselves. They care—deeply.

If you think you want to be a Transformer and discover your next most radiant self, then get ready to have more fun, but also, to get hurt more. There is no safety from pain—just a commitment to learning and growing from it. Radiance can take the form of laughter—many Transformers report their sense of humor increasing and that they laugh more, both at themselves and with others. Your next most radiant self will also be more open and less defensive and resistant, so you'll experience more flow and aliveness. You'll become increasingly real, sharing your pain and your joy, your anger and your fear, your gifts and your foibles. By continually developing emotional and social intelligence, you negotiate life's inevitable knocks and problems with greater ease and benefit. In your next bright incarnation, you will still experience losses, illness, and tough breaks, but you'll have a greater capacity to deal with them. You will have developed what psychological researchers call "mature adaptations."

Transformers continually step into the unknown, courageously creating their next most radiant selves. As a result, expect to live a life rich with meaning and purpose and create ever-expanding consciousness, ever-greatening potential, and ever-broadening possibilities for ourselves and for the world.

Transformers live the truth of the statement by Paulo Coelho, the beloved Brazilian writer and author of *The Alchemist:* "When we strive to become better than we are, everything around us becomes better too."

BEING HERE, NOW—A PATH OF CONSCIOUSNESS

If you go back to Bob's story about the Impressionists and recall his epiphany, you might now understand that he required full consciousness in order for that epiphany to take place. By being acutely aware of what was going on around him and inside of him, he discovered radiance. Ultimately, the path of Transformation, as revealed by our research, is a path of consciousness—it requires consciousness and it also develops consciousness. Neuroscience research has shown that our attention density—that is, what we put our attention on consistently—is what shapes our brains, shapes our reality, and guides how we create who we are and the world we see. It is novelty, attention density, and a surge of emotion that wakes up our brain, cues it to pay attention, and activates our neuroplasticity. The process brings us to consciousness, and consciousness brings the process into being.

Being conscious means becoming aware of our matrix, realizing that our unconscious mind is the dominant force that formed us and influences us, and using critical thinking to consciously choose our values and beliefs and make conscious choices beyond our foundational matrix to create our future.

The phases of transformation all require consciousness—being aware and staying awake, and making intentional choices. You must be present to sense the stirrings of your yearning—and to consciously engage to meet those yearnings. Revelating is an ongoing act of consciousness—being aware of our emotions, thoughts, motivations, belief systems, matrix, what is coloring our world—and being able to see things in new, liberating ways. Liberating is consciously chosen action in response to our revelating, just as rematrixing is a conscious rewiring and re-creation of our beliefs, values, and ways of being and acting. Dedicating is consciously choosing to make transforming your way of life. Transformation is consciously engaging in our own evolution—a journey of turning the unimaginable into the possible.

BELIEVE IN POSSIBILITIES

In calling for you to transform and release your next radiant self, we're calling on many years of research as well as many years of living. We are both children of the '60s, and we witnessed the positive changes in consciousness that occurred during that time. We need to share a brief bit of history with you so you can grasp why we believe in the possibility of transformation. Back in the '60s, movements of awareness and action spawned the civil rights movement, the feminist movement, the rising belief in human potential for all beings in all walks of life. This included a wellspring of personal development technologies, a growing consciousness of the power of being in the moment, and the green movement—a developing awareness of the sanctity of our planet. We're not suggesting that all these events and movements stayed on track or were simon-pure, but that cumulatively, they raised consciousness in all walks of life—activating the yearning to make a difference, and the belief that we can.

The spirit of those times was fueled by the belief that human emergence was not only possible, but critical to the survival of our world. Buckminster Fuller, the futurist, inventor, and visionary, said that we were poised on a precipice of either Utopia or Oblivion and called us to make a conscious choice to tip the balance to the positive.

The call to consciousness isn't just from the 1960s. It is the call from leaders throughout history to awaken to the universe of unrealized possibilities. The call is to one of greatness, to the possibility of facilitating what is good in life, and to seeing the value in all—the truth and promise of our potential.

We have had the privilege of learning from and studying with spiritual teachers all over the world for the past four decades—Christian, Hindu, Buddhist, Jewish, mystical Kabbalists, Sufis, Jains, Sikhs, and more. We have had the honor of being introduced to dedicated spiritual and economic communities from Damanhur to Mondragon, Focolare to Mantak Chia's Daoist community in Thailand, Parmarth Niketan and Gayatri Pariwar on the banks of the Ganges, to the Jerusalem monks in Paris. We've worked with, hosted, and attended events with world thought leaders, including Nobel Peace and Economics laureates, some of the most dedicated leaders of major world corporations, and thousands of people who yearn and work for better lives for themselves and others, with missions in an array of disciplines, from education to economics. What we all have in common is heeding the call to consciousness, the awareness of possibilities, and the yearning to transform, to be our best selves, and to create just, fair, mutually-empowering, sustainable living on our planet.

This is what is activated as we transform, releasing our next most radiant selves . . . and the next, and the next.

MAY THE FORCE BE WITH YOU ON THE HERO'S JOURNEY OF TRANSFORMATION

It is this sense of inner radiance that is evoked in us when we envision . . .

. . . Star Wars.

. . . King Arthur.

. . . Harry Potter.

We are thrilled as Luke discovers that The Force is strong in him; when Arthur finds the strength to pull the sword from the stone; and when Harry Potter discovers his magical ability. These stories and myths resonate with us because they echo a calling we sense from within: that we have gifts within us awaiting discovery, a more powerful "us" that is waiting to be released. Who has not secretly related to these characters and felt the hint of greatness within? This is the prompting of our yearning seeking the emergence of our next most radiant self, the releasing of our inner power. We yearn to go on our own transformational journey, honing our gifts in the same way both our real-life and fictional heroes have done—embarking on their quests, honing their gifts, shaping their characters, and pursuing their destinies.

Often our heroes discover their power when they are children or adolescents—at the ages when we more readily believe in the possibility that there is greatness within us and have not yet lost the faith in our potential. Tapping into our yearning evokes the essence of our childlike selves, when we saw our possibilities as endless—inviting us to suspend our disbelief and recapture our hopeful essence.

Our young heroes aren't "done" once they discover their power. Like the tasks of rematrixing, there is rigorous training they must undertake to harness, develop, and utilize their power. Luke trains first with Obi-Wan-Kenobi and then Yoda. Arthur is mentored by Merlin. Harry Potter is under the demanding tutelage of the instructors at Hogwarts, Dumbledore, and other magical beings. And they too, must practice—deeply and deliberately. Like all Transformers, they are also supported on their journeys by allies—Luke by Han Solo, Chewbacca, and the rebel force; Arthur by the Knights of the Round Table; Harry Potter by Hermione and Ron.

Our heroes' journeys aren't about goals. Luke Skywalker didn't start off with a goal to save the universe from darkness. While he did initially have a goal, to get off the planet and become a pilot, that shifted as he discovered the Force. Arthur didn't have a goal to become a king—in fact, he supplanted others who did. And Harry Potter didn't have a goal of becoming a magician and slaying He-Who-Must-Not-Be-Named. Their lives weren't shaped by a goal. They were shaped by discovering their inner radiance, their gifts, and their power; practicing hard; and transforming. This is what shaped their destinies.

Their journeys are echoed in the stories of the saints and spiritual adepts who answered an inner call, their yearning, and put in years of practice praying and meditating, developing their spiritual gifts, becoming adept at martial arts, triumphing over trials in the deserts—to facilitate the emergence of their next most radiant selves.

Like them, you are designed to transform, to release your next most radiant self and live your own unique hero's journey—the stuff of poetry and myth, now proven by science: you are designed to follow the stirring in your heart that is awakened by heroic stories. To fulfill your potential and pursue your destiny—to take your place in the world—is part of your design and the design for humanity.

CHAPTER ELEVEN

WHAT IF. . .
THE TRANSFORMATIONAL
IMPERATIVE REALIZED

WE ARE DESIGNED TO BE VISIONARIES—to see the as-yet unseeable. As we transform, we activate the design element that leads to vision. As we dedicate and expand our capacity to operate in our frontal lobe, the place of possibilities, we imagine greater opportunities and envision new futures. As we consciously shift our awareness, we expand our consciousness. It's like we shine a bigger beacon and discover treasures that had been hidden in the dark. We perceive more of the previously unrecognized stimuli that our brain receives. We vision, both near and far. Moment-by-moment, we recognize our deeper yearning and engage in new possibilities, discovering elements of our world and ourselves. This leads us to see possibilities that invite us into a world of possibilities. Doing this consistently, we rematrix with dedication.

We touch others more deeply and are much more available to be touched by them. Our vision of what we are capable of expands as we discover more options in every area of our lives. Gradually, we become accustomed to expanding our reality, and we perceive ways to enhance our relationships with our families, work, community, and the larger world. We can recognize data to which we had previously been blind.

Growing in awareness, our consciousness expands. We find ourselves articulating insights—ideas and truths that previously were denied us. Engaging in broader and deeper ways, we relish more fully the adventure of our lives. We begin relating ideas to others, inspiring them and surprising ourselves. At first we are delighted, and then we begin to notice that we are not only seeing life with greater perspective, but perceiving with greater sensitivity.

It is as if we are now able to receive more wisdom from the universe, from the web of life. The illusion of separation becomes a thin veil when we are truly focused and fully aware. We open our minds to receiving new information, rather than just processing what we already know. Our frontal lobes love to create bigger models of ideas and possibilities. We start to see that we are part of this expanding universe, that we are part of the big bang, continually expanding from its source. Opening our minds and hearts helps us to transform, and transforming opens us to visioning, contemplating greater possibilities, and imagining greater futures.

We begin to feel a sense of connection to a larger whole. We suspect that we are designed to imagine big possibilities and potential futures for ourselves and our world. And when we envision the grand design, or the big bang, or God, or creation, we change our brains. Science is revealing that the more we think about cosmic themes, possibilities for humanity, or creation, the more we permanently alter and restructure the neural circuits in specific parts of our brains that control our moods, form our conscious notions of ourselves, and shape our sensory perceptions of the world. Contemplating God or other spiritual values sends incredible bursts of neural activity in different parts of the brain, and as we think about big questions, our brains grow, changing not only our brains but also our essential selves.

Imagine a world of Evolators, developing visionaries . . . creating a world that champions the right of all human beings to fulfill their potential, to continually transform—to consciously engage in their own transformation—leading great lives and empowering others to fulfill their potential. Imagine a world where families, schools, organizations, churches, neighborhoods, businesses, and even cities and countries see it as their mission to foster the fulfillment of human potential. Imagine that the *Transformed!* process is taught to schoolchildren; that they learn to follow their yearning and engage in life according to the desires of their hearts; that they continually expand their awareness to learn, grow, revelate, liberate, rematrix, and dedicate. Imagine a world where schools see their job as fostering the emergence of the next most radiant self of every child, where every family supports each member to be his or her best. Businesses' successes goes far beyond making a profit— they see it as their responsibility and privilege to foster the emergence of each of their employees. Friendships are mutually empowering and inspiring, and marriages are dynamic partnerships of growth, intimacy, and connection.

What will these couples, families, individuals, and organizations look like as they learn to live from a radically different set of values, being genuine and authentic? Basic needs are more easily met, and problems are solved through the interconnectivity and resources of all beings.

Imagine humanity evolving, creating a world where all people engage in transforming and supporting one another to transform and actualize their potential.

Imagine the expanding consciousness of humanity, all human beings connected to one another, drawing from the rich resources of seven billion brothers and sisters, harnessing the collective gifts, wisdom, and experience of the entire human family, a family that is continually evolving.

Like the millions of connected SETI computers collectively assembling data from outer space, envision all of humanity connected through our expanded consciousness, computing the well-being and potential of individuals and the planet alike.

We transform ourselves, our families, our communities, businesses, organizations, and our world—a world that not only works for all, but that also fosters the transformation of all beings to become who they can become: their most conscious, loving selves. It all starts with you.

The transformational force is strong in you.

Just start with a simple urge, a deep yearning, and let it drive you inward, outward, and to places you never imagined, even in your wildest dreams. May you transform into your next most radiant self and be a blazing beacon in the world.

SPECIAL OFFER:
FREE BONUS GIFT

GET THE MOST OUT OF THIS BOOK . . . and out of your life! If you've made it this far, you've already made the decision to invest in your own growth—but your odds of being able to follow through, dedicate, and sustain your gains over the long haul increase exponentially with experiential learning and ongoing support.

That's why we are extending this special offer to you and a friend to join us for an impactful, complimentary weekend training:

Transform! Training:
The Heart and Science of Spectacular Living

Collect your gift for two worth $1600! With your purchase of this book, you and a friend may be our guests at this weekend training ($800 value/each) for only the materials and facilities fee ($98.40) per person. To hold your spot, register now at www.wrightliving.com/transformed.

Do you want even greater success or fulfillment than you have now? Do you have a pressing problem you need to solve? One of these yearnings led you to buy the book. Whichever it is, please know that within you resides a vast potential you have not yet fully tapped. The *Transform!* Training provides an opportunity to live the skills taught in the *Transformed!* book and to tap that hidden potential.

Through interactive lectures, small group learning, fun and challenging assignments, and personal support, you will deepen and apply your understanding of the Evolating model. Your life can be dramatically different by Sunday evening.

With the guidance of Dr. Judith and Dr. Bob Wright and powerful exercises not included in this book, you will:

- Uncover your deepest YEARNINGS and learn techniques to meet them directly—both independently and in relationships.

- Learn to ENGAGE more fully and more often than you thought possible. Working with your small group, you will see ways that you empower and disempower others, discover gifts and gaps in your social and emotional intelligence, and rehearse new habits in your communication and way of being that will impact every area of your life—both personal and professional.

- REVELATE on how your unconscious mind runs the show. Identify the primary core mistaken beliefs and the constellation of rules, myths, and beliefs that prevent you from having more career success, quality relationships, and impact wherever you are.

- LIBERATE through the Assignment Way of Living, stepping outside your cage of limiting beliefs with each Wright Performative Learning activity you choose to participate in. Particularly relevant assignments focus on truth, genuineness, and authenticity with those closest to you.

- Begin REMATRIXING core mistaken beliefs, expanding your vision of what's possible in your life by trying new behaviors yourself and being inspired by others' examples. Learn simple but powerful steps for having a life with increased genuineness, authenticity, and truth.

- Join and tap into the powerful network of high-quality individuals who DEDICATE themselves to making a difference in the world by transforming themselves, their families, and their workplaces.

The weekend training will not only immerse you in a proven process for personal transformation and success but also lead you to discover why other changes you've desired haven't lasted and how to make future changes stick for long-term success.

Be our guest at the *Transform!* Training and join countless others who have found support and inspiration on the journey to realizing their full potential!

Dr. Judith Wright &
Dr. Bob Wright

For details, see the certificate on the following page or visit wrightliving.com/transformed.

TESTIMONIALS
FROM COMPLIMENTARY
TRANSFORM! TRAINING

As a physician working in a high-level health-care setting, I've found that applying the Transform! concepts has made me more productive, more satisfied, and contributed significantly to me being rated as one of the top physicians in Chicago.
—MARILYN, PHYSICIAN

A magna cum laude graduate from a top law school, I had a high-powered job, great salary, and good marriage, all before age thirty. But I learned there was much more available to me. I've combined my drive with my love of service to create a thriving law practice and a deeper, closer, and more loving relationship with my wife.
—BILAL, ATTORNEY

I was already a highly successful career woman, but now I am experiencing new excitement and possibilities for my relationships and work life. I'm taking on more responsibilities and increasing my compensation while I do it.
—VAL, GLOBAL SR. DIRECTOR, HUMAN RESOURCES

I work in the not-for-profit field. Now, with the Transform! Training, rather than just thinking, dreaming, and wanting to make a difference in the world, I am out making changes, influencing others, and powerfully contributing to my family, my work, and society.
—MOLLY, ATTORNEY

ENDNOTES

CHAPTER 1
The Transformational Imperative

3   *This sentiment has echoed throughout the millennia*
For a more detailed discussion on this historical inquiry, see Dr. Judith Wright, *Living a Great Life: The Theory of Evolating* and Dr. Bob Wright and Dr. Judith Wright, *Foundations of Lifelong Learning and Personal Transformation* (Chicago: Evolating Press, 2012). For more on the concepts of *eudaimonia* and *areté* refer to the Stanford Encyclopedia of Philosophy http://plato.stanford.edu.

3   *The existential philosophers from Kierkegaard to Nietzsche*
See more on existentialism at the Stanford Encyclopedia of Philosophy http://plato.stanford.edu/search/searcher.py?query=existentialism.

4   *Inspired by Nietzsche's will to power*
For more on the concept of will to power see Friedrich Nietzsche and Walter Kaufmann, *Beyond Good and Evil,* (New York: Vintage Books, 1989), and Friedrich Nietzsche, Walter Kaufmann, and R. J. Hollingdale, *The Will to Power* (New York: Vintage, 1968).

4   *Alfred Adler, founder of the school of individual psychology*
Alfred Adler, *The Individual Psychology of Alfred Adler: A Systematic Presentation in Selections from his Writings,* ed. and annotated by Heinz L. Ansbacher and Rowena R. Ansbacher (New York: Basic, 1956).

4   *Abraham Maslow, the father of humanistic psychology*
Maslow, *Motivation and Personality* (New York: Harper, 1954, 1970), 15–31.

4 *Positive psychologists and economists alike study the good life*
For an overview from one of the fathers of positive psychology see Martin Seligman, *Flourish* (New York: Free Press, 2011). For economists' perspective on the good life see the works of one of the founders of behavioral economics, Nobel Laureate Daniel Kahneman, of behavioral economists such as Daniel Ariely, and of members of the field of Happiness economics.

4 *We have the amazing gift of neuroplasticity*
For inspiring examples of the implications of neuroplasticity and also the pioneering brain plasticity research of neuroscientist Michael Merzenich, see Norman Doidge, *The Brain That Changes Itself* (New York: Viking, 2007) and also Sharon Begley, *Train Your Mind, Change Your Brain* (New York: Ballantine Books, 2007).

5 *Our transformation circuits are only activated, however, with our conscious choice*
See Merzenich's work as described in Doidge, *The Brain That Changes Itself.*

5 *Such attention not only rewires the circuitry of our brains*
See Richard Davidson, "The Heart-Brain Connection: The Neuroscience of Social, Emotional, and Academic Learning," lecture, at http://www.Edutopia. Org/Richard-Davidson-Sel-Brain-Video. Also see Richard Davidson and Sharon Begley, *The Emotional Life of Your Brain* (New York: Hudson Street Press, 2012).

5 *our seeking circuits are firing, activating one of the pleasure centers in our brains*
See Jaak Panksepp, "Brain Emotional Systems and Qualities of Mental Life." in *The Healing Power of Emotion*, eds. Diana Fosha, Daniel J. Siegel, and Marion Solomon (New York: W. W. Norton & Company, 2009). Also see Emily Yoffe, "Seeking: How the Brain Hard-wires Us to Love Google, Twitter, and Texting. And Why That's Dangerous," *Slate*, posted Aug. 12, 2009, http://www.slate. com/id/2224932/pagenum/all/.

5 *the other pleasure center of our brains—our satisfaction center*
See Doidge, *The Brain That Changes Itself,* for a discussion of satisfaction and pleasure centers.

5 *It is the novelty, not the outcome*
See Gregory Berns, *Satisfaction: The Science of Finding True Fulfillment* (New York: Henry Holt, 2005).

5 *Our brains respond with a flurry of neuronal activity*

Doidge, *The Brain That Changes Itself;* Joe Dispenza, *Evolve Your Brain: The Science of Changing Your Mind* (Deerfield Beach, FL: Health Communications, Inc., 2007).

5   *The frontal lobe is the seat of our intention, our will*
See Dispenza, *Evolve Your Brain,* and David Perlmutter and Alberto Villoldo, *Power Up Your Brain: The Neuroscience of Enlightenment* (Carlsbad, CA: Hay House, 2011).

6   *But the transformational design changes in adulthood.*
For more on the capacity of the adult brain to change its speed and functioning see Michael Merzenich's work in Norman Doidge, "Redesigning the Brain," in *The Brain That Changes Itself.*

6   *what we call* evolating
For the grounded theory study that led to the theory of evolating, see Dr. Judith Wright, *Living a Great Life: The Theory of Evolating.*

11   *At Wright, a personal and professional development organization*
The assignment way of living is a key component of Wright Performative Education. See Dr. Bob Wright and Dr. Judith Wright, *Foundations of Lifelong Learning and Personal Transformation,* and Dr. Judith Wright, *Living a Great Life: The Theory of Evolating,* for a more detailed discussion on the assignment way of living and Wright Performative Education.

13   *We then took this initial data and dug deeply on our own to discover*
To generate data for our study we used grounded theory methodology—a powerful inductive research method used for data and knowledge generation. Unlike traditional sociological methodologies in which the researcher begins with a theory developed from a review of relevant literature, in grounded theory the researcher systematically generates theories from data. These theories can then be tested using traditional methodologies. The data from which the theory of Evolating emerged was generated by just such a grounded research project. For more on grounded research theory, see Barney G. Glaser, *Theoretical Sensitivity* (Mill Valley, CA: Sociology Press, 1978). Also see B. G. Glaser & Anselm Strauss, *The Discovery of Grounded Theory: Strategies for Qualitative Research* (New York: Hawthorne, 1967). See also Dr. Judith Wright, *Living a Great Life: The Theory of Evolating.*

CHAPTER 2
Transformed: The Science of Personal Change and Transformation

17   *Transformation feels as if some basic architecture*
See "Emotion as Integration," in *The Healing Power of Emotion*, eds. Diana Fosha, Daniel J. Siegel, Marion F. Solomon (New York: Norton, 2009), 148.

19   *The Groundbreaking, Eye-Opening Study*
Dr. Judith Wright's doctoral dissertation used grounded theory research methods to study a group of exceptional performers at the Wright Institute. The data that emerged from this study was used to generate the theory of Evolating, which described the generalizable process that accounted for their success. The results of the study and the extensive research that supported the results are described in *Living a Great Life: The Theory of Evolating.*

20   *human emergence technologies*
"Human emergence technologies" is our term for the processes and methodologies which facilitate the development of human potential.

21   *positive deviance research*
See William Seidman and Michael McCauley, "Your Organization's Secret Sauce," article, at http://www.cerebyte.com/articles/Pt%201%20-%20 Discovering%20the%20Secret%20Sauce.pdf. Also see Richard Pascale, Richard Tanner, and Jerry Sternin, "Your Company's Secret Change Agents," *Harvard Business Review* 83, no. 5 (May 2005): 72–81 and Richard Pascale, Jerry Sternin, and Monique Sternin, *The Power of Positive Deviance: How Unlikely Innovators Solve the World's Toughest Problems* (Boston: Harvard Business, 2010).

28   *Dr. Diana Fosha, a leader in the new field of interpersonal neurobiology*
Fosha calls this fundamental need for transformation "transformance." See Diana Fosha, "Emotion and Recognition at Work: Energy, Vitality, Pleasure, Truth, Desire, and the Emergent Phenomenology of Transformational Experience," in *The Healing Power of Emotion*, eds. Diana Fosha, Daniel J. Siegel, Marion F. Solomon (New York: Norton, 2009), 172–204. Also see Fosha, "Transformance, Recognition of Self by Self, and Effective Action," in *Existential-Integrative Psychotherapy: Guideposts to the Core of Practice,* ed. Kirk J. Schneider (New York: Routledge, 2008), 290–320. Also see Dr. Judith Wright, *Living a Great Life: The Theory of Evolating*, which describes the innate drive as the "longing for MORE" and traces the historical roots of the concept through both Eastern and Western philosophical and psychological traditions.

28   *"ontological guilt"*
Existentialists called the inner sense that comes from knowing that we did not choose to become what we could have become ontological guilt. Alternatively, human beings have a choice between ontological guilt and existential anxiety —the term used by Kierkegaard to describe the sense of upset that all human beings share when they confront their freedom to choose. Sartre described the denial of our choice bad faith. For more on the concept of ontological guilt, see R. Firestone, "The 'Voice': The Dual Nature of Guilt Reactions," *The American Journal of Psychoanalysis* 47, no 3: 210-229. Also see Dr. Bob Wright and Dr. Judith Wright, *Foundations of Lifelong Learning and Transformational Leadership.* For a discussion of the relationship between lifestyle adaptations and responses to ontological guilt and bad faith see Dr. Judith Wright, *The Soft Addiction Solution* (New York: Penguin/Tarcher, 2007).

29   *In 2008, 2.6 million kids played Little League baseball*
http://en.wikipedia.org/wiki/Little_League_Baseball
http://espn.go.com/mlb/standings

29   *The Transformative Process: The Six Phases*
See Dr. Judith Wright, *Living a Great Life: The Theory of Evolating* for a full discussion on the six phases and sub-phases of Evolating and the research supporting its structuring.

32   *brain plasticity*
Or neuroplasticity is the property of the brain that allows us to learn, grow, change, and fulfill our potential. For a detailed discussion of brain plasticity see the work of Dr. Michael Merzenich in Doidge, *The Brain That Changes Itself* (New York: Viking, 2007), 46–48.

36   *Daniel Siegel, an expert in interpersonal neurobiology*
Daniel J. Siegel, *Mindsight: The New Science of Personal Transformation* (New York: Bantam Books, 2010).

37   *Neuropsychiatrist Dr. Jeffrey Schwartz reinforces this concept with what he calls "attention density."*
For more on attention density, see "A Brain-Based Approach to Coaching," *Journal of Coaching in Organizations* 4, no. 2 (2006): 32–43.

37   *IQ can be raised by 21 points over four years.*
See Sharon Begley, "Buff Your Brain," *Newsweek*, 1 January 2012. http://www.thedailybeast.com/newsweek/2012/01/01/buff-your-brain.html.

37   *Studies of monks found that the more they meditated, the more gray matter they developed*
In *Train Your Mind, Change Your Brain* (New York: Ballantine Books, 2008), Begley documents numerous studies—including much additional material on Richard Davidson's research on meditating monks. In *How God Changes Your Brain* (New York: Ballantine Books, 2010), Dr. Andrew Newberg and Mark Robert Waldman offer a detailed treatment of the relationship between meditation and brain change. For additional material on the study of meditating monks see Davidson and Begley's *The Emotional Life of Your Brain* (New York: Hudson Street Press, 2012).

38   *Numerous studies demonstrate that brain plasticity can be increased even in aging adults.*
See Merzenich's work described in Norman Doidge, *The Brain That Changes Itself* (New York: Viking, 2007) and the case of Dr. Bach-y-Rita described in Chapter 1.

39   *Cultural evolutionists such as Andrew Cohen and Ken Wilber*
For a more detailed discussion on this topic see Andrew Cohen's *Evolutionary Enlightenment* (New York: Select Books, 2011) and issues of *EnlightenNext* for conversations between Cohen and Wilber at http://magazine.enlightennext.org/.

CHAPTER 3
Yearn: Ignite Your Transformation

42   *Maslow's hierarchy of needs*
Abraham Maslow, *Motivation and Personality* (New York: Harper, 1954, 1970), 15–31.

45   *as positive psychologists Daniel Gilbert and Timothy Wilson have noted*
Daniel T. Gilbert and Timothy D. Wilson, "Miswanting: Some Problems in the Forecasting of Future Affective States," in *Feeling and Thinking: The Role of Affect in Social Cognition,* ed. J. Forgas (New York: Cambridge University Press, 2000), 178–197.

45   *Neuroscientists have identified different pleasure centers in the brain*
See Doidge, *The Brain That Changes Itself* for a discussion of excitatory, satisfaction, and pleasure centers. Daniel Nettle provides a discussion of the distinction between liking and wanting in *Happiness* (New York: Oxford University Press, 2005); for more on liking, rewards, and opioids see Susana

Pecina, Kyle S. Smith, and Kent C. Berridge, "Hedonic Hot Spots in the Brain," *The Neuroscientist* 12, no. 6 (2006): 500–51, and Kent C. Berridge and Terry E. Robinson, "What Is the Role of Dopamine in Reward: Hedonic Impact, Reward Learning, or Incentive Salience?" *Brain Research Reviews* 28 (1998): 309–369. For a related discussion of Jaak Panksepp's work on seeking see also Yoffe, "Seeking: How the Brain Hard-wires Us to Love Google, Twitter, and Texting. And Why That's Dangerous," *Slate,* posted Aug. 12, 2009, http://www.slate.com/id/2224932/pagenum/all/.

46   *poor affective forecasting*
See Timothy D. Wilson and Daniel T. Gilbert, "Affective Forecasting: Knowing What to Want," *Current Directions in Psychological Science* 14, no. 3 (June 2005): 131–134. Also see John Gertner's article "The Futile Pursuit of Happiness," *New York Times,* 7 September 2003, for a discussion of the impact of miswanting and poor affective forecasting on our decision-making.

50   *intrinsic motivators result in higher achievement and enjoyment than extrinsic ones do*
Daniel H. Pink, *Drive: The Surprising Truth about What Motivates Us* (New York: Riverhead Books, 2009), 77–81; R. M. Ryan and E. L. Deci, "Self-determination Theory and the Facilitation of Intrinsic Motivation, Social Development, and Well-being," *American Psychologist* 55 (2000): 68–78.

54   *Urges originate in a deeper place*
 A discussion of urges and cravings and their relationship to satisfaction can be found in "Fulfill Your Spiritual Hungers," in J. Wright, *The Soft Addiction Solution.* Also see "The Desire," in Dr. Judith Wright, *The One Decision* (New York: Penguin/Tarcher, 2005).

58   *Soft addictions*
The term "soft addiction" was coined by Dr. Judith Wright. See *The Soft Addiction Solution.*

58   *Loss aversion*
The term "loss aversion" refers to the phenomenon in human nature whereby awareness of the pain of loss outweighs the prospect of the joy of experiencing a gain. For more on loss aversion see the Nobel Peace Prize–winning research of Daniel Kahneman and Amos Tversky in "Prospect Theory: An Analysis of Decision Under Risk," *Econometrica* 47, no. 2 (1979): 263–292 and "Loss Aversion in Riskless Choice: A Reference-dependent Model," *Quarterly Journal of Economics* 106 (1991): 1039–1061.

CHAPTER 4
Engage: Translate Yearning into Action

67   *engaging continuum*
This is a copyrighted model of engagement constructed by Dr. Judith Wright
and Dr. Bob Wright. For a similar model, see Ori and Rom Brafman's *Click:
The Magic of Instant Connections* (New York: Broadway, 2010).

68   *Research from the relatively new field of positive psychology*
Martin E. P. Seligman, *Flourish: A Visionary New Understanding of Happiness
and Well-Being* (New York: Free Press, 2011) provides a discussion of engaging
as a key element of authentic happiness. Also see Mihaly Csikszentmihalyi,
Flow: The Psychology of Optimal Experience (New York: HarperCollins, 1990).

68   *the key to being happy at work can be seen as intentional engaging*
See Amy Wrzesniewski "Ten Things Science Says Will Make You Happy,"
in *yes!* at http://www.yesmagazine.org/pdf/48/Happiness_Poster11x17.
pdf. Also see Amy Wrzesniewski and Jane E. Dutton, "Crafting a Job:
Revisioning Employees as Active Crafters of Their Work," *The Academy of
Management Review* 26, no. 2 (April 2001): 179–20. Also at http://www.jstor.
org/stable/259118.

68   *our brains light up in ways that result in positive experiences*
Gregory Berns, *Satisfaction: The Science of Finding True Fulfillment* (New
York: Henry Holt, 2005).

68   *the property of the brain that allows us to learn, grow, change, and
fulfill our potential*
See discussion of the work of Michael Merzenich in Norman Doidge, *The
Brain That Changes Itself.*

68   *being aware, paying attention, and intentionally doing new things*
David Rock and Jeffrey Schwartz, "The Neuroscience of Leadership," *Strategy +
Business Magazine* 43 (2006): 1–10 .

68   *engaging in novel experiences, and not just being focused on the
outcomes*
Gregory Berns, *Satisfaction: The Science of Finding True Fulfillment* (New
York: Henry Holt and Company, 2005).

68   *deep engagement at work leads to enhanced productivity*
For more on the effects of engagement at work see, David Rock and Dr. Yiyuan

Tang, "The Neuroscience of Engagement," *NeuroLeadershipJournal,*2009 http://www.davidrock.net/files/A2_NOE_US.pdf and David Rock and Jeffrey Schwartz. "The Neuroscience of Leadership," *Strategy+Business Magazine* 43 (2006): 1-10.

68 *"grit"—the perseverance needed for long-term goals*
Angela Duckworth first identified this personality trait, which accounts for differences in individual success. See Angela L. Duckworth, Christopher Peterson, Michael D. Matthews, and Dennis R. Kelly, "Grit: Perseverance and Passion for Long-Term Goals," *Journal of Personality and Social Psychology* 92, no. 6 (2007): 1087–1101.

69 *that's because your actions aren't designed to satisfy a yearning*
Daniel T. Gilbert and Timothy D. Wilson, "Miswanting: Some Problems in the Forecasting of Future Affective States," in *Feeling and Thinking: The Role of Affect in Social Cognition,* ed. J. Forgas (New York: Cambridge University Press, 2000), 178–197.

71 *soft addiction*
See Dr. Judith Wright, *The Soft Addiction Solution* (New York: Penguin/Tarcher, 2007).

71 *continuous partial attention*
Also referred to as continuous partial engagement. For more on continuous partial attention, see Linda Stone, "Fine Dining with Mobile Devices" in *The Huffington Post,* 9 January 2008, http://huffingtonpost.com/linda-stone/fine-dining-with-mobile-d_b_80819.html.

71 *develop true grit*
In "Love is the Opposite of Underwear," Jonah Lehrer calls the property of persevering "grit," at http://www.wired.com/wiredscience/2011/08/love-is-the-opposite-of-underwear/. Also see Jonah Lehrer, "Which Traits Predict Success?" in *Wired,* http://www.wired.com/wiredscience/2011/03/what-is-success-true-grit/.

74 *People who Engage on the right side of the continuum possess another quality*
Carol S. Dweck, *Mindset: The New Psychology of Success* (New York: Random House, 2006).

74 *Stanford psychology researcher Carol Dweck, which is a "growth mindset."*

Carol S. Dweck, *Mindset: The New Psychology of Success* (New York: Random House, 2006).

77   *If you need further evidence that real engaging is worth the effort*
See Daniel Goleman, *Emotional Intelligence* (New York: Bantam, 1995) and Richard Boyatzis and Annie McKee, *Primal Leadership* (Boston: Harvard Business Review Press, 2004). Also see Diana Fosha, Ph.D., "Emotion and Recognition at Work: Energy, Vitality, Pleasure, Truth, Desire, and the Emergent Phenomenology of Transformational Experience," in *The Healing Power of Emotion*, eds. Diane Fosha, Daniel J. Siegel, Marion F. Solomon (New York: Norton, 2009), 172–204.

77   *Peter Senge*
Peter Senge is the founding Chairman of the Society for Organizational Learning. See his book, *The Fifth Discipline: The Art and Practice of the Learning Organization* (New York: Doubleday/Currency, 1990).

78   *Russian psychologist and educational theorist Lev Vygotsky*
See Lev Vygotsky, *Mind in Society: The Development of Higher Psychological Processes* (Cambridge, MA: Harvard University Press, 1978). For a more detailed discussion of learning by doing, see Dr. Bob Wright and Dr. Judith Wright, *Foundations of Lifelong Learning and Personal Transformation* (Chicago: Evolating Press, 2012) as well as Dr. Judith Wright, *Living a Great Life: The Theory of Evolating* for an extended discussion of the educational theories of Lev Vygotsky, John Dewey, Jerome Bruner, and Jack Mezirow and their relationship to Wright Performative Education.

78   *Current neuroscience research shows that neurons are continually wiring together*
For more on the importance of learning from mistakes to achieve top performance see Daniel Coyle, *The Talent Code: Greatness Isn't Born. It's Grown. Here's How.* (New York: Bantam, 2009); Geoffrey Colvin, *Talent Is Overrated: What Really Separates World-class Performers from Everybody Else* (New York: Portfolio, 2008); Carol Dweck, *Mindset*; and Norman Doidge, *The Brain That Changes Itself.* Also see Jonah Lehrer, *How We Decide* (Boston: Houghton Mifflin, 2009).

80   *poor affective forecasting*
For a discussion of poor affective forecasting see Timothy D. Wilson and Daniel T. Gilbert, "Affective Forecasting: Knowing What to Want," *Current Direction in Psychological Science* 14, no. 3 (June 2005): 131–134.

80   *dread*

See Diana Fosha, "Emotion and Recognition at Work" *in The Healing Power of Emotions* for a discussion on dread. Also see Gregory Berns, *Iconoclast* (Boston: Harvard Business Press, 2010) for an account of experiments involving "extreme dreaders" and the manifestations of dread in brain activity.

80   *loss aversion*

The phenomenon in human nature whereby awareness of the pain of loss outweighs the prospect of the joy of experiencing a gain. See the work of Daniel Kahneman and Amos Tversky, "Prospect Theory: An Analysis of Decision Under Risk," *Econometrica* 47, no. 2 (March 1979): 263–292 and "Loss Aversion in Riskless Choice: A Reference-dependent Model," *The Quarterly Journal of Economics* 106, no. 4 (November, 1991): 103–1061.

80   *lack of self-efficacy*

For a discussion of self-efficacy refer to Albert Bandura, *Social Foundations of Thought and Action: A Social Cognitive Theory* (Englewood Cliffs, NJ: Prentice-Hall, 1986) and Carol Dweck, *Mindset*.

84   *assignment way of living*

The assignment way of living is a key component of Wright Performative Education. See Dr. Bob Wright and Dr. Judith Wright, *Foundations of Lifelong Learning and Personal Transformation* and Dr. Judith Wright, *Living a Great Life: The Theory of Evolating* for a more detailed discussion on the assignment way of living and Wright Performative Education.

87   *He talked about living his life as an experiment*

See R. B. Fuller, *Critical Path* (New York: St. Martin's Press, 1981). See also his *Guinea Pig B: The 56-Year Experiment* (Clayton, CA: Critical Path Press, 2004) and James T. Baldwin's *Buckyworks: Buckminster Fuller's Ideas for Today* (New York: John Wiley, 1996).

CHAPTER 5
Revelate: Discover Your Program, Unleash Your Potential

92   *they are neurons firing and wiring together and forming hubs*

This concept is known as Hebbian learning. It was first introduced by Canadian behavioral psychologist Donald Hebb in 1949. For more on this see Dispenza, *Evolve Your Brain*, 184–185. Also see Norman Doidge, *The Brain That Changes Itself*, for an account of Merzenich's pioneering work in this area.

92   *largely formed shortly after birth based on their relationships and experiences with primary caregivers*
For more on what we call matrix formation in terms of early attachment schema see Louis Cozolino, *The Neuroscience of Human Relationships* (New York: W. W. Norton & Company, 2006) and Daniel J. Siegel, *The Developing Mind: How Relationships and the Brain Interact to Shape Who We Are* (New York: Guildford, 2012).

92   *what neuroscientists call "experience-dependent neurogenesis."*
A discussion of neurogenesis can be found in Doidge, *The Brain That Changes Itself.*

94   *a matrix (our term) of core beliefs about ourselves and the world*
See Siegel, *The Developing Mind.* Also see Cozolino, *The Neuroscience of Human Relationships,* and "Healing the Social Brain," in *The Neuroscience of Psychotherapy* (New York: W. W. Norton & Company, 2010).

94   *As Robert A. Heinlein said, "Man is not a rational animal, he is a rationalizing animal."*
Assignment in Eternity (New York: New American Library, 1953).

94   *An experiment cited in* Sway: The Irresistible Pull of Irrational Behavior *took place at MIT*
See Ori Brafman and Ram Brafman, *Sway: The Irresistible Pull of Irrational Behavior* (New York: Doubleday, 2008), 71–73.

95   *if your name is Dennis or Denise*
See David Brooks, *The Social Animal: The Hidden Sources of Love, Character, and Achievement* (New York: Random House, 2011).

95   *Freud and Adler and their followers believe that the unconscious drives behaviors*
For concise reviews of Freudian thought see Calvin Hall, *A Primer of Freudian Psychology* (Cleveland, OH: World Publishing, 1954), and for Adlerian thought, see Harold H. Mosak and Michael Maniacci, *A Primer of Adlerian Psychology: The Analytic-behavioral-cognitive Psychology of Alfred Adler* (Philadelphia: Brunner/Mazel, 1999).

95   *Personality psychologist Otto Rank*
See Otto Rank, *Art & Artist: Creative Urge and Personality Development* (New York: W. W. Norton & Company, 1989). Rank urged us to "step out of the frame of the prevailing ideology," 70.

95   *The existential philosophers—Heidegger, Kierkegaard, Nietzsche, and Sartre*
See more on existentialist thought on breaking through cultural norms in Dr. Bob Wright and Dr. Judith Wright, *Foundations of Lifelong Learning and Personal Transformation.*

95   *"We are born in the 'they'. . ."*
See Martin Heidegger, *Being and Time,* trans. John Macquarrie and Edward Robinson (New York: Harper and Row, 1962), 312–313; also see the version translated by Joan Stambaugh (Albany: State University of New York Press, 1996), 248.

95   *Jack Mezirow, the originator of Transformative Learning Theory*
Read more in *Learning as Transformation: Critical Perspectives on a Theory in Progress* (San Francisco: Jossey-Bass, 2000).

99   *here is what happens when we gain an insight about our programming*
See the work of Merzenich cited in Doidge, *Evolve Your Brain.* Also see J. Kounios & M. Jung-Beeman, "Aha! The Cognitive Neuroscience of Insight," *Current Directions in Psychological Science* 18 (2009): 210–216.

99   *We feel an adrenaline rush . . . motivates us to act*
See David Rock and Jeffrey Schwartz, "The Neuroscience of Leadership" *Strategy+Business Magazine* 43 (2006): 1–10.

103   *Daniel Coyle speaks about ignition*
For an account of examples of ignition in top performers see *The Talent Code,* 97–120.

104   *The Johari window is a good tool*
Joseph Luft and Harry Ingham created the Johari window as a technique for self-awareness, personal development, interpersonal relationships, group dynamics, and team development.

107   *One Segment of a Matrix Mapped*
Wright and Wright, original copyrighted diagram. The concepts of core mistaken beliefs, related beliefs, and consequent rules draw heavily upon Alfred Adler's idea of limiting beliefs and how they develop into a lifestyle. See Alfred Adler, *The Individual Psychology of Alfred Adler: A Systematic Presentation in Selections from His Writings* (New York: Basic, 1956).

109   *self-fulfilling prophecy*
Sociologist Robert K. Merton is credited with coining the term "self-fulfilling

prophecy." See his book, *Social Theory and Social Structure* (New York: Free Press, 1968), 477.

114   *It is very difficult to gain and maintain the insights that revelating provides*
K. Subramaniam, J. Kounios, E. M. Bowden, T. B. Parrish, and M. Jung-Beeman, "Positive Mood and Anxiety Modulate Anterior Cingulate Activity and cognitive preparation for insight," *Journal of Cognitive Neuroscience* 21 (2012): 415–432. See also Barbara Frederickson, *Positivity* (New York: Crown, 2009).

CHAPTER 6
Liberate: Break Free and Launch Your Spectacular Life

120   *Nietzsche viewed freedom and the responsibility it holds as your true power*
See Friedrich Nietzsche and Walter Kaufmann, *Beyond Good and Evil* (New York: Vintage Books, 1989), and Friedrich Nietszsche, Walter Kaufmann, and R. J. Hollingdale, *The Will to Power* (New York: Vintage, 1968).

121   *What the existentialists mean by "ontological guilt"*
See R. Firestone. "The 'Voice': The Dual Nature of Guilt Reactions," *The American Journal of Psychoanalysis* 47, no. 3 (1987): 210–229. Also see Dr. Bob Wright and Dr. Judith Wright, *Foundations of Lifelong Learning and Transformational Leadership.*

121   *that authenticity isn't being true to who you've been*
Martin Heidegger, *Being and Time,* trans. John MacQuarrie and Edward Robinson (San Francisco: Harper, 1927, 1962). Jean-Paul Sartre, *Being and Nothingness* (New York: Citadel Press, 1956); see also Gordon Medlock, "The Evolving Ethic of Authenticity: From Humanistic to Positive Psychology," *The Humanistic Psychologist* 40, no. 1 (February 2012): 38–57.

121   *who we wound up being*
See Werner Erhard, Michael C. Jensen, and Steve Zaffron, "Integrity: A Positive Model that Incorporates the Normative Phenomena of Morality, Ethics, and Legality," from *The Transformational Experiences that Leave Ordinary People Being Leaders and Access to a Context that Uses You and Education as Stretching the Mind,* Harvard Business School NOM Working Paper No. 10-061, Landmark Education LLC. Revised 7 March 2010; See also Werner Erhard, Michael C. Jensen, Steve Zaffron, and Kari Granger, "Introductory

Reading for Being a Leader and The Effective Exercise of Leadership: An Ontological Model" from *Harvard Business School Negotiation, Organizations and Markets Research Papers*, July 5, 2012.

124   *step squarely into your existential anxiety*
See Søren Kierkegaard, *The Concept of Anxiety: A Simple Psychologically Orientating Deliberation on the Dogmatic Issue of Hereditary Sin* (Princeton, NJ: Princeton University Press, 1980). For more on existential anxiety, see Dr. Bob Wright and Dr. Judith Wright, *Foundations of Lifelong Learning and Transformational Leadership*. See also Paul Tillich, *The Courage to Be* (New Haven, CT: Yale University Press, 1952).

124   *Søren Kierkegaard, the existential Christian minister and philosopher*
See his *Purity of Heart Is to Will One Thing* (New York: Harper, 1938).

124   *Abraham Maslow, the father of humanistic psychology*
Abraham Maslow, "A Theory of Human Motivation," *Psychological Review* 50, no. 4 (1943): 370–96.

127   *Dr. Michael Merzenich, a well-respected University of California professor*
For more on Merzenich's work see Norman Doidge, *The Brain That Changes Itself*.

127   *Brain plasticity is activated by doing something new and different*
For more on brain plasticity and neural plasticity see Daniel Siegel, *Mindsight*; Norman Doidge, *The Brain That Changes Itself*; Daniel Coyle, *The Talent Code*; and Geoffrey Colvin, *Talent Is Overrated*.

128   *With focused attention and repetition*
For more on this subject see Daniel Siegel, *Mindsight*; Norman Doidge, *The Brain That Changes Itself*; Daniel Coyle, *The Talent Code*; and Geoffrey Colvin, *Talent Is Overrated*.

128   *Our brain learns better when challenged*
See Gregory Berns, *Satisfaction*, and *Iconoclast*.

128   *Stanford psychologist Carol Dweck*
Refer to Carol Dweck, *Mindset*.

128   *Dr. Philip Zimbardo runs the Shyness Clinic at Stanford University*
See Philip Zimbardo, *Shyness: What It Is, What to Do About It* (Reading, MA: Addison-Wesley, 1977).

129   *research regarding our brain chemistry*
See Dispenza, *Evolve Your Brain.*

130   *Walt Disney was once fired from a job*
From an article by Melinda Beck, "If at First You Don't Succeed, You're in Good Company," *Wall Street Journal*, 29 April 2008.

130   *Neuroscience research backs up the power of making mistakes*
See Jonah Lehrer, *How We Decide* (Boston: Houghton Mifflin Harcourt, 2009), Coyle, *The Talent Code*, and Colvin, *Talent Is Overrated.*

130   *worrying about making mistakes, rather than just going for it*
See Sian Beilock, *Choke: What the Secrets of the Brain Reveal About Getting It Right When You Have To* (New York: Free Press, 2010).

130   *Name It to Tame It.*
See Matthew D. Lieberman, Naomi I. Eisenberger, Molly J. Crockett, Sabrina M. Tom, Jennifer H. Pfeifer, Baldwon M. Way, "Putting Feelings into Words: Affect Labeling Disrupts Amygdala Activity in Reponse to Affective Stimuli." *Psychological Science* 18 (2007): 421–428 at http://www.scn.ucla.edu/pdf/AL(2007).pdf and http://www.scn.ucla.edu/pdf/Lieberman-Todorov-Ch13.pdf. See also Siegel, *Mindsight.*

131   *Writing down the feeling, or even composing a poem*
See Richard Alleyne, "AAAS: Writing Poems Helps Brain Cope with Emotional Turmoil, Say Scientists," in *The Telegraph,* at http://www.telegraph.co.uk/culture/culturenews/4630043/AAAS-Writing-poems-helps-brain-cope-with-emotional-turmoil-say-scientists.html.

132   *what Russian psychologist and educator Lev Vygotsky calls MKOs*
See Lev Vygotsky, *Mind in Society: The Development of Higher Psychological Processes* (Cambridge, MA: Harvard University Press, 1978). For a more detailed discussion of learning by doing see Dr. Bob Wright and Dr. Judith Wright, *Foundations of Lifelong Learning and Personal Transformation* (Chicago: Evolating Press, 2012) as well as Dr. Judith Wright, *Living a Great Life: The Theory of Evolating* for an extended discussion of the educational theories of Lev Vygotsky.

133   *Adopt the assignment way of living*
For a more detailed discussion of the assignment way of living see Dr. Bob Wright and Dr. Judith Wright, *Foundations of Lifelong Learning and Personal Transformation* (Chicago: Evolating Press, 2012) as well as Dr. Judith Wright,

Living a Great Life: The Theory of Evolating which details the educational theories supporting the technology of the assignment way of living.

137   *The brain is a predictive organ*
See Berns, *Iconoclast.*

138   *eye contact, physical touch, the reassurance of a soothing voice*
The research of Dr. James Coan, Director of the University of Virginia Affective Neuroscience Lab, shows that holding the hand of a loving partner literally calms jittery neurons in our brains. See J. A. Coan, H. S. Schaefer, and R. J. Davidson, "Lending a Hand: Social Regulation of the Neural Response to Threat," *Psychological Science* 17 (2006): 1032–1039. Also see Benedict Carey, "Evidence That Little Touches Do Mean So Much," *The New York Times,* 23 February 2010. Also see Siegel, *Mindsight,* and Bonnie Badenoch, *Being a Brainwise Therapist: A Practical Guide to Interpersonal Neurobiology* (New York: W. W. Norton, 2008).

138   *"Human beings do not realize the extent to which their own sense of defeat . . ."*
Colin Wilson in an interview by Paul Newman in Abraxas Unbound & the Colin Wilson Newsletter http://abrax7.stormloader.com/interview.htm.

139   *fixed versus a growth mindset*
See Dweck, *Mindset.*

142   *Maslow talked about "peak experiences" as a trait of a self-actualized person*
See Maslow, *Toward a Psychology of Being* (New York: Van Nostrand Reinhold, 1968) and his *The Farther Reaches of Human Nature* (New York: Penguin, 1993), 44–45.

CHAPTER 7
Rematrix: Reprogram Your Mind, Transform Your Life

146   *meet the conditions for lasting change*
See Coyle, *The Talent Code,* Doidge, *The Brain That Changes Itself,* and Colvin, *Talent Is Overrated.*

148   *Children's bodies release brain-derived neurotrophic factor (BDNF)*
See Doidge, "Redesigning the Brain," in *The Brain That Changes Itself,* which details Merzenich's work.

148   *Merzenich and other neuroscientists have found that the brain's ability to grow new nerve cells*
For further discussion of Merzenich's work, see also Sharon Begley, *Train Your Mind, Change Your Brain* (New York: Ballantine Books, 2007) and Norman Doidge, *The Brain That Changes Itself.*

149   *you've run into the work of K. Anders Ericsson*
Malcolm Gladwell, *Outliers: The Story of Success* (New York: Little, Brown and Company, 2008). *The Talent Code* provides more detailed information on Ericsson's studies on deliberate practice, performance, and myelin science. See also K. Anders Ericsson, "The Influence of Experience and Deliberate Practice on the Development of Superior Expert Performance," in *The Cambridge Handbook of Expertise and Expert Performance,* eds. K. Anders Ericsson, Neil Charness, Paul J. Feltovich, and Robert R. Hoffman (New York: Cambridge University Press, 2006). *Talent Is Overrated* provides further specifics on Ericsson's work and what constitutes deliberate practice.

149   *Asked why he practices so much, world-class pianist Vladimir Horowitz*
As related in *The Talent Code,* p. 88. This quote has also been attributed to other world-class musicians including Luciano Pavarotti and Ignace Paderewski, according to Colvin in "What It Takes to Be Great," *Fortune* (October 2006) at http://money.cnn.com/magazines/fortune/fortune_archive/2006/10/30/8391794/index.htm.

149   *Colvin details the requirements of deliberate practice*
See Colvin, *Talent Is Overrated* and "What It Takes to Be Great."

150   *Meadowmount School of Music*
For more on Meadowmount School of Music see Coyle, *The Talent Code.* Also see Meadowmount website http://www.meadowmount.com/.

151   *In fact, by the time we are about 35, we are rarely learning and growing*
See Merzenich's work as discussed in Doidge, *The Brain That Changes Itself.* Also see Dispenza, *Evolve Your Brain,* and John Assaraff's interview with Dispenza from March 12, 2007, at http://www.johnassaraf.com/resources/Joe_Dispenza-Evolve_Your_Brain_the_Science_of_Changing_Your_Mind.pdf.

151   *And by the time we are 70, we may not have systematically engaged the systems in the brain to trigger neuroplasticity*
See more on this in Merzenich work on rebuilding the brain's plasticity as discussed in Doidge's *The Brain That Changes Itself.* Joe Dispenza also discusses this in *Evolve Your Brain.*

151 *Having years of "experience" doesn't give us mastery*
See Colvin, *Talent Is Overrated* and "What It Takes to Be Great."

151 *we won't retrain the circuits in our brain and be free of the neurochemical fix*
See Dispenza *Evolve your Brain,* and also the John Assaraff interview of March 12, 2007, with Dispenza cited above.

152 *Daniel Coyle calls the "razor edge of our ability"*
See *Practice Makes Perfect?* at http://www.abc.net.au/radionational/programs/allinthemind/practice-makes-perfect/3611212.

152 *what researchers term learning velocity*
See Coyle, *The Talent Code.*

152 *As Coyle says, "It's literally like installing broadband in your brain."*
See "Growing Talent; Interview with Daniel Coyle: Myelin, Skill and the Brain" http://www.superconsciousness.com/topics/knowledge/growing-talent-interview-daniel-coyle. Also see Coyle, *The Talent Code.*

152 *Transformers don't stop with small change*
See Coyle, *The Talent Code,* for further discussion of the importance of pushing on to further goals.

153 *Transformation doesn't take place only in your thoughts*
See more on this in Diana Fosha's "Emotion and Recognition at Work" in *The Healing Power of Emotion* (Diana Fosha, Daniel Siegel, and Marion F. Solomon eds.).

153 *Transformation produces an acute tension between hope and fear*
See more on this in Diana Fosha's "Emotion and Recognition at Work" in *The Healing Power of Emotion.*

154 *because our brains also have* competitive plasticity
See Merzenich's work as discussed in Doidge, *The Brain That Changes Itself,* 58–60.

155 *In* The Power of Habit, *for instance, author Charles Duhigg cites a study of a woman*
Charles Duhigg, *The Power of Habit* (New York: Random House, 2012), xiv.

157 *As Dr. Barbara Fredrickson points out in her broaden-and-build theory*
See Fredrickson, *Positivity.*

161   *Jump off the OK Plateau*
Joshua Foer, *Moonwalking with Einstein: The Art and Science of Remembering Everything* (New York: Penguin Press, 2011).

161   *Jim Collins' assertion, "Good is the enemy of great,"*
Good to Great: Why Some Companies Make the Leap . . . and Others Don't (New York: HarperBusiness, 2001).

161   *K. Anders Ericsson's groundbreaking research on expertise*
See K. Anders Ericsson, "The Influence of Experience and Deliberate Practice on the Development of Superior Expert Performance" in *The Cambridge Handbook of Expertise and Expert Performance*, K. Anders Ericsson, Neil Charness, Paul J. Feltovich, and Robert R. Hoffman, eds. (New York: Cambridge University Press, 2006). For more on deliberate practice see Geoff Colvin, *Talent Is Overrated* and Daniel Coyle's treatment of deep practice in *The Talent Code.*

163   *The legendary cellist Pablo Casals was in his nineties*
Doidge, *The Brain That Changes Itself,* 257.

164   *Change Your Self-fulfilling Prophecy Cycle*
Sociologist Robert K. Merton, *Social Theory and Social Structure* (New York: Free Press, 1968), is credited with coining the term "self-fulfilling prophecy." This concept is frequently applied in Wright Performative Education in the context of the existential principle of personal responsibility and choice.

167   *Geoffrey Colvin states that the answers to two questions are the foundation*
Colvin, *Talent Is Overrated.*

CHAPTER 8
Dedicate: Change for the Better Forever

172   *We are tapping into a massive evolutionary energy source.*
http://www.personalbrandingblog.com/personal-branding-interview-daniel-coyle/. Interview with Coyle, *The Talent Code.*

172   *a fascinating study by Gary McPherson demonstrates how this works*
Gary McPherson, "Commitment and Practice: Key Ingredients for Achievement During the Early Stages of Learning a Musical Instrument." *Council for Research in Music Education* 147 (2001): 122–127. Also see Coyle, *The Talent Code,* 102–106.

172 *They did the deep practice that is the hallmark of rematrixing*
See references on deep and deliberate practice in Coyle and Colvin above.

173 *were more likely to engage in more demanding deliberate practice*
See references on deep and deliberate practice in Coyle and Colvin above.

173 *having transformation be part of your identity is where you tap its power*
Practice Makes Perfect? Natasha Mitchell interviewing K. Anders Ericcson, Daniel Coyle, Maria Tickle, Georia Wheeler. Australian Broadcasting Corporation, 5 November 2011. http://www.abc.net.au/radionational/programs/allinthemind/practice-makes-perfect/3611212. See also K. Anders Ericsson, "The Influence of Experience and Deliberate Practice on the Development of Superior Expert Performance," in K. Anders Ericsson, Neil Charness, Paul J. Feltovich, and Robert R. Hoffman, eds., *The Cambridge Handbook of Expertise and Expert Performance* (New York: Cambridge University Press, 2006).

173 *Dedicating and living with intent activates the most highly evolved part of our brain*
David Perlmutter, M.D., and Alberto Villoldo, Ph.D., *Power Up Your Brain: The Neuroscience of Enlightenment* (New York: Hay House, 2011), 19–20, 23–31. See also Dispenza, "Taking Control: The Frontal Lobe in Thought and Action" in *Evolve Your Brain,* 337–380.

175 *Signs of Not Dedicating*
For further discussion and more on the role of the frontal lobe in decision-making and intention see Joe Dispenza's discussion in "Taking Control" from *Evolve Your Brain: The Science of Changing Your Mind.*

175 *develop "attention density"—a laser-like focus on challenging objectives*
See Rock and Schwartz, "The Neuroscience of Leadership," *Strategy+Business Magazine* 43 (2006): 1–10.

176 *the famous Stanford University marshmallow experiment in the 1960s*
See Jonah Lehrer, "Don't! The Secret of Self Control," *The New Yorker,* 18 May 2009, 26–32. Walter Mischel, the Stanford professor of psychology, conducted experiments using marshmallows to test the ability of children to delay gratification—see http://www.newyorker.com/reporting/2009/05/18/090518fa_fact_lehrer.

177 *Biographer Walter Isaacson called Franklin "the most accomplished American of his age"*
Walter Isaacson, *Benjamin Franklin: An American Life* (New York: Simon &

Schuster, 2003) and H. W. Brands, *The First American: The Life and Times of Benjamin Franklin* (New York: Anchor Books, 2000).

178   *". . . yet I was, by the endeavour, a better and a happier man . . ."*
Benjamin Franklin, *Autobiography* (New York: SoHoBooks, 2012).

180   *let's examine the six components of this phase*
See Dr. Judith Wright, the chapter on Dedicating, in *Living a Great Life: The Theory of Evolating* for more details on the properties and stages of the Dedicating phase of Evolating.

180   *the growth choices over the safe choices*
See Maslow, *Motivation and Personality*.

181   *don't allow rejection to derail your dreams, and see mistakes as just a problem to solve.*
Brooks reminds us that "You can develop a resilient mindset at any age." For more, see Melinda Beck, "If at First You Don't Succeed, You're in Excellent Company" In *The Wall Street Journal*, 29 April 2008.

182   *Flip on the Up*
Flipping on the Up draws from Kahneman and Tversky's *Prospect Theory: An Analysis of Decision-Making Under Risk* (Eugene, OR: Decision Research, Perceptronics, 1977). The term "flipping on the up" refers to the concept of investing resources and committing to maximize gains when things are going well, rather than holding one's breath or waiting for things to get bad before investing to change it. Most people wait until odds are not good, when things are on the downturn. A smaller percentage "flip on the up," investing when things are going well, which maximizes payout. For a more detailed discussion of concepts related to flipping up on the up, see the chapter on Dedicating in Dr. Judith Wright, *Living a Great Life: The Theory of Evolating*, which describes in greater detail the level of investment of people who choose a transformational path.

183   *Live Purposefully*
Refer to "The Keys to the Kingdom" chapter in Dr. Judith Wright's *The One Decision* for a more in-depth guide to principled living. For a treatment of these principles with respect to cycles of human development, refer to the "Wright Model of Human Growth and Development." A more detailed description of the philosophical and psychological theories integrated in this model is contained in Dr. Bob Wright and Dr. Judith Wright, *Foundations of Lifelong Learning and Personal Transformation*. For a more detailed treatment of life purpose and developing a personal and business mission, see

Robert J. Wright, *Business with Purpose: Beyond Time Management* (Boston: Butterworth-Heinemann, 1997).

185   *motivation explodes when we identify with others who are performing*
Dr. Geoffrey Cohen's work on choice, motivation, and goals discussed in Coyle, *The Talent Code*, 109. Also see Coyle's discussion of primal cues and ignition and their role in motivation, goals, and choice in the same book.

187   *Cézanne didn't just have help. He had a dream team in his corner.*
Malcolm Gladwell, "Late Bloomers: Why Do We Equate Genius with Precocity?" *The New Yorker*, 19 October 2006, at
http://www.newyorker.com/reporting/2008/10/20/081020fa_fact_gladwell.
For a moving account of Camille Pissaro's influence on fellow Impressionist painters and theirs on him, read *Depths of Glory* by Irving Stone.

CHAPTER 9
The Heart of Transformation

193   *the remarkable benefits that research shows we derive from emotional intelligence*
For more on emotional intelligence see Daniel Goleman, *Emotional Intelligence: Why It Can Matter More Than IQ*, as well as his *Working with Emotional Intelligence* (New York: Bantam, 1998), both of which make a strong business case for the development of social and emotional intelligence. See also B. Fredrickson, *Positivity* and Richard Davidson, "The Heart-Brain Connection: The Neuroscience of Social, Emotional, And Academic Learning" at http://www.edutopia.org/richard-davidson-sel-brain-video. For more on the health benefits of enhancing our personal social and emotional intelligence, see S. Cohen and Sarah D. Pressman, "Does Positive Affect Influence Health?" *Psychological Bulletin* 131, no. 6 (2005): 925–971 and Sonja Lyubomirsky, Laura King, and Ed Diener, "The Benefits of Frequent Positive Affect: Does Happiness Lead to Success?" *Psychological Bulletin* 131, no. 6 (November 2005): 803-855. See also Ed Diener, Carol Nickerson, Richard Lucas, and Ed Sandvik, "Dispositional Affect and Job Outcomes," *Social Indicators Research, ProQuest Social Science Journals* 59, no. 3 (September 2002): 229–259, which shows that people with positive emotions earn more over the course of their lifetimes. For research on the relationship between positive emotions and satisfying life outcomes such as marriage and well-being, see L. Harker and D. Keltner, "Expressions of Positive Emotion in Women's College Yearbook Pictures and Their Relationship to Personality and Life Outcomes Across Adulthood," *Journal of Personality and Social Psychology* 80, no. 1 (2001): 112–124.

194   *a field of neuroscience is dedicated to the study of emotions—affective neuroscience*
For some studies in the field, see Jaak Panksepp, "Affective Neuroscience: The Foundations of Human and Animal Emotion," in *The Healing Power of Emotion: Affective Neuroscience, Development and Clinical Practice*.

195   *Primary emotions are fear, anger, hurt, sadness, and joy*
For more on primary and secondary emotions see Dr. Bob Wright and Dr. Judith Wright, *Foundations of Lifelong Learning and Personal Transformation*.

196   *Secondary emotions are based on our own unique internal experience base*
See Antonio Damasio, *Descartes' Error: Emotion, Reason, and the Human Brain* (New York: Putnam, 1994).

198   *Each emotion is evolutionarily dedicated to give us the resources*
See Nico H. Frijda, *The Laws of Emotion* (Mahwah, NJ: Lawrence Erlbaum Associates, 2007). See also Frijda, *The Emotions* (Cambridge, UK: Cambridge University Press, 1986).

198   *Neuroscience research shows that our emotions anticipate our needs*
See W. G. Parrot and J. Schulkin, "Neuropsychology and the Cognitive Nature of the Emotions," in *Cognition and Emotion* 7 (1993): 43–59, and Edward W. Taylor, "Transformative Learning Theory: A Neurobiological Perspective of the Role of Emotions and Unconscious Ways of Knowing" in *International Journal of Lifelong Education* 20, no. 3 (May–June 2001): 218–236.

198   *arbiters of our pleasure-pain mechanism*
See Dr. Bob Wright and Dr. Judith Wright, *Foundations of Lifelong Learning and Personal Transformation*.

198   *they are accompanied by a sense of energy and vitality, broader awareness, openness, and a sense of well-being*
See Barbara Frederickson, *Positivity*, and Barbara Fredrickson and Marcial Losada, "Positive Affect and the Complex Dynamics of Human Flourishing," *American Psychologist* 60, no. 7 (2005): 678–686. See also Diana Fosha's "Emotion and Recognition at Work" in *The Healing Power of Emotion* (Diana Fosha, Daniel Siegel, and Marion F. Solomon eds.).

198   *Emotions . . . are essential to rationality*
Antonio Damasio, *The Feeling of What Happens: Body, Emotion, and the Making of Consciousness* (New York: Harcourt Brace, 1999).

199   *David Brooks, the* New York Times *columnist and author of* The Social Animal
David Brooks, TED Talk, "The Social Animal," filmed and posted March 2011, http://www.ted.com/talks/david_brooks_the_social_animal.html.

199   *Damasio found that people with a tumor on their emotional centers*
See more on this in Lehrer, *How We Decide.*

199   *"the banks of rigidity and chaos."*
Daniel J. Siegel, *Mindsight: The New Science of Personal Transformation* (New York: Bantam Books, 2010).

199   *Daniel Goleman's article on emotional intelligence*
The popularity of Daniel Goleman's 1998 *Harvard Business Review* article "What Makes a Leader" led the *Harvard Business Review* to reexamine the data on emotional intelligence, and in April 2003 published "Breakthrough Ideas for Tomorrow's Business Agenda," which contains this quote.

200   *They need to be expressed in order for you to fully experience their transformational power.*
Metaphor borrowed from James Twyman, *Love, God, and the Art of French Cooking* (Carlsbad, CA: Hay House, 2011).

200   *sensing and feeling our emotions within our bodies in conjunction with our cognition*
See E. T. Gendlin, *Focusing-oriented Psychotherapy: A Manual of the Experiential Method* (New York: Guildford Press, 1996). See also L. S. Greenberg & S. C. Paivio, *Working with Emotions in Psychotherapy* (New York: Guildford Press, 1997). Also see P. Levine, *Waking the Tiger: Healing Trauma* (Berkeley, CA: North Atlantic Books, 1997). See also Fosha, "Emotion, True Self, True Other, Core State: Toward a Clinical Theory of Affective Change Process," *Psychoanalytic Review* 92, no. 4 (2005): 513–552.

201   *a sense of empowerment, inner strength, and assertiveness*
See Fosha, "Emotion, True Self."

202   *Dan Siegel's research shows that when we share emotional experiences like these*
See Siegel, *Mindsight* and his *The Developing Mind.*

202   *experiences of "aliveness, hope, faith, clarity, agency, simplicity, compassion, truth, self, and beauty."*

See Diana Fosha's "Emotion and Recognition at Work" in *The Healing Power of Emotion* (Diana Fosha, Daniel Siegel, and Marion F. Solomon eds.).

202   *it actually changes our brains, shifting the gene expression*
See Richard Davidson, "The Heart-Brain Connection: The Neuroscience of Social, Emotional, and Academic Learning" at http://www.edutopia.org/richard-davidson-sel-brain-video.

203   *Neuroscientist Candace Pert's research*
See Pert, *Molecules of Emotion: Why You Feel the Way You Feel* (New York: Scribner, 1997).

204   *It degrades our ability to recall information and limits our cognitive performance*
See David Rock, *Your Brain at Work: Strategies for Overcoming Distraction, Regaining Focus, and Working Smarter All Day Long* (New York: Harper Business, 2009) *and Jane M.* Richards and James J. Gross, "Emotion Regulation and Memory: The Cognitive Costs of Keeping One's Cool," *Journal of Personality and Social Psychology* 79, no. 3 *(*2000): 410–424. See also Philippe R. Goldin, Kateri McRae, Wiveka Ramel, and James J. Gross, "The Neural Bases of Emotion Regulation: Reappraisal and Suppression of Negative Emotion," *Biological Psychiatry* 63 (2008): 577–586.

205   *Ins and Outs and Ups and Downs of Emotional Facility*
Emotional facility and emotional regulation are key skills of social and emotional intelligence. The in-out-up-down model is part of the emotional facility curriculum of the Certificate in Emotional Intelligence offered at the Wright Graduate Institute, which is part of the Wright Foundation for the Realization of Human Potential.

212   *But there is another fear that emerged and became increasingly important*
See Naomi I. Eisenberger and Matthew D. Lieberman, "Why Rejection Hurts: A Common Neural Alarm System for Physical and Social Pain," *Trends in Cognitive Sciences* 8, no. 7 (July 2004): 294–300. See also Matthew D. Lieberman and Naomi I. Eisenberger, "Pains and Pleasures of Social Life," *Science* 323, no. 5916 (13 February 2009): 890–891. Also refer to Rock, *Your Brain at Work.*

212   *we feel the social pain of rejection in the same brain area where we feel physical pain*
See Naomi I. Eisenberger and Matthew D. Lieberman, "Why Rejection Hurts: A Common Neural Alarm System for Physical and Social Pain," *Trends in Cognitive Sciences* 8, no. 7 (July 2004): 294–300. See also Matthew D. Lieberman

and Naomi I. Eisenberger, "Pains and Pleasures of Social Life," *Science* 323, no. 5916 (13 February 2009): 890–891. Also refer to Rock, *Your Brain at Work*.

216   *Our capacity for being soothed comes from our early childhood attachment*
See Cozolino, *Neuroscience of Human Relationships*, and Siegel, *Developing Mind* and *Mindsight*. See also Bonnie Badenoch, *Being a Brainwise Therapist: A Practical Guide to Interpersonal Neurobiology*.

217   *Studies have shown that when people experience the anxiety of an MRI*
See Jim Coan's study referenced in Sue Johnson's *Hold Me Tight* (New York: Little, Brown and Company, 2008).

219   *As we open our hearts and feel our feelings, we nourish ourselves*
Refer to "The Four Loving Truths" in Dr. Judith Wright's *The Soft Addiction Solution* and also "The Way of the Heart" in her *The One Decision*.

CHAPTER 10
Your Next Most Radiant Self

228   *What to Expect—The Manifestations of Transforming*
The manifestations of transformation were based on data gathered from the grounded research study of positive deviants which formed the basis of Dr. Judith Wright's doctoral dissertation, *Living a Great Life: The Theory of Evolating*. For more details on the research study and the participants' experiences, see Chapter Four "Introduction to Living a Great Life: The Theory of Evolating."

230   *Abraham Maslow observed that self-actualized people experience things fully*
Abraham Maslow, *Toward a Psychology of Being* and *Motivation and Personality*.

230   *one of the fathers of positive psychology, Mihály Csíkszentmihályi*
See Mihály Csíkszentmihályi, *Flow* (New York: Harper and Row, 1990).

236   *what psychological researchers call "mature adaptations"*
See Ana Freud, *Ego and Mechanisms of Defence* (New York: International Universities Press, 1946). See also George E. Vaillant, *Adaptation to Life* (Boston: Little, Brown, 1977). Also see Joshua Wolf Shenk, "What Makes Us Happy?" *The Atlantic* (June 2009): 36–53.

236   *Transformers live the truth of the statement by Paulo Coelho*
See Paulo Coelho, *The Alchemist* (San Francisco: Harper, 1993).

239   *that there is greatness within us and have not yet lost the faith in our potential*
The faith in human potential is a consistent theme from existentialist to humanistic philosophers and psychologists. For more on human potential see Dr. Bob Wright and Dr. Judith Wright, *Foundations of Lifelong Learning and Transformational Leadership*. Also revisit Chapter 1 of this book, "The Transformational Imperative," for a historical perspective on human potential.

CHAPTER 11
What If . . . The Transformational Imperative Realized

242   *frontal lobes*
See Dispenza, *Evolve Your Brain,* and Perlmutter and Villoldo, *Power Up Your Brain.*

242   *when we envision the grand design, or the big bang, or God*
See Andrew B. Newberg and Mark Robert Waldman, *How God Changes Your Brain: Breakthrough Findings from a Leading Neuroscientist* (New York: Ballantine, 2009).

INDEX

ACKNOWLEDGMENTS

IN ADDITION TO THE TRANSFORMERS whose stories are reflected in this book, we wish to acknowledge transformers and positive deviants throughout history—from the ancient Greeks who imagined the ideal man to present-day scientists who are discovering and seeking ways to maximize the magic of neuroplasticity.

In our work, we stand on the shoulders of giants—among them Alfred Adler, Friedrich Nietszche, Sigmund Freud, Paul Tillich, Carl Rogers, Lev Vygotsky, their followers, and too many others to mention. Adding significantly to the developing vision of human emergence that has fostered the work studied in *Transformed!* are Drs. Jane Loevinger, Clare W. Graves, Don Beck, and Jim Morningstar.

Special mention goes to Robert Postel for his significant advancements in the realization of human potential, combining individual and group work in his Contemporary Adlerian Primary Relationship Training using what we have further developed into The Assignment Way of Living.

To those whose research appears in these pages, thank you for your contribution. We apologize in advance for any errors we may have inadvertently made in applying your work, and as a learning organization, we hope you'll let us know if this has occurred.

Dr. Gordon Medlock has been a thought partner in much of the research and development of the Wright Model of Human Emergence. Angela Kezon, Barb Burgess, Kate Holmquest, and John Aquilina have spent countless hours on this book and untold all-nighters for this and other projects. Also dedicating their lives to the realization of human potential are Jillian Eichel, Beryl Stromsta, and Gertrude Lyons. Their partnership cannot be adequately acknowledged—all-nighters, whatever it takes, meeting impossible deadlines, and so much more. None of them believed us when we told them before hiring them that they would work twice as hard for half the money they could earn elsewhere, but that the fulfillment was priceless. Well, they will likely agree with the fulfillment, but say that we were wrong on the hours—they work three times as hard.

Dr. Michael Zwell has fostered the birth of the graduate institute and much more. Jennifer Stephen and Mike were the first student leaders of many who now make our advanced curriculum more widely available. Other board members and supporters of our foundation—many of whom also serve as adjunct faculty or staff—include Dr. Stan V. Smith, Dr. Denise and Dr. Don Delves, John and Jacki Davidoff, Rich and Gertrude Lyons, and Scott and Jen Stephen.

Deepest thanks to our students, with whom we are honored to share the exciting journey of transformation, as well as the audiences at our speaking and media events, and readers of our books. Generosity and dedication abound in many forms at Wright. Our work is truly a community activity.

Specifically, we want to single out Karen Wilson Smithbauer who provided, among other gifts, the matching grant that enabled the birth of the Wright Graduate Institute for the Realization of Human Potential's master's program. Also donating to the Foundation for Transformational Leadership and founding our doctoral program, The Terry Human Emergence Research Institute, are Karen and Tom Terry. Another benefactor and the grandfather of our leadership programs is Art Silver. Special thanks to Janet and Brad Anderson and the other sponsors of the most recent Transformational Leadership Symposium.

Dr. Bernie Luskin has shepherded us through our doctoral studies, which led to *Transformed!*, while Dr. Robert Moore has provided invaluable support to Bob. Dr. Bill Seidman provided the initial research of our positive deviants. Other research and academic support came from Dr. Judy Witt, Dr. Toni Gregory, Dr. Odis Simmons, and Dr. Lee Mahon. Many participated in the research and production; however, special acknowledgment goes to Collin and Christina Canright, Dee Danner, Dr. Marilyn Pearson, Eric Masi (cover design), the women of SOFIA (The Society of Femininity in Action), and all of our Summer Leadership Training participants who contributed their hearts, minds, and resources. Getting the book to the publisher would have been infinitely more difficult and probably less effective without the belief, strategizing, and expert editing of Bruce Wexler. Our publisher, Todd Bottorff, deserves a great deal of credit along with acquiring editor Diane Gedymin; our editor and production partner, Christina Huffines; and the shepherd of the process, our agent, Carol Mann.

There are so many people to thank that we would need to write another book to mention everyone who deserves acknowledgment. As our dear Spiritual Grandmother, Virginia Rogers, says when praying, "Lord, A,B,C, . . . X, Y, Z. Please read my heart and bless everyone whose name starts with one of these letters who resides there." For us, we too need to repeat the alphabet, and ask that all contributors with names beginning with one of these letters be acknowledged.

Finally, we give our greatest thanks to the Divine Source of all.

ABOUT THE AUTHORS

DR. JUDITH WRIGHT AND DR. BOB WRIGHT have trained and coached thousands of individuals through a myriad of challenges and opportunities from career to relationship, self-esteem to transformational leadership—taking some from the point of graduating from business school to being top executives in multi-national public corporations. In addition, the Wrights co-founded the Graduate Institute for the Realization of Human Potential, offering master's degrees in transformational coaching, leadership, and learning. With its sister organization, the Terry Human Emergence Research Institute, the Graduate Institute offers doctoral degrees in Transformational Learning, Leadership, and Coaching. Dr. Judith and Dr. Bob Wright have become two of the country's foremost experts on transformational leadership, having established the Foundation for Transformational Leadership as well as the Transformational Leadership Symposium, which convened leadership experts from around the nation to recognize cutting-edge leaders including Brad Anderson, former CEO of Best Buy, as well as the 2012 Award recipient, Dr. Muhammad Yunus.

DR. JUDITH WRIGHT

A media favorite, sought-after speaker, respected leader, bestselling author, world-class coach, and corporate consultant, Dr. Judith

Wright (www.drjudithwright.com) wrote *There Must Be More Than This* (Random House/Broadway Books), *The One Decision,* and *The Soft Addiction Solution* (Penguin/Tarcher) to share her proven personal transformation methodologies with a broader audience. She is a sought-after expert who has appeared as a featured lifestyle expert and coach on ABC's *20/20, Oprah, Good Morning America,* the *Today* show and hundreds of radio and television shows. Called the "world's ultimate expert," her work has appeared in over 80 magazines and newspapers around the globe including *Marie Claire, Fitness Magazine, Health, Better Homes and Gardens, Shape,* the *New York Daily News,* the *Chicago Tribune,* the *Boston Herald,* and the *San Francisco Chronicle.*

A pioneer in the field of human development, Dr. Judith Wright first rose to national recognition developing a model program for barrier-free college education and continued her national recognition winning national demonstration grants for innovative education and early childhood development programs for those with developmental disabilities and their families. These experiences revealed the essential elements for the triumph of the human spirit that fuels her passion for developing human potential based on her deep-rooted commitment to help people live great lives, whatever their circumstances.

Dr. Judith Wright's most recent work, the culmination of a comprehensive ten-year research initiative, forms the basis for the Evolating Process, which is the foundation for this book. Dr. Wright is the founder of SOFIA (Society of Femininity in Action), providing revolutionary leadership training for women. She has her BA in psychology, her MA in education and counseling, and her doctorate in Educational Leadership and Change.

DR. BOB WRIGHT

Considered by many to be one of the leading thinkers in human development, Dr. Bob Wright (www.drbobwright.com) is an internationally recognized visionary, educator, program developer, author, speaker, entrepreneur, consultant, and executive coach. Coaching CEOs across the country from leading-name public companies to entrepreneurial startups, he is recognized as a top executive coach by *Crain's Chicago Business.* Dr. Bob Wright's revolutionary *Wright Model of Human Emergence,* called the most powerful comprehensive model of its kind, provides a much-needed practical application of theory into everyday life. Forming the core of the curriculum at Wright, which he co-founded with his wife Judith, Dr. Bob Wright's revolutionary personal and professional training and development methodology leads not only to significant professional success, but also to fulfillment in all life areas.

Dr. Bob Wright has demonstrated success in a wide variety of areas. He is an outstanding radio and television personality, delivering what author Andrew Harvey calls his "hard light." Writing books on purpose in business and people skills, his work has been translated into multiple languages and has sold over 200,000 copies around the globe. And his nationally acclaimed employee assistance and managed mental health firm, Human Effectiveness, Inc., was rated top in the nation by Mercer Meidinger Medical Audit as well as Arthur Andersen. In addition to his environmental restoration work, Dr. Bob Wright has founded the Men's Guild, a powerful men's organization for a new model of manhood; and established Be Heard, an organization to promote environmentally conscious political action.

Dr. Bob Wright's education, coaching, and leadership training and research led to the development of what he named Grounded Leadership, an invaluable facilitative part of the transformational leader's tool box. Dr. Bob founded the Graduate Institute for the Realization of Human Potential and the Foundation for Transformational Leadership. Dr. Bob Wright's degrees include a BA in Sociology, MA in Communications, MSW in Clinical Social Work, and a Doctorate in Education, Leadership, and Change.

ABOUT WRIGHT

Our purpose is to live spectacular lives and to support others to unleash their potential by consciously engaging in their own transformation and leadership, for the advancement of humanity and conscious, sustainable living on the planet.
—Wright Statement of Purpose

WRIGHT

WRIGHT APPLIES BOTH TRADITIONAL AND CUTTING-edge human emergence technologies to leadership, career, relationship, and personal development. Through a unique synergy of seminars, coaching, and small group training, participants in their programs generally discover and realize visions far beyond their original hopes. Ninety-seven percent report living successful lives of purpose, meaning, and fulfillment both personally and professionally.

With an accomplished team of faculty, adjunct faculty, staff, and coaches, Wright provides world-class coaching, training, learning laboratories, research, and graduate education that help students and clients develop a vision to surpass their goals and live their dreams as they maximize their contribution to their worlds.

As a result, Wright is the hub of a powerful and diverse student network—from CEOs to stay-at-home moms, from artists to M.D.'s. These students represent varied religious backgrounds, ethnicities, and walks of life, but what they have in common is a powerful intent to lead great lives filled with purpose, meaning, and contribution. From impacting national policy to transforming education and health care, you can recognize Wright students and consulting clients by their results, as well as their way of being—they have potent and powerful relationships that last, families that work, and businesses that contribute to staff, industry, and their communities. They are responsible, open, contributory, creative participants in whatever they are doing.

This client network of outstanding individuals represents a significant aspect of the research data that revealed the powerful process revealed in *Transformed!*

THE GRADUATE INSTITUTE

The Graduate Institute for the Realization of Human Potential offers master's degrees in Transformational Leadership, Learning, and Coaching as well as certificates in Transformational Leadership, Transformational Coaching, Social Intelligence, and Emotional Intelligence. The Terry Research Institute for the Study of Human Emergence is a sister organization offering doctoral degrees.

A 501(c)3 nonprofit organization, The Graduate Institute bridges the divide between academic research and popular approaches to human development—the intersection of traditional educational philosophy, human process, business theory, organizational development, traditional and positive psychology, theology, and neuroscience.

The Graduate Institute's mission is twofold: providing transformational education for transformational leaders, while fostering the integration, development, and dissemination of the best human development technologies available through research and education. Students develop their cognitive, leadership, and people skills in a wide variety of professions from human services to business, education, public service, consulting, organizational development, communications, and training.

This unique, groundbreaking educational model not only facilitates students' professional development but only awards degrees to students who can demonstrate their personal transformation as well as their contribution to the transformation of others, applying their academic learning in powerful ways that enhance their lives and the lives of those they touch.

The Graduate Institute establishes this foundation for personal transformation through the technology of Wright Performative Education—a highly personalized course of study that blends traditional cognitive learning and academic rigor with a practical regimen of daily personal and applied experiments and application—leading to personal and professional growth, self-knowledge, and skill development.

RECOMMENDED RESOURCES

WRIGHT PROGRAMS AND PRODUCTS

BELOW YOU'LL FIND A SELECTION of programs and resources to help you live a spectacular life. At Wright, we offer a wide variety of both paid and complimentary transformative products and services. To check out the most current offering, visit the *Transformed!* area of our website at www.wrightliving.com/transformed.

FREE PRODUCTS AND SERVICES

FREE *Transformed!* Toolkit
A complimentary robust downloadable toolkit that is the perfect companion to the *Transformed!* book. This toolkit gives you technology to better understand and leverage the concepts you learn in *Transformed!*.

FREE Newsletter: *Transform!*: a Weekly Guide to a Spectacular Life Project
A weekly inspirational tool with valuable insights, tips, education, humor, and technology that will keep you moving on your transformational journey. Information and tips are shared from Dr. Judith Wright, Dr. Bob Wright, and from individual students who are applying what they are learning to their careers, families, and communities.

FREE Introductory Coaching Session

Explore how you could use coaching to maximize your performance and satisfaction in every area of life during this complimentary thirty-minute session with a Wright faculty member.

WRIGHT PROGRAMS AND SERVICES

Speaking Engagements

Dr. Judith Wright, Dr. Bob Wright, or one of the individuals from the Wright speakers bureau would be delighted to speak to your organization, association, or business. Their dynamic, engaging, powerful, and entertaining keynotes cover diverse topics from *Transformed!* and others customized to your situation and needs. Popular topics include transformational leadership, employee engagement, social and emotional intelligence, soft addictions, relationships, purposeful living, and more.

Year of Transformation

Our signature program, the Year of Transformation, combines the best of human emergence technologies to empower individuals to create exponential results in their lives—proven results that really last. A combination of weekend trainings, individual coaching, and laboratory learning, this in-depth program teaches the *Transformed!* process through the lens of four impactful life areas: Nourishment & Self-Care, Personal Power, Family & Intimacy, and Purposeful Living & Spiritual Development. Whether you are a CEO looking to become a more effective transformational leader, a single person wanting the most out of life in career and relationships, or a parent wanting to more powerfully empower your children, this program gives you the foundational skills you need. The program starts with the *Transform! Training*. As a reader of this book, you can use the complimentary certificate found online to attend this introductory training.

Coaching

A perfect way to start your journey of transformation, coaching with Wright faculty offers quality, depth, and proven results. Whether your short-term desire is to jump-start your career or business or to improve the relationships in your life, we have a coach that will work for you. Call Wright today at 312.645.8300 for your first vision coaching session by phone, video, or in-person—complimentary with your purchase of *Transformed!: The Science of Spectacular Living*.

Consulting & Executive Coaching

Dr. Bob Wright and Dr. Judith Wright are available for consulting and executive coaching for your company or organization. They have coached top performers and organizations across a wide range of disciplines from finance to health care, publishing to technology. If you are serious about a transformational level of success for yourself, your employees, or your organization, contact us to learn more. Here is what a few of their clients have said.

"I am living proof that the Wrights are all about results. My business grew from a small shop of number-crunchers to a 200-member force for excellence in the actuarial profession until I sold it to a Fortune 50 company. I'm now leading my profession internationally and have been at the forefront of the public debate about retirement security in this country—all while using the techniques and perspectives described in *Transformed!* to fundamentally and forever alter the quality of every aspect of my life—my marriage, my relationships with my children, my quality of contact with those I do business with, and my sense of purpose in the world."

—Tom Terry, President Elect 2014, American Association of Actuaries & Former CEO, JP Morgan Compensation & Benefit Strategies

"Judith Wright is one of my secret weapons in life. Through her one-on-one coaching with me and through my participation in many of her courses, I have learned to appreciate the many gifts I have and to share those gifts with clients and friends. Judith is definitely the wind in my sails."

—John Davidoff, Founder & Managing Director, Davidoff Communications

"Bob Wright's ongoing coaching was a key factor for me in unlocking critical insights about individuals and groups within the challenging dynamics of a public company. By methodically listening and teasing out information, he helped me build working models of situations that made it possible to tackle seemingly overwhelming problems. Bob's value as a coach is multiplied by both his wide range of professional contacts and his broad understanding of business, technology, and entertainment, yet he also has a very mutual approach to looking at situations through the same views and constraints that I have to navigate in the day-to-day reality of my work. His coaching has been invaluable to me."

—MATT BOOTY, FORMER PRESIDENT AND CEO OF
MIDWAY GAMES, INC.

"The Wrights are expert coaches who are dedicated to ensuring that their clients become great people who create a positive impact in teams, organizations, and the world. Because of their commitment to staying on their professional edge, their coaching is infused with up-to-date technologies and strategies. For individuals who are looking for someone who will stand shoulder to shoulder with them as they navigate business complexities, operate from a high degree of character and integrity, and be a straight shooter who is wholeheartedly invested in your development—Bob and Judith Wright are the coaches for you."
—WENDY MANNING, MARKETING EXECUTIVE, AEROSPACE INDUSTRY

"Bob Wright is by far the best in his field. My business has grown from 500K to a multimillion-dollar company. SMS has most recently been recognized in *Inc. Magazine* as one of the 500 fastest-growing privately held companies in America and this is due to the leadership he has provided me personally and professionally. I continue and will continue to hire Bob as my coach to lead me into new and risky undertakings that will help me develop as an individual as well as a businesswoman. I've never encountered anyone like Bob—he is truly an expert in his field. He's a Great Leader."

—PAMELA ZASTROW, PRINCIPAL, SMS DISPLAY GROUP, INC.

CPSIA information can be obtained
at www.ICGtesting.com
Printed in the USA
LVOW11s1946311017

554461LV00002BA/141/P